Contents

Printed by Woods of Perth
Front Cover Design by Tiger Chick

Rensburg
Sheppards

INVESTMENT LED
WEALTH MANAGEMENT

We are delighted to continue our sponsorship of Scotland's Gardens Scheme guidebook for 2010. We would also like to congratulate all the garden owners for the dedication and hard work involved in preparing their gardens for the public to enjoy. Your reward is not only the admiration of your visitors, but the knowledge that takings at the garden gate will help to fund many vital charitable projects.

To all readers of this guidebook, we express our thanks for being part of this process by visiting some of the many inspirational gardens that can be found within these pages. All of us at Rensburg Sheppards are very proud to be associated with an organisation that continues to work so effectively to provide financial support for charities small and large in Scotland, all of which will be close to the hearts of garden owners and visitors alike.

Steve Elliott

Steve Elliott
Chief Executive
Rensburg Sheppards

SCOTLAND'S GARDENS SCHEME

Created as a registered charity in 1931 Scotland's Gardens Scheme's objective was to raise funds for the Queen's Nurses, a charity that supported community nurses in primary care, by opening country house gardens to the public for a nominal charge.

Today Scotland's Gardens Scheme has a small management team and approximately two hundred volunteers in twenty seven Scottish districts who organise the opening each year of about 475, mostly private gardens of all kinds ranging from formal castle gardens to groups of small village gardens.

The Queen's Nursing Institute (as it has become) remains one of the Scheme's three principal beneficiaries. The others are The Gardens Fund of The National Trust for Scotland and Maggie's Cancer Caring Centres. Perennial (The Gardeners' Royal Benevolent Society) and The Royal Fund for Gardeners' Children also receive support annually. These five charities receive 60% net of the money raised from the garden openings whilst 40% gross is allocated to charities of each garden owner's choice.

At most garden openings there are homemade teas and a plant stall and for both of these Scotland's Garden Scheme is renowned. At many there are other attractions and stalls to make the openings as enjoyable as possible for all visitors.

CHAIRMAN'S MESSAGE

"These are extraordinary times we live in. When I last wrote the financial world was in crisis and indeed much hardship has come in the wake of that, which means that help for our many charities is needed more than ever. All the more splendid then that Scotland's Gardens Scheme managed a record year in 2008 and at the time of writing we have hopes that 2009 will be very close to that.

We have so many people to thank for this success; our team of volunteers who keep the wheels turning, our garden owners without whom we would not exist, all their wonderfully varied helpers who make openings happen and of course all those of you who, in ever increasing numbers, visit these fantastic gardens. On a different level we must not forget our small dynamic employed team of two plus one part time!

Thank you for buying this book. Please do visit as many of these very special gardens as you can, every one has its own individual character and special charm and every one will give you the warmest of welcomes whatever the weather! "

Trine Kennedy

SPONSORSHIP

We would like to both thank and acknowledge the following organisations for their 2010 sponsorship. Their support is appreciated greatly by everyone involved with Scotland's Gardens Scheme and the charities that benefit from our work.

Rensburg Sheppards Investment Management Limited

Corney & Barrow

Lycett, Browne Swinburn Douglas Ltd

Johnstons

Brodie Melrose Drysdale & Co. Ltd.

Adam & Company Investment Management

Savills (L&P) Ltd

The Macallen Single Malt Whisky

The Edinburgh International Conference Centre

In addition we would like to say how grateful we are to the many private donors who support us.

Maggie's Cancer Caring Centres provide a programme of support that empowers people to live with, through and beyond a diagnosis of cancer.

One in three of us will develop cancer over the course of our lives and the number of diagnoses is predicted to rise by 30% by 2020. Maggie's Centres offer people somewhere to turn to for help. People can go there if they've been recently diagnosed or have been living with cancer for some time. The centres are also open to friends and family members supporting those with cancer. We work together with these people to help them overcome the isolation and despair often caused by a cancer diagnosis.

Our founder, Maggie Keswick Jencks, recognised that moving from 'passive victim' to 'active participant' was the most important step that anyone diagnosed with cancer could take. Furthermore, Maggie, loved gardens and placed great emphasis on the therapeutic benefits of landscape and outdoor space in creating a relaxing environment with the emphasis on stress reduction and healing. The gardens at Maggie's Centres are peaceful and uplifting outside rooms that are intrinsic to the overall function of the buildings, which are themselves designed by some of the world's most prominent architects.

In 2008 we launched our groundbreaking Online Centre which provides live support group sessions with a Clinical Psychologist, allowing us to work with and care for people who are unable to visit a centre due to location, work or travel commitments.

All our services are provided free of charge to centre visitors and we rely on fundraising to both build and run our centres. We have a number of centres across Scotland, (in Edinburgh, Glasgow, Dundee, the Highlands, Fife and Lanarkshire) and it is because of this that we are so very grateful for the fantastic support of Scotland's Gardens Scheme, the garden owners who open their gardens to the public as part of the scheme and the thousands of people who visit them each year.

On behalf of everyone at Maggie's, including the thousands of people who visit our centres each year, I thank you for your support.

Laura Lee
Chief Executive

www.maggiescentres.org

THE QUEEN'S NURSING INSTITUTE SCOTLAND
Patron: Her Majesty The Queen
31 Castle Terrace, Edinburgh EH1 2EL
Tel: 0131 229 2333 Fax: 0131 228 9066
Registered Scottish Charity No: SC005751

The Queen's Nursing Institute Scotland (QNIS) is a registered independent charity. The main aim is to promote excellence in community nursing in Scotland and provide support to nurses through: education, research grants and scholarships, training events and conferences throughout Scotland and funding nurse led innovative projects. In addition QNIS provides welfare support to retired Queen's Nurses.

In 2009 QNIS celebrated 150 years of District Nursing.

QNIS works closely with the National Health Service and associated professional bodies. As a charity and a non political organisation QNIS is uniquely placed to listen to and support nurses working at grass roots level.

QNIS has a long and valued relationship with Scotland's Garden Scheme and is extremely grateful to be a beneficiary of the scheme. Donations received are used to fund nurse led projects.

Examples of current projects include:

The provision of a **sensory garden** in Kirkintilloch, coordinated by a nurse who works with older people. The garden is next to a new Health and Community Care centre and will be open to local people, elderly people who attend the Centre and nursing staff. The garden will be fully accessible for disabled people.
This is an exciting project where all will benefit from the effect on wellbeing that a garden can provide.

Dementia Care
This highly relevant project involves a nurse working with Dundee University to explore the contribution that community nurses make to the care of people with dementia and to find out which models of care most help people with dementia and their carers.

Tobacco and Alcohol Use in people with a learning disability (Glasgow, Ayrshire and Arran) Group discussions and training are being undertaken to establish best practice and ensure that community nurses are equipped with the correct information and special skills.

When a project is completed the emphasis is on sharing good practice throughout Scotland.

None of this would be possible without the generosity of Scotland's Gardens Scheme.

We take this opportunity to say a very big thank you to organisers, garden owners, and the visiting public.

Merrill Whalen
Trustee QNIS

the National Trust
for Scotland

On behalf of the Council and Board for the National Trust for Scotland, I would like to thank all of Scotland's Gardens Scheme owners for their continuing support and commitment to the National Trust for Scotland and its own gardens.

During 2009 the Trust opened its garden gates at 30 properties to raise money for Scotland's Gardens Scheme, with events such as guided walks and plant sales happening throughout the year. We are especially looking forward to 2010's Annual Gardens Days which will include, for the first time, the garden at Canna House, Inner Hebrides where the Head Gardener will lead garden tours on the last Wednesday of each month from April to August, meeting visitors from the Small Isles' ferry. A number of gardens will be hosting practical demonstrations and talks and the Trust's Gardens & Designed Landscape Services team will host a special Master Class on garden conservation management in March 2010 in aid of Scotland's Gardens Scheme.

Along with other garden owners in 2009, we continued to suffer the effects of the outbreaks of Phytophthora ramorum and P. Kernoviae which has impacted significantly on our west coast gardens. Challenges of this nature emphasise the importance of good training and further research in all aspects of gardening. Our Centre for Excellence in Heritage Horticulture now provides a framework to support training for gardeners throughout the Trust with placements at Threave Garden Kellie Castle and Inverewe Garden. This also allows us to enhance our apprenticeship programme in general and to develop other initiatives such as workshops and exchanges for all gardeners and more opportunities for volunteers. In 2009, Scotland's Gardens Scheme support enabled Gerald Thornton to attend the School of Practical Horticulture at Threave.

Your support has helped us enormously during the year. We have been able to purchase much needed replacement equipment for many of our gardens affected by the recent staff losses and financial cut backs.

We look forward to continuing our work with you and hope that 2010 will be a productive year for gardeners.

Kate Mavor
Chief Executive

THE ROYAL FUND FOR GARDENERS' CHILDREN

Registered Charity 248746

Our Fund, which was established in commemoration of the Golden Jubilee of Queen Victoria, has been helping the orphaned children of professional horticulturists since 1887, and in recent years this assistance has been extended so that we can offer help to all needy children whose parents are, or have been, employed in horticulture.

Over the past year we have helped 18 orphaned and needy children in Scotland. Two of these are young men, just embarking upon their college educations and to whom we have given regular financial assistance since the death of their father in 1992. Such a long term commitment is not unusual in our work and thus the support of Scotland's Gardens Scheme, which continues even through difficult times such as the current economic recession, is especially welcomed.

The support we give is, we know, invaluable to our beneficiaries, and we would like to thank Scotland's Gardens Scheme for the annual donation it gives, enabling us to meet the demand for our assistance in Scotland.

The Royal Fund for Gardeners' Children
10 Deards Wood
Knebworth
Herts SG3 6PG
Tel: 01438 813939
Web: www.rfgc.org.uk
Email: rfgc@btinternet.com

"Gardens of Scotland" 2010

may now be purchased

on-line at our website

www.gardensofscotland.org

on the Garden Handbook Page

PERENNIAL
GARDENERS' ROYAL BENEVOLENT SOCIETY
Helping Horticulturists In Need Since 1839

Perennial is the only charity dedicated to helping the 500,000 people in the UK who work, or have previously worked, in the horticultural professions. With the drastic downturn in the financial climate Perennial is needed more than ever before, and in the past year our UK-wide casework team has offered assistance and support to almost 1,000 individuals in need. We rely on the involvement and generosity of our donors to continue – we receive no government support, and must raise vital funds to support all aspects of our work with those in need. To mark our 170th year a special appeal – the Heart of Perennial – has been launched, to raise funds for our Good Samaritan Welfare Fund. The fund was originally established in our founding year, and today channels vital support for our core services for elderly people and those facing financial crises – the very groups we were first established to help. We would like to thank Scotland's Gardens Scheme for its annual donation which allows us to continue our work here in Scotland. If you would like to find out more about Perennial and our work her in Scotland please contact Alexandra Rutherford at **arutherford@perennial.org.uk** or 0141 334 6523 or check out our website at www.perennial.org.uk

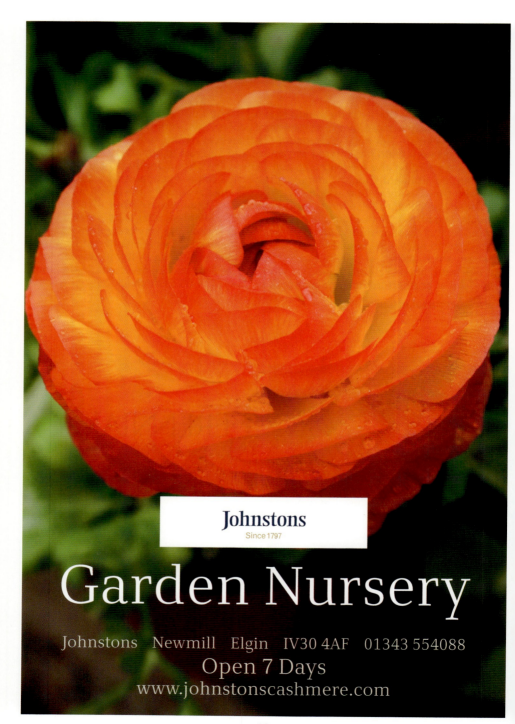

Inspiring gardeners since 1865

The Garden Experts

Dobbies has been inspiring gardeners since 1865. Since then our name has been synonymous with quality horticulture, providing the very best products and expert advice to gardeners everywhere for more than 140 years. And to assure you that you are not just getting great advice, but excellent products, we offer a 5 year guarantee on all hardy plants.

For great savings and rewards throughout the year, join Dobbies Gardening Club and enjoy:

- **10% off** all full price plants, bulbs and seeds – every day!
- **Collect reward points** with money back rewards twice a year
- **24 FREE** tea/filter coffee vouchers, worth over £30
- **Plus even more exclusive offers** and events for members

Annual membership is only £12

Join in-store or online for the discounted price of £10 at www.dobbies.com

Dobbies Garden World | Melville Nursery | Lasswade
Edinburgh | EH18 1AZ | Tel: 0131 663 1941 | OPEN 7 DAYS
Contact us for opening times or visit www.dobbies.com

Dobbies
GARDEN WORLD
it's in our nature
www.dobbies.com

Also at: Aberdeen | Ayr | Cumbernauld | Dalgety Bay | Dunfermline | Edinburgh | Kinross | Milngavie | Paisley | Perth | Sandyholm | Stirling

Banking and Investment Management for Private Clients

Focusing on the things that matter to you

Turcan Connell offers a comprehensive service to private individuals and their families; charities; and the owners and managers of land. Our focus has always been on providing trusted counsel over the long term. Our combination of legal and financial expertise allows us to provide focused and tailored advice on the issues that really matter.

- Asset Protection
- Charity Law
- Dispute Resolution
- Employment Law
- Family Law
- Family Office
- Financial Planning
- Investment Management
- Land & Property
- Pensions
- Tax Services
- Trust and Succession

Edinburgh   London   Guernsey

Princes Exchange, I Earl Grey Street
Edinburgh EH3 9EE

Tel: 0131 228 8111

enquiries@turcanconnell.com
www.turcanconnell.com

TURCAN CONNELL
SOLICITORS AND ASSET MANAGERS

Turcan Connell is authorised and regulated by the
Financial Services Authority for investment business.

the National Trust
for Scotland
a place for everyone

Arduaine

A unique and precious treasure

With rich and diverse plant collections, a breathtaking location and a remarkable history, Arduaine is a haven of tranquillity that demands our care and support.

For more information about how you can help secure the future of this garden, please contact the National Trust for Scotland Development Department on **0844 493 2408**, email **information@nts.org.uk** or **visit www.nts.org.uk**

www.nts.org.uk

The National Trust for Scotland Wemyss House, 28 Charlotte Square Edinburgh, Scotland United Kingdom EH2 4ET

The National Trust for Scotland for Places of Historic Interest or Natural Beauty is a charity registered in Scotland, Charity Number SC 007410

GARDENS OPEN ON A SPECIFIC DATE

Dates to be Confirmed
Edinburgh & West Lothian   Dalmeny Park, South Queensferry

Kirkcudbrightshire   Danevale Park, Crossmichael

Saturday 06 February
Ayrshire   Blair House, Dalry

Sunday 07 February
Ayrshire   Blair House, Dalry

Stirlingshire   West Plean House, Denny Road, By Stirling

Sunday 14 February
Ayrshire   Caprington Castle, Kilmarnock

Stirlingshire   West Plean House, Denny Road, By Stirling

Wigtownshire   Kirkdale, Carsluith, Newton Stewart

Thursday 18 February
Perth & Kinross   Rossie House, Forgandenny

Saturday 20 February
Ettrick & Lauderdale   Bowhill Country Park, Selkirk

Sunday 21 February
Ayrshire   Blairquhan, Straiton, Maybole

East Lothian   Shepherd House, Inveresk

Peeblesshire   Drumelzier Place, Broughton

Renfrewshire   Lochside, Lochwinnoch

Stirlingshire   West Plean House, Denny Road, By Stirling

Sunday 28 February
Kincardine & Deeside   Ecclesgreig Castle, St Cyrus

Midlothian   Kevock Garden, 16 Kevock Road, Lasswade

Peeblesshire   Kailzie Gardens, Peebles

Stirlingshire   Kilbryde Castle, Dunblane

Thursday 18 March
Perth & Kinross   Rossie House, Forgandenny

GARDENS OPEN ON A SPECIFIC DATE

Sunday 04 April

Edinburgh & West Lothian	61 Fountainhall Road, Edinburgh

Sunday 11 April

East Lothian	Winton House, Pencaitland
Edinburgh & West Lothian	61 Fountainhall Road, Edinburgh
Edinburgh & West Lothian	Dean Gardens, Edinburgh
Perth & Kinross	Megginch Castle, Errol
Stirlingshire	Milseybank, Bridge of Allan
Wigtownshire	Smithy Hill Cottage, Leswalt

Thursday 15 April

Perth & Kinross	Rossie House, Forgandenny
Ross, Cromarty, Skye & Inverness	Dundonnell House, Little Loch Broom

Saturday 17 April

Midlothian	Kevock Garden, 16 Kevock Road, Lasswade

Sunday 18 April

Aberdeenshire	Auchmacoy, Ellon
Dunbartonshire	Kilarden, Rosneath
Ettrick & Lauderdale	Bemersyde, Melrose
Midlothian	Kevock Garden, 16 Kevock Road, Lasswade
Stirlingshire	Avonmuir House, Muiravonside

Sunday 25 April

Angus	3 Balfour Cottages, Menmuir
Argyllshire	Benmore Botanic Garden, Benmore
East Lothian	Shepherd House, Inveresk
Edinburgh & West Lothian	Moray Place & Bank Gardens, Edinburgh
Edinburgh & West Lothian	Redhall Walled Garden, 97 Lanark Road, Edinburgh
Kirkcudbrightshire	Walton Park, Castle Douglas

Saturday 01 May

Argyllshire	Drim na Vullin, Blarbuie Road, Lochgilphead
Argyllshire	Strachur House Flower & Woodland Gardens, Strachur
Midlothian	Mount Ceres, 3 Lower Broomieknowe, Lasswade

Sunday 02 May

Argyllshire	Drim na Vullin, Blarbuie Road, Lochgilphead
Argyllshire	Strachur House Flower & Woodland Gardens, Strachur

Berwickshire	Charterhall, Duns
Dumfriesshire	Portrack House, Holywood
Lanarkshire	The Scots Mining Company House, Leadhills, Biggar
Perth & Kinross	Glendoick, by Perth
Stirlingshire	The Pass House, Kilmahog, Callander
Wigtownshire	Logan House Gardens, Port Logan, By Stranraer
Wigtownshire	Smithy Hill Cottage, Leswalt, By Stranraer

Friday 07 May

Fife	St. Andrews Botanic Garden, Canongate, St. Andrews

Saturday 08 May

Argyllshire	Knock Cottage, Lochgair
Edinburgh & West Lothian	Roscullen, 1 Bonaly Road, Edinburgh

Sunday 09 May

Angus	Brechin Castle, Brechin
Argyllshire	Arduaine, Kilmelford,
Argyllshire	Knock Cottage, Lochgair
Dunbartonshire	Ardchapel and Seven The Birches, Shandon
Edinburgh & West Lothian	Roscullen, 1 Bonaly Road, Edinburgh
Fife	Craigrothie Village Gardens
Isle of Arran	Brodick Castle & Country Park, Brodick
Lanarkshire	20 Smithycroft, Hamilton
Perth & Kinross	Branklyn, 116 Dundee Road, Perth
Stirlingshire	Kilbryde Castle, Dunblane
Wigtownshire	Smithy Hill Cottage, Leswalt

Thursday 13 May

Perth & Kinross	Rossie House, Forgandenny

Saturday 15 May

Argyllshire	Knock Cottage, Lochgair

Sunday 16 May

Aberdeenshire	Haddo House, Methlick
Angus	Dunninald, Montrose
Argyllshire	Crarae Garden, Inveraray
Argyllshire	Knock Cottage, Lochgair
Ayrshire	Kirkhill Castle, Colmonell
Dumfriesshire	Dalswinton House, Dalswinton

GARDENS OPEN ON A SPECIFIC DATE

Dunbartonshire	Geilston Garden, Main Road, Cardross
East Lothian	Tyninghame House, Dunbar
Edinburgh & West Lothian	61 Fountainhall Road, Edinburgh
Edinburgh & West Lothian	Hunter's Tryst, 95 Oxgangs Road, Edinburgh
Fife	Tayfield, Forgan
Fife	Willowhill, Forgan
Glasgow & District	44 Gordon Road, Netherlee
Kirkcudbrightshire	Threave Garden, Castle Douglas
Moray & Nairn	Bents Green, 10 Pilmuir Road West, Forres
Perth & Kinross	Glendoick, by Perth
Perth & Kinross	Pitcurran House, Abernethy
Stirlingshire	Touch, Stirling
Stirlingshire	Yellowcraig Wood Bluebell Walk, Nr. Causewayhead
Wigtownshire	Smithy Hill Cottage, Leswalt, By Stranraer

Wednesday 19 May

Aberdeenshire	Cruickshank Botanic Gardens, 23 St. Machar Drive, Aberdeen

Saturday 22 May

Glasgow & District	Kirklee Circus Pleasure Garden and Beyond, Glasgow
Ross, Cromarty, Skye & Inverness	Attadale, Strathcarron

Sunday 23 May

Angus	Dalfruin, Kirktonhill Road, Kirriemuir
Ayrshire	Blair House, Dalry
Berwickshire	Lennel Bank, Coldstream
Dunbartonshire	Ross Priory, Gartocharn
Edinburgh & West Lothian	61 Fountainhall Road, Edinburgh
Fife	Kirklands, Saline
Fife	Strathairly House, Upper Largo
Glasgow & District	Kilsyth Gardens, Allanfauld Road, Kilsyth
Isle of Arran	Strabane, Brodick
Kincardine & Deeside	Inchmarlo House Garden, Inchmarlo
Kirkcudbrightshire	Spottes, Haugh of Urr
Lochaber & Badenoch	Camusdarach, Arisaig
Perth & Kinross	Dowhill, Kelty
Renfrewshire	Duchal, Kilmacolm
Stirlingshire	Glenorchard, Auchenlay Road, Dunblane
Wigtownshire	Smithy Hill Cottage, Leswalt

Tuesday 25 May

Ross, Cromarty, Skye & Inverness	Inverewe, Poolewe

Wednesday 26 May

Ross, Cromarty, Skye & Inverness	House of Gruinard, Laide

Thursday 27 May

Aberdeenshire	Leith Hall, Huntly

Saturday 29 May

Ayrshire	Holmes Farm, Drybridge

Sunday 30 May

Ayrshire	Holmes Farm, Drybridge
Dumfriesshire	Cowhill Tower, Holywood
Dunbartonshire	Milton House, Milton
East Lothian	Stenton Village
Fife	Earlshall Castle, Leuchars
Fife	St. Monans Village Gardens
Isle of Arran	Strabane, Brodick
Kincardine & Deeside	The Burn House & The Burn Garden House, Glenesk
Kirkcudbrightshire	Corsock House, Corsock
Peeblesshire	Baddinsgill, West Linton
Peeblesshire	Haystoun, Peebles
Perth & Kinross	Achnacloich, Balhomais, by Aberfeldy
Perth & Kinross	Cloan, by Auchterarder
Perth & Kinross	Farleyer Field House, by Aberfeldy
Ross, Cromarty, Skye & Inverness	Croc na Boull, Muir of Ord
Wigtownshire	Logan Botanic Garden, Port Logan
Wigtownshire	Smithy Hill Cottage, Leswalt

Tuesday 01 June

Midlothian	Mount Ceres, 3 Lower Broomieknowe, Lasswade
Ross, Cromarty, Skye & Inverness	Inverewe, Poolewe

Thursday 03 June

Ross, Cromarty, Skye & Inverness	Dundonnell House, Little Loch Broom

GARDENS OPEN ON A SPECIFIC DATE

Saturday 05 June

Argyllshire	Strachur House Flower & Woodland Gardens, Strachur
Caithness, Sutherland & Orkney	Amat, Ardgay
East Lothian	St Mary's Pleasance, 28 Sidegate, Haddington
Edinburgh & West Lothian	101 Greenbank Cresent, Edinburgh
Fife	Kellie Castle, Pittenweem
Glasgow & District	Kew Terrace Secret Gardens, 19 Kew Terrace, Glasgow
Perth & Kinross	Murthly Castle, Murthly

Sunday 06 June

Aberdeenshire	Kildrummy Castle Gardens, Alford
Aberdeenshire	Tillypronie, Tarland
Angus	Cortachy Castle, Cortachy
Argyllshire	Strachur House Flower & Woodland Gardens, Strachur
Caithness, Sutherland & Orkney	Amat, Ardgay
Dumfriesshire	Glenae, Amisfield
East Lothian	Inveresk Village, Musselburgh
East Lothian	Shepherd House, Inveresk
Fife	Westfield Road Gardens, Cupar
Glasgow & District	46 Corrour Road, Newlands
Kincardine & Deeside	Kincardine, Kincardine O'Neil
Lochaber & Badenoch	Aberarder, Kinlochlaggan
Lochaber & Badenoch	Ardverikie, Kinlochlaggan
Midlothian	Penicuik House, Penicuik
Ross, Cromarty, Skye & Inverness	Field House, Belladrum
Roxburghshire	Stable House, Maxton, St Boswells
Stirlingshire	Bridge of Allan Gardens, Bridge of Allan
Wigtownshire	Smithy Hill Cottage, Leswalt

Saturday 12 June

Argyllshire	Lip Na Cloiche, Ballygown, Nr Ulva Ferry
East Lothian	Dirleton Village, North Berwick
Midlothian	Cousland Smiddy and Village Gardeners, Cousland
Ross, Cromarty, Skye & Inverness	Applecross Walled Garden, Strathcarron

Sunday 13 June

Aberdeenshire	Dunecht House Gardens, Dunecht
Aberdeenshire	Esslemont, Ellon
Angus	Ethie Castle, By Arbroath
Argyllshire	Lip Na Cloiche, Ballygown, Nr Ulva Ferry
Caithness, Sutherland & Orkney	Pentland Firth Gardens, Dunnet
Dumfriesshire	Dunesslin, Dunscore
East Lothian	Dirleton Village, North Berwick
Fife	Culross Palace, Culross
Kirkcudbrightshire	Arndarroch, St John's Town of Dalry
Lochaber & Badenoch	Conaglen, Ardgour
Moray & Nairn	Carestown Steading, Deskford
Moray & Nairn	Castleview, Auchindoun
Peeblesshire	West Linton Village Gardens, West Linton
Perth & Kinross	Bradystone House, Murthly
Perth & Kinross	Explorers Garden, Pitlochry
Ross, Cromarty, Skye & Inverness	Novar, Evanton
Stirlingshire	Kilbryde Castle, Dunblane

Saturday 19 June

Argyllshire	Crarae Garden, Inveraray
Argyllshire	Seafield, 173 Marine Parade, Hunter's Quay
Ayrshire	Gardens of West Kilbride and Seamill
Edinburgh & West Lothian	9 Osborne Terrace, Edinburgh
Fife	Blebo Craigs Village Gardens, Cupar
Ross, Cromarty, Skye & Inverness	Cardon, Balnafoich

Sunday 20 June

Argyllshire	Seafield, 173 Marine Parade, Dunoon
Ayrshire	Gardens of West Kilbride and Seamill
Dunbartonshire	Kirkton Cottage, Cardross
East Lothian	Inveresk Lodge Garden, 24 Inveresk Village
East Lothian	Tyninghame House, Dunbar
Edinburgh & West Lothian	61 Fountainhall Road, Edinburgh
Fife	Blebo Craigs Village Gardens, Cupar
Fife	Scotlandwell Community Allotments, Young's Moss
Kincardine & Deeside	Ecclesgreig Castle, St Cyrus
Kirkcudbrightshire	Cally Gardens, Gatehouse of Fleet

GARDENS OPEN ON A SPECIFIC DATE

Lanarkshire	Dippoolbank Cottage, Carnwath
Lanarkshire	New Lanark Roof Garden, New Lanark Mills
Moray & Nairn	Knocknagore, Knockando
Perth & Kinross	Carig Dhubh, Bonskeid
Renfrewshire	Greenock Gardens, Greenock
Stirlingshire	King's Park Gardens, Southfield Crescent, Stirling
Wigtownshire	Castle Kennedy & Gardens, Stranraer

Thursday 24 June

Aberdeenshire	Leith Hall, Huntly
Edinburgh & West Lothian	Malleny Garden, Balerno

Friday 25 June

Ross, Cromarty, Skye & Inverness	Brackla Wood, Culbokie

Saturday 26 June

Argyllshire	The Shore Villages, by Dunoon
East Lothian	North Berwick Coastal Gardens, North Berwick
Fife	Balcarres, Colinsburgh
Perth & Kinross	Blair Castle Gardens, Blair Atholl

Sunday 27 June

Aberdeenshire	Ploughman's Hall, Old Rayne
Angus	Edzell Village, Edzell
Argyllshire	The Shore Villages, by Dunoon
Ayrshire	Largs Gardening Club
Berwickshire	Anton's Hill and Walled Garden, Leitholm
Caithness, Sutherland & Orkney	Bumblebee Cottage, Embo Street, Dornoch
Dumfriesshire	The Garth, Tynron
East Lothian	Clint, Stenton
Edinburgh & West Lothian	61 Fountainhall Road, Edinburgh
Edinburgh & West Lothian	Merchiston Cottage, 16 Colinton Road, Edinburgh
Edinburgh & West Lothian	Midmar Allotments Association, Midmar Drive, Edinburgh
Ettrick & Lauderdale	Harmony Garden, St. Mary's Road, Melrose
Ettrick & Lauderdale	Priorwood Gardens, Melrose
Fife	Earlshall Castle, Leuchars
Isle of Arran	Dougarie
Kincardine & Deeside	Crathes Castle, Banchory
Kincardine & Deeside	Finzean House, Finzean

Kirkcudbrightshire	The Waterhouse Gardens at Stockarton
Lanarkshire	Symington House, By Biggar
Midlothian	The Old Sun Inn, Newbattle
Moray & Nairn	Applegrove Primary School, Orchard Road, Forres
Perth & Kinross	Lands of Loyal Hotel, Loyal Road, Alyth, Blairgowrie
Perth & Kinross	The Cottage, 36 Main Street, Longforgan
Ross, Cromarty, Skye & Inverness	House of Aigas and Field Centre, by Beauly
Stirlingshire	Coldoch, Blairdrummond, Stirling

Tuesday 29 June

Glasgow & District	Greenbank Garden, Flenders Road, Clarkston

Thursday 01 July

Midlothian	Mount Ceres, 3 Lower Broomieknowe, Lasswade
Ross, Cromarty, Skye & Inverness	Dundonnell House, Little Loch Broom

Saturday 03 July

Aberdeenshire	Hillockhead, Glendeskry, Strathdon
Angus	6 Strathview, Forfar
Roxburghshire	Corbet Tower, Morebattle

Sunday 04 July

Aberdeenshire	Mansefield, Alford
Angus	6 Strathview, Forfar
Ayrshire	Glenhaven, Kirkmichael
Berwickshire	Netherbyres, Eyemouth
East Lothian	Gifford Village, Gifford
Ettrick & Lauderdale	Lowwood House Garden, Melrose
Fife	Craigfoodie, Dairsie
Kincardine & Deeside	Findrack, Torphins
Kirkcudbrightshire	The Old Manse, Crossmichael
Lanarkshire	Auchlochan House, New Trows Road, Lesmahagow
Perth & Kinross	Glenlyon House, Fortingall
Renfrewshire	Lochwinnoch Gardens, Lochwinnoch
Roxburghshire	West Leas, Bonchester Bridge
Stirlingshire	32 Ledcameroch Gardens, Dunblane
Stirlingshire	Dunblane Gardens, Dunblane

Wednesday 07 July

Caithness, Sutherland & Orkney	The Castle & Gardens of Mey, Mey

GARDENS OPEN ON A SPECIFIC DATE

Saturday 10 July
Ayrshire	Barr Village Gardens, By Girvan
Ross, Cromarty, Skye & Inverness	Applecross Walled Garden, Strathcarron
Roxburghshire	St Boswells Village Gardens, St Boswells

Sunday 11 July
Aberdeenshire	23 Don Street, Old Aberdeen
Aberdeenshire	Bruckhills Croft, Rothienorman
Angus	Gallery, Montrose
Ayrshire	Barr Village Gardens, By Girvan
Dumfriesshire	Woodend Cottage, Closeburn
East Lothian	Inwood, Carberry, Musselburgh
Fife	Wormistoune House, Crail
Glasgow & District	Beanscroft, Fluchter Road, Ballmore
Isle of Arran	Brodick Castle & Country Park, Brodick
Kirkcudbrightshire	Southwick House, Southwick
Perth & Kinross	Wester Cloquhat, Bridge of Cally
Renfrewshire	Sma' Shot Cottages Heritage Centre, 11/17 George Place, Paisley
Stirlingshire	Drumbroider Moss, Easter Greencraigs

Monday 12 July
Kirkcudbrightshire	Southwick House, Southwick

Tuesday 13 July
Kirkcudbrightshire	Southwick House, Southwick

Wednesday 14 July
Kirkcudbrightshire	Southwick House, Southwick

Thursday 15 July
Caithness, Sutherland & Orkney	The Castle & Gardens of Mey, Mey
Kirkcudbrightshire	Southwick House, Southwick

Friday 16 July
Kirkcudbrightshire	Southwick House, Southwick

Sunday 18 July

Ayrshire	Carnell, Hurlford
Edinburgh & West Lothian	Hunter's Tryst, 95 Oxgangs Road, Edinburgh
Fife	Scotlandwell Community Allotments, Young's Moss
Kincardine & Deeside	Douneside House, Tarland
Kirkcudbrightshire	Glensone Walled Garden, Southwick
Lanarkshire	Baitlaws, Lamington, Biggar
Midlothian	Newhall, Carlops
Perth & Kinross	Auchleeks House, Calvine
Roxburghshire	Yetholm Village Gardens, Town Yetholm

Tuesday 20 July

Ayrshire	Culzean, Maybole

Saturday 24 July

Edinburgh & West Lothian	9 Braid Farm Road, Edinburgh
Fife	Crail: Small Gardens in the Burgh

Sunday 25 July

Dumfriesshire	Berscar House, Closeburn
Edinburgh & West Lothian	9 Braid Farm Road, Edinburgh
Edinburgh & West Lothian	Annet House Garden, 143 High Street, Linlithgow
Fife	Crail: Small Gardens in the Burgh
Lanarkshire	Dippoolbank Cottage, Carnwath
Moray & Nairn	Bents Green, 10 Pilmuir Road West, Forres
Perth & Kinross	Boreland, Killin
Renfrewshire	Paisley Gardens, Paisley
Ross, Cromarty, Skye & Inverness	House of Aigas and Field Centre, By Beauly
Stirlingshire	The Tors and 33 High Station Road, Falkirk

Tuesday 27 July

Stirlingshire	The Gean House, Tullibody Road, Alloa

Wednesday 28 July

Ross, Cromarty, Skye & Inverness	House of Gruinard, Laide

Thursday 29 July

Aberdeenshire	Leith Hall, Huntly

GARDENS OPEN ON A SPECIFIC DATE

Saturday 31 July

Caithness, Sutherland & Orkney	House of Tongue, Tongue
Edinburgh & West Lothian	2 Houstoun Gardens, Uphall
Edinburgh & West Lothian	45 Northfield Crescent, Longridge
Edinburgh & West Lothian	Dr Neil's Garden, Duddingston Village
Glasgow & District	Garscube Allotments, Maryhill Road

Sunday 01 August

Ayrshire	Skeldon, Dalrymple
Edinburgh & West Lothian	2 Houstoun Gardens, Uphall
Edinburgh & West Lothian	45 Northfield Crescent, Longridge
Edinburgh & West Lothian	Dr Neil's Garden, Duddingston Village
Fife	Ladies Lake, The Scores
Kincardine & Deeside	Glenbervie House, Drumlithie
Midlothian	Mount Ceres, 3 Lower Broomieknowe, Lasswade
Midlothian	Silverburn Village, Silverburn Village
Moray & Nairn	Castleview, Auchindoun
Perth & Kinross	Mount Tabor House, Mount Tabor Road, Perth

Saturday 07 August

Perth & Kinross	Scone Palace, Perth
Ross, Cromarty, Skye & Inverness	Applecross Walled Garden, Strathcarron

Sunday 08 August

Aberdeenshire	5 Rubislaw Den North, Aberdeen
Angus	Airlie Castle, Airlie
Caithness, Sutherland & Orkney	Langwell, Berriedale
Glasgow & District	Ingadi Enhle, 9 Brooklime Drive, Stewartfield
Kirkcudbrightshire	Threave Garden, Castle Douglas
Lanarkshire	Culter Allers, Coulter
Perth & Kinross	Drummond Castle Gardens, Crieff
Perth & Kinross	Scone Palace, Perth
Stirlingshire	Thorntree, Arnprior

Thursday 12 August

Ross, Cromarty, Skye & Inverness	Dundonnell House, Little Loch Broom

Saturay 14 August

Caithness, Sutherland & Orkney	The Castle & Gardens of Mey, Mey
Fife	Falkland's Small Gardens

Sunday 15 August

Argyllshire	Glecknabae, Rothesay
Caithness, Sutherland & Orkney	Langwell, Berriedale
Fife	Falkland's Small Gardens
Fife	Scotlandwell Community Allotments, Young's Moss

Monday 16 August

Fife	Willowhill, Forgan

Tuesday 17 August

Fife	Willowhill, Forgan

Wednesday 18 August

Fife	Willowhill, Forgan

Thursday 19 August

Fife	Willowhill, Forgan

Friday 20 August

Fife	Willowhill, Forgan

Sunday 22 August

Aberdeenshire	Pitmedden Garden, Ellon
East Lothian	Johnstounburn House, Humbie
Fife	Kirklands, Saline
Glasgow & District	Greenbank Garden, Flenders Road, Clarkston
Kirkcudbrightshire	Broughton House Garden, 12 High Street, Kirkcudbright
Renfrewshire	Barshaw Park Walled Garden, Paisley

Friday 27 August

Aberdeenshire	Fyvie Castle, Fyvie

Saturday 28 August

Caithness, Sutherland & Orkney	Bighouse Lodge, By Melvich

GARDENS OPEN ON A SPECIFIC DATE

Sunday 29 August

Aberdeenshire	Castle Fraser, Sauchen
Aberdeenshire	Tillypronie, Tarland
Kirkcudbrightshire	Cally Gardens, Gatehouse of Fleet
Moray & Nairn	Gordonstoun, Duffus, Near Elgin
Ross, Cromarty, Skye & Inverness	Woodview, Highfield

Sunday 05 September

Dunbartonshire	The Hill House, Helensburgh
Edinburgh & West Lothian	61 Fountainhall Road, Edinburgh
Kirkcudbrightshire	Arndarroch, St John's Town of Dalry
Stirlingshire	Avonmuir House, Muiravonside

Sunday 12 September

Edinburgh & West Lothian	61 Fountainhall Road, Edinburgh
Fife	Tayfield, Forgan
Fife	Willowhill, Forgan

Sunday 26 September

Stirlingshire	Gargunnock House, Gargunnock

Sunday 03 October

Edinburgh & West Lothian	61 Fountainhall Road, Edinburgh
Fife	Hill of Tarvit
Peeblesshire	Dawyck Botanic Garden, Stobo

Sunday 10 October

Angus	Cortachy Castle, Cortachy

Sunday 17 October

Fife	Cambo House, Kingsbarns
Peeblesshire	Stobo Japanese Water Garden, Home Farm, Stobo

Sunday 24 October

Kincardine & Deeside	Inchmarlo House Garden, Inchmarlo

HEBRIDEAN ISLAND CRUISES

Hebridean Island Cruises has been setting the benchmark for luxury cruising since 1989. Our small, five star luxury cruise ship Ð Hebridean Princess Ð affords our guests the highest standards of luxury cruise ship accommodation, together with a level of service from an almost forgotten era.

Each all-inclusive cruise is carefully planned by our own highly experienced researchers, whose brief is to capture the cultural essence and historical significance of each port of call.

For your cruise around the Western Isles of Scotland, Hebridean Island Cruises can take you there in unrivalled style.

Garden Highlights 2010

Achamore House Gardens
Isle of Gigha

Ardgowan House Gardens
Farlie

Armadale Castle Gardens
Isle of Skye

Benmore Botanical Gardens
Holy Loch

Crarae Woodland Gardens
Loch Fyne

Inveraray Castle Gardens
Inveraray

Jura House Walled Garden
Isle of Jura

Inverewe Gardens
Loch Ewe

Torosay Castle Gardens
Isle of Mull

www.hebridean.co.uk
01756 704704

Hebridean Island Cruises
Kintail House
Carleton New Road
Skipton
BD23 2DE

HEBRIDEAN PRINCESS

4th – 6th June

ROYAL HIGHLAND CENTRE, INGLISTON, EDINBURGH

GARDENING SCOTLAND 2010

SCOTLAND'S NATIONAL
CELEBRATION OF GARDENING AND OUTDOOR LIVING

Book early and save money

The Wonderful Floral Hall

Hundreds of Exhibitors

Beautiful Show and Pallet Gardens

Gardening Advice

Free Entry for Children

Plant Village

www.gardeningscotland.com
tel: 0131 333 0965

the National Trust
for Scotland
a place for everyone

HOLIDAY accommodation

For your next holiday or short break in Scotland, the Trust's self-catering properties provide a perfect place to get away from it all. There are over 60 to choose from and many are ideally located for exploring the Trust's picturesque gardens.

Find out more and book online at www.nts.org.uk or call 0844 493 2108 to request a brochure.

The National Trust for Scotland for Places of Historic Interest or Natural Beauty is a charity registered in Scotland, Charity Number SC 007410.

INCHMARLO

Retirement living around 'a garden paradise' on Royal Deeside.

Discover the many benefits of the *'Inchmarlo way of life'*

The opening of the Inchmarlo Continuing Care Retirement Community in 1986 pioneered a new way of living in Scotland for those over 55 years old. We are proud that 250 people call Inchmarlo "home"

We offer services that will enable you to live independently in your own home and if, or when, health patterns change we provide additional services, which can be tailored to enable you to continue living in your own home longer than might be the case elsewhere. By postponing a permanent move into a Care Home, significant savings can be made of £28, 000 per year.

- 24-hour security warden • care support
- help call system • home delivery of meals
- customer liaison officer
- priority entry to Inchmarlo Care Home
- respite care • social committee and events programme • Private Function Room

1 and 2 bedroom apartments and 2 – 4 bedroom houses are available for resale throughout the year from £95,000 to £350,000. For more information please contact Phyllis Barclay on 01330 826242 or visit www.inchmarlo-retirement.co.uk

New 'Rainbow Garden'
Group Tours welcome
See listing page

Scotland's Gardens Scheme Autumn Lecture

The Albert Hall, Stirling

Tuesday 14th September 2010

10.30am – 4.00pm

3 Keynote Speakers
(to be announced)

Morning Coffee, Sandwich Lunch, Wine & Stalls

Tickets £45.00

Please contact - Lady Edmonstone

Duntreath Castle, Blanefield, Glasgow, G63 9AJ

Telephone: 01360 770215

Email: juliet@edmonstone.com

GARDENS OPEN BY ARRANGEMENT

When attending a garden that is open by arrangement, please discuss any specific requirements with the garden in advance

Aberdeenshire

5 Rubislaw Den North, Aberdeen	On request
Blairwood House, S. Deeside Rd, Blairs	21 June - 7 September
Grandhome, Aberdeen	On request
Greenridge, Craigton Road, Cults	01 July - 31 August
Gregellen House, Banchory-Devenick	10 May - 13 June
Hatton Castle, Turriff	On request
Howemill, Craigievar	On request
Lochan House, Blackchambers	On request
Mansefield, Alford	On request
Ploughman's Hall, Old Rayne	On request
Tillypronie, Tarland	On request

Angus

6 Strathview, Forfar	On request
Kirkside of Lochty, Menmuir	On request

Argyllshire

Fairwinds, 14 George St, Hunter's Quay	Spring - Autumn
Kilbrandon, Balvicar	April - October
Kinlochlaich House Gardens, Appin	Christmas and New Year
Knock Cottage, Lochgair	Mid April - Mid June

Ayrshire

Caprington Castle, Kilmarnock	February

Berwickshire

Anton's Hill and Walled Garden	On request
Lennel Bank, Coldstream	On request
Netherbyres, Eyemouth	May - September: For groups of 10 or more

Caithness, Sutherland & Orkney

Langwell, Berriedale	On request

Dumfriesshire

Peilton, Moniaive	April and May

East Lothian

Inwood, Carberry, Musselburgh	Groups Welcome
Shepherd House, Inveresk	Groups Welcome

Edinburgh & West Lothian

36 Morningside Drive, Edinburgh	12 - 20 June and 14 - 22 August
Newliston, Kirkliston	1 May - 4 June Wednesday to Saturday

Fife

Barham, Bow of Fife	24 February - 29 September - Weds
Micklegarth, Aberdour	01 May - 31 July
Teasses Gardens, Nr. Ceres	All Year: Individuals or Groups

Glasgow & District

5 Broomknowe, Balloch	On request

Kincardine & Deeside

4 Robert Street, Stonehaven	01 - 31 July
Inchmarlo House Garden, Inchmarlo	For Charities and Groups

Kirkcudbrightshire

Arndarroch, St John's Town of Dalry	July - September
Corsock House, Corsock	April - June & Autumn
Danevale Park, Crossmichael	Until 1 June
Manor Cottage, Ross	June & July
Stockarton, Kirkcudbright	May, June and July

Lanarkshire

Baitlaws, Lamington	June - August
Biggar Park, Biggar	May - July - Groups Welcome
Carmichael Mill, Hyndford Bridge	On request
The Scots Mining Company House, Leadhills	On request

Midlothian

Mount Ceres, 3 Lower Broomieknowe, Lasswade	Private Viewing for Large Groups
Newhall, Carlops	June, July and August

Moray & Nairn

Bents Green, 10 Pilmuir Rd West, Forres	15 February - 14 March
	02 May - 19 September

GARDENS OPEN BY ARRANGEMENT

Perth & Kinross

Auchleeks House, Calvine	01 June - 30 September
Carig Dhubh, Bonskeid	01 May - 31 August
Easter Meikle Fardle, Meikleour	Large Groups Welcomed
Glendoick, by Perth	For dates not listed (See main entry)
Glenlyon House, Fortingall	01 June - 30 September
Parkhead House, Parkhead Gdns, Perth	03 May - 30 September

Ross, Cromarty, Skye & Inverness

Brackla Wood, Culbokie	03 - 31 July (other dates may be possible)
Dundonnell House, Dundonnell	On request
Dunvegan Castle and Gardens, Isle of Skye	16 October - 31 December, Weekdays Only (ex Christmas & New Year)
House of Aigas and Field Centre, by Beauly	For Groups of a Minimum of 8 People
Leathad Ard, Upper Carloway	Call to arrange a suitable time (Not Sundays)
Novar, Evanton	For Groups of a Minimum of 8 People
West Lodge, Kilravock	20 May - 20 August

Roxburghshire

Stable House, Maxton	For Groups

Stirlingshire

Arndean, By Dollar	Mid May - Mid June
Culbuie, Buchlyvie	May - October Groups Welcome
Duntreath Castle, Blanefield	On request
Gargunnock House, Gargunnock	For Groups
Kilbryde Castle, Dunblane	On request
Lochdochart, Crianlarich	01 May - 30 September
Milseybank, Bridge of Allan	On request
The Linns, Sheriffmuir	01 February - 11 March and 19 May - 29 June
Thorntree, Arnprior	On request

Wigtownshire

Castle Kennedy & Gardens, Stranraer	November - January
Smithy Hill Cottage, Leswalt	On request
Woodfall Gardens, Glasserton	1 May - 31 August

GARDENS OPEN ON A REGULAR BASIS

Aberdeenshire

Kildrummy Castle Gardens, Alford	April - October For Groups
Pitmedden Garden, Ellon	01 May - 30 September

Angus

Dunninald, Montrose	01 July - 01 August
Gagie House, Duntrune	13 February – 31 May
Melgam House, Lintrathen	April - October
Pitmuies Gardens, House of Pitmuies	21 March - 31 October

Argyllshire

Ardkinglas Woodland Garden, Cairndow	All year
Ardmaddy Castle, By Oban	All year
Barguillean's "Angus Garden", Taynuilt	All year
Jura House, Ardfin	All year
Torosay Castle & Gardens, Craignure	All year
Benmore Botanic Garden, Benmore	March & October
Achnacloich, Connel, Oban	31 March - 31 October
An Cala, Ellenabeich	01 April - 31 October
Ardchattan Priory, North Connel	01 April - 31 October
Ascog Hall, Isle of Bute	Easter - October (ex. Mondays & Tuesdays)
Druimneil House, Port Appin	April - October
Kinlochlaich House Gardens, Appin	April – September Daily and October - March (Mondays to Saturdays)
Crinan Hotel Garden, Crinan	01 May - 31 August
Oakbank, Ardrishaig	01 May - 31 August
Inveraray Castle Gardens, Inveraray	16 May - 12 June

Berwickshire

Bughtrig, Near Leitholm, Coldsteam	01 June - 01 September

Caithness, Sutherland & Orkney

The Castle & Gardens of Mey, Mey	02 April - 05 April, 01 May - 29 July and 10 August - 30 September

Dunbartonshire

Glenarn, Glenarn Road, Rhu	21 March - 21 September

GARDENS OPEN ON A REGULAR BASIS

East Lothian

Shepherd House, Inveresk	09 February - 04 March (Tues & Thurs) & 01 April - 29 June (Tues & Thurs)
Inwood, Carberry, Musselburgh	01 April to 30 Sept. (Tues, Thurs & Sats)
St Mary's Pleasance, 28 Sidegate, Haddington	All Year

Edinburgh & West Lothian

'Avant - Gardens Festival' at New Hopetoun Gdns, Newton Village	May - October
Kirknewton House, Kirknewton	June - Tuesdays & Thursdays

Kirkcudbrightshire

Threave Garden, Castle Douglas	02 April - 31 October
Cally Gardens, Gatehouse of Fleet	03 April - 26 September (Ex Mondays)
Broughton House Garden, 12 High Street, Kirkcudbright	Summer Openings

Lanarkshire

New Lanark Roof Garden, New Lanark Mills, Lanark	All Year - Ex. 25 Dec & 1 Jan Groups Welcome

Lochaber & Badenoch

Ardtornish, By Lochaline, Morvern	All Year
Canna House Walled Garden, Isle of Canna	Apr – Aug Last Wed. each month and May – Aug First Saturday each month

Peeblesshire

Kailzie Gardens, Peebles	Woodland & Wild Garden: All Year Walled Garden: Mid March - 31 Oct

Perth & Kinross

Ardvorlich, Lochearnhead	01 May – 31 May
Blair Castle Gardens, Blair Atholl	05 Jan - 23 March (Tues & Sats) & Sun 14 March
Braco Castle, Braco	01 February - 31 October
Cluny House, Aberfeldy	20 February - 14 March
Scone Palace, Perth	20, 21, 26, 27 & 28 February 01 April - 31 October Nov - Mar (Grounds only open Fri)
Cluny House, Aberfeldy	15 March - 31 October
Blair Castle Gardens, Blair Atholl	28 March - 29 October
Bolfracks, Aberfeldy	01 April - 31 October

Explorers Garden, Pitlochry	01 April - 31 October
Easter Meikle Fardle, Meikleour	05 April - 31 July (Mons and Fridays)
Glendoick, by Perth	15 February - 19 February
	22 February - 26 February
	05 April - 11 June
	Daily for Garden Centre
Drummond Castle Gardens, Crieff	01 May - 31 October
Lands of Loyal Hotel, Loyal Road, Alyth	All Year Plant Sales

Ross, Cromarty, Skye & Inverness

Armadale Castle Gardens, Armadale	All Year
Attadale, Strathcarron	01 April - 31 Oct. (except Sundays)
Dunvegan Castle and Gardens, Isle of Skye	01 April - 15 October
Leckmelm Shrubbery & Arboretum, By Ullapool	01 April - 31 October
Abriachan Garden Nursery, Loch Ness Side	01 February - 30 November
An Acarsaid, Ord, Sleat, Isle of Skye	01 April - 31 October
Applecross Walled Garden, Strathcarron	01 March - 31 October
Balmeanach House, Struan, Isle of Skye	02 May - 31 October (Weds & Sats)
Duirinish Lodge & Gardens, Kyle of Lochalsh	31 May - 05 June
Leathad Ard, Upper Carloway, Isle of Lewis	05 June - 28 Aug. (Tues, Thurs & Sats)
Coiltie Garden, Divach, Drumnadrochit	18 June - 18 July

Roxburghshire

Monteviot, Jedburgh	01 April - 31 October
Floors Castle, Kelso	02 April - 05 April & 01 May - 31 Oct

Stirlingshire

Gargunnock House, Gargunnock	01 February - 11 March (Weds & Suns)
	Mid April - Mid June (Wednesdays)
	15 May - 13 June (Sats & Suns)
	01 Sept. - 31 Oct. (Wednesdays)

Wigtownshire

Ardwell House Gardens, Ardwell, Stranraer	01 April - 30 September
Castle Kennedy & Gardens, Stranraer	February - March (Saturdays & Sundays)
	01 April – 30 October
Logan House Gardens, Port Logan	02 February – 31 August
	03 May – 31 August

Snowdrop Openings

In early springtime properties with snowdrops are extremely popular. The following snowdrop openings will be taking place:

Blairquhan, Ayrshire © Andrea Jones

Kirkdale, Wigtownshire © Andrea Jones

Once again VisitScotland will be including the "Snowdrop Festival" in their 2010 "Winter White" campaign. This campaign has been hugely successful in recent years and the "Snowdrop Festival" will do much to boost visitor numbers for participating properties and these include most opening for SGS.

PLANT SALES

Glasgow & District

Glasgow Botanic Gardens,	Saturday 12 June	11:00am - 4:00pm
Great Western Road, Glasgow		

Dunbartonshire

The Hill House Plant Sale,	Sunday 05 September	11:00am - 4:00pm
Helensburgh		

Renfrewshire

St Fillan's Episcopal Church,	Saturday 18 September	10:00am - 1:00pm
Moss Road, Kilmacolm		

Stirlingshire

Gargunnock House,	Sunday 26 September	2:00pm - 5:00pm
Gargunnock		

Fife

Hill of Tarvit Annual	Sunday 03 October	10:30am - 4:00pm
SGS Plant Sale and Fair, Cupar		

East Lothian/Midlothian

SGS Plant Sale	Saturday 09 October	9:30am - 1:30pm
Oxenfoord Mains, Near Pathhead		

PLANT DONATIONS

Donations of plants for each of the Plant Sales are always welcome. Please contact the Local Organisers or those responsible for Plant Sales as indicated in the appropriate District entries later in this book.

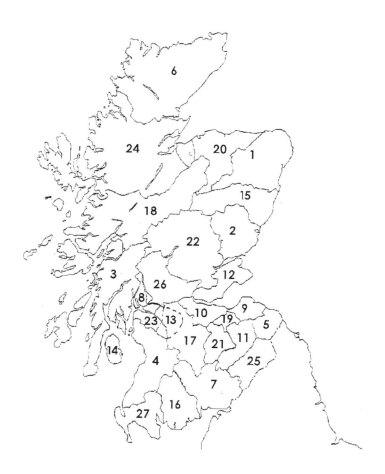

1. Aberdeenshire
2. Angus
3. Argyllshire
4. Ayrshire
5. Berwickshire
6. Caithness, Sutherland
   & Orkney
7. Dumfriesshire
8. Dunbartonshire
9. East Lothian

10. Edinburgh &
    West Lothian
11. Ettrick & Lauderdale
12. Fife
13. Glasgow & District
14. Isle of Arran
15. Kincardine & Deeside
16. Kircudbrightshire
17. Lanarkshire
18. Lochaber & Badenoch

19. Midlothian
20. Moray & Nairn
21. Peeblesshire
22. Perth & Kinross
23. Renfrewshire
24. Ross, Cromarty,
    Skye & Inverness
25. Roxburghshire
26. Stirlingshire
27. Wigtownshire

General Information

Maps: the maps show the *approximate* locations of gardens. Directions can be found in the garden descriptions

Houses: are not open unless specifically stated; where the house or part of the house is shown, an additional charge is usually made.

Lavatories: Private gardens do not normally have outside lavatories. For security reasons owners have been advised not to admit visitors into their houses.

Professional Photographers: No photographs taken in a garden may be used for sale or reproduction without the prior permission of the garden owner.

NEW
Garden opening this year for the first time or re-opening after a break of six years or more.

Wheelchair access to at least the main features of the garden.

B&B
Accommodation and breakfast available on request.

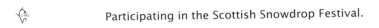
Dogs on a lead welcomed. PLEASE NOTE: WHERE NO DOG SYMBOL IS SHOWN DOGS, EXCEPT GUIDE DOGS, ARE NOT ALLOWED.

NCCPG
Gardens that hold an NCCPG National Plant Collection.

Plant stall.

Teas normally available at a charge. When there are cream or special teas this is stated after the symbol.

Participating in the Scottish Snowdrop Festival.

Children are always welcome but must be accompanied by an adult. Children's activities are often available at openings.

Aberdeenshire

'Gardens of Scotland' 2010 is sponsored by **Rensburg Sheppards Investment Management**

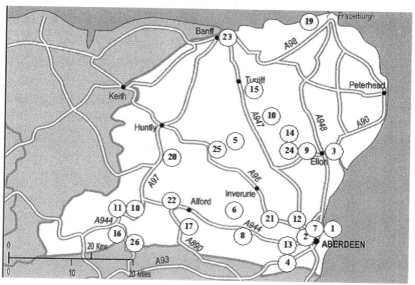

District Organiser:	**Mrs V Walters** Tillychetly, Alford AB33 8HQ
Area Organisers:	**Mrs H. Gibson** 6 The Chanonry, Old Aberdeen AB24 1RP
	Mrs C Hamilton Ardneidly, Monymusk, Inverurie AB51 7HX
	Mrs F G Lawson Asloun, Alford AB33 8NR
	Mrs A Robertson Drumblade House, Huntly AB54 6ER
	Mrs F M K Tuck Stable Cottage, Allargue, Gorgarff AB36 8YP
Treasurer:	**Mr J Ludlow** St. Nicholas House, Banchory AB31 5YT

Gardens Open On a Specific Date

Auchmacoy, Ellon	Sunday 18 April	1:30pm - 4:00pm
Haddo House, Methlick	Sunday 16 May	10:00am - 5:00pm
Cruickshank Botanic Gardens, Aberdeen	Wednesday 19 May	6:30pm - 8:30pm
Leith Hall, Huntly	Thursday 27 May	7:00pm
Kildrummy Castle Gardens, Alford	Sunday 06 June	10:00am - 5:00am
Tillypronie, Tarland	Sunday 06 June	2:00pm - 5:00pm
Dunecht House Gardens, Dunecht	Sunday 13 June	1:00pm - 5:00pm
Esslemont, Ellon	Sunday 13 June	1:00pm - 4:30pm
Leith Hall, Huntly	Thursday 24 June	7:00pm
Ploughman's Hall, Old Rayne	Sunday 27 June	1:30pm - 6:00pm
Hillockhead, Glendeskry	Saturday 03 July	2:00pm - 5:00pm

ABERDEENSHIRE

Mansefield, Alford	Sunday 04 July	2:00pm - 5:00pm
23 Don Street, Old Aberdeen	Sunday 11 July	1:30pm - 6:00pm
Bruckhills Croft, Rothienorman	Sunday 11 July	12:00am - 5:00pm
Leith Hall, Huntly	Thursday 29 July	7:00pm
5 Rubislaw Den North, Aberdeen	Sunday 08 August	2:00pm - 5:00pm
Pitmedden Garden, Ellon	Sunday 22 August	10:00am - 5:30pm
Fyvie Castle, Fyvie, Turriff	Friday 27 August	7:00pm - 10:00pm
Castle Fraser, Sauchen	Sunday 29 August	1:00pm - 4:30pm
Tillypronie, Tarland	Sunday 29 August	2:00pm - 5:00pm

Gardens Open By Arrangement

When organising a visit to a garden open by arrangement, please enquire if there are facilities and catering available

5 Rubislaw Den North, Aberdeen	On request	Tel: 01224 317345
Blairwood House, Blairs	21 June - 07 Sept.	Tel: 01224 868301
Grandhome, Aberdeen	On request	Tel: 01224 722202
Greenridge, Cults	01 July - 31 August	Tel: 01224 860200 or Fax 01224 860210
Gregellen House, Banchory-Devenick	10 May - 13 June	Tel: 01224 861090
Hatton Castle, Turriff	On request	Tel: 01888 562279
Howemill, Craigievar	On request	Tel: 01975 581278
Lochan House, Blackchambers	On request	Tel: 01224 791753
Mansefield, Alford	On request	Tel: 019755 63086
Ploughman's Hall, Old Rayne	On request	Tel: 01464 851253
Tillypronie, Tarland	On request	Tel: 01339 881529

Gardens Open Regularly

Kildrummy Castle Gardens, Alford	April – Oct. (groups)	10:00am - 5:00pm
Pitmedden Garden, Ellon	01 May - 30 Sept.	10:00am - 5:30pm

1. 23 DON STREET Old Aberdeen AB24 1UH

Miss M and Mr G Mackechnie

Atmospheric walled garden in historic Old Aberdeen. Wide range of rare and unusual plants and old-fashioned scented roses.

Route: Park at St. Machar Cathedral, short walk down Chanonry to Don Street, turn right. City plan ref: P7.

Admission: £4.00 Concessions £3.50

SUNDAY 11 JULY 1:30pm - 6:00pm

Cat Protection receives 40%, the net remaining to SGS Beneficiaries.

✿ ♿ ☕ Homemade

2. 5 RUBISLAW DEN NORTH Aberdeen AB15 4AL

Dr. Tom Smith

Featured in the RHS magazine, this is a beautiful and complex garden of sculptural design with many rare and exotic plants not usually found in north-east Scotland. It reflects the owner's passion for form, science and philosophy, as well as for plants.

Route: Turn North off Queen's Road into Forest Road; Rubislaw Den North is second on left.

Admission: £7.00

SUNDAY 08 AUGUST 2:00pm - 5:00pm
ALSO BY ARRANGEMENT ON REQUEST

Telephone: 01224 317345

St James' Church Roof Fund receives 40%, the net remaining to SGS Beneficiaries.

☕ Available at Gordon Highlanders Museum in Nearby Viewfield Road

3. AUCHMACOY Ellon AB41 8RB

Mr and Mrs Charles Buchan

Auchmacoy House's attractive policies feature spectacular displays of thousands of daffodils.

Route: A90 from Aberdeen. Turn right to Auchmacoy/Collieston.

Admission: £3.00 Concessions £2.00 Children under 12 free

SUNDAY 18 APRIL 1:30pm - 4:00pm

Royal National Mission to Deep Sea Fishermen receives 40%, the net remaining to SGS Beneficiaries.

Tombola, Produce and Homemade Jam for Sale   ☕ Homemade

4. BLAIRWOOD HOUSE South Deeside Road, Blairs AB12 5YQ

Ilse Elders

A ten year old garden of approx. ½ acre. It has been designed to sit easily in the surrounding countryside and to provide colour over a long season, without requiring too much maintenance. Herbaceous borders, some new ones planted up last year. Small beautiful herb garden packed with well over a hundred medicinal and culinary herbs, pebble mosaics and sunken patio area. One garden 'room' has been grown on a landfill site.

Route: Blairs, on the B9077, 5 mins. by car from Bridge of Dee, Aberdeen. Very close to Blairs Museum.

Admission: £3.00

BY ARRANGEMENT 21 JUNE - 7 SEPTEMBER

Telephone: 01224 868301

Email Address: elders@talk21.com

Elvanfoot Trust receives 40%, the net remaining to SGS Beneficiaries.

🐕 ☕ Light Refreshments   Available in Several Local Hotels

ABERDEENSHIRE

5. BRUCKHILLS CROFT Rothienorman, Inverurie AB51 8YB

Mrs Helen Rushton

A slate built croft-house is surrounded by an informal country cottage garden. There is an orchard, a productive fruit and vegetable patch, herbaceous borders and rabbit proof mixed planting areas. A new walk around the wildflower meadow and wildlife pond opened in 2009. The more unusual plants include Cardiocrinum Giganteum, Onopordium Acanthium and Cardoon. Produce from the garden will be available to purchase in the form of homemade jams and preserves.

Route: From Rothienorman take the B9001 north, just after Badenscoth Nursing Home (approx 2.5 miles) turn left, after 1 mile you will be directed into a field behind the Croft

Admission: £3.00 Concessions £2.50 Children Free

SUNDAY 11 JULY 12:00pm - 5:00pm

Telephone: 01651 821596 Email Address: helenrushton1@aol.com

Advocacy Service Aberdeen receives 40%, the net remaining to SGS Beneficiaries.

⌘ Homebakes and Homemade Jams and Preserves   ☕ Homemade

6. CASTLE FRASER Sauchen, Inverurie AB51 7LD

The National Trust for Scotland

Castle Fraser is one of the most spectacular of the Castles of Mar built between 1575 and 1635 with designed landscape and parkland, the work of Thomas White in 1794. Includes exciting new garden developments. A traditional walled garden including trees, shrubs and new herbaceous borders. Also a medicinal and culinary border, organically grown fruit and vegetables. A newly constructed woodland garden with adventure playground.

Route: Near Kemnay, off A944

Admission: £3.00

SUNDAY 29 AUGUST 1:00pm - 4:30pm

Web Site: www.nts.org.uk

Telephone: 0844 493 2164 Email Address: castlefraser@nts.org.uk

Donation to SGS Beneficiaries

♿ Live Music, Childrens Entertainment, Raffle   ☕ Light Refreshments

7. CRUICKSHANK BOTANIC GARDENS 23 St. Machar Drive, Aberdeen AB24 3UU

Cruickshank Botanic Garden Trust/Aberdeen University

An evening tour with Head Gardener, Richard Walker. The garden is named after a bequest by Miss Anne Cruickshank. It is funded partly by the University of Aberdeen and partly by the Cruickshank Botanic Garden Trust and supported by an active Friends group. It has an area of 4 hectares located less than 2 kilometres from the North Sea. Comprises: a sunken garden with alpine lawn, a rock garden built in the 1960s complete with waterfalls and pond system, a long unbroken herbaceous border, a formal rose garden with drystone walling, and an arboretum. Has a large collection of flowering bulbs and rhododendrons, and many unusual shrubs and trees including 2 mature Camperdown Elms. It is sometimes known as The Secret Garden of Old Aberdeen.

Route: Come down St Machar Drive over the mini-roundabout, at the next set of traffic lights turn left. The Garden entrance lies within the Chanonry. Park by St Machar's Cathedral, at end of Chanonry.

Admission: £4.00 includes light refreshments

WEDNESDAY 19 MAY 6:30pm - 8:30pm

Web Site: http://www.abdn.ac.uk/biologicalsci/pss/gardens.sh

Cruickshank Botanic Garden receives 40%, the net remaining to SGS Beneficiaries.

 ♿ ☕ Light Refreshments

8. DUNECHT HOUSE GARDENS Dunecht AB32 7AW

The Hon Charles A Pearson

A magnificent copper beech avenue leads to Dunecht House built by John and William Smith with a Romanesque addition in 1877 by G Edmund Street. Highlights include rhododendrons, azaleas and a wild garden.

Route: Dunecht 1 mile, routes: A944 and B977.

Admission: £3.00 Concessions £2.50

SUNDAY 13 JUNE 1:00pm - 5:00pm

Riding for the Disabled, Gordon District, receives 40%, the net remaining to SGS Beneficiaries.

🐕 ☕ Proceeds in Aid of Dunecht Village Hall

9. ESSLEMONT Ellon AB41 8PA

Mr and Mrs Wolrige Gordon of Esslemont

Victorian house set in wooded policies above River Ythan. Roses and shrubs in garden with double yew hedges (17th and 18th centuries).

Route: A920 from Ellon. On Pitmedden/Oldmeldrum Road.

Admission: £3.00 Concessions £2.00

SUNDAY 13 JUNE 1:00pm - 4:30pm

Boys Brigade, Ellon, receives 40%, the net remaining to SGS Beneficiaries.

🐕 ☕ Homemade Light Refreshments

10. FYVIE CASTLE Fyvie, Turriff AB53 8JS

The National Trust for Scotland

The 18th century walled garden has been developed as a garden of Scottish fruits and vegetables. There is also the American Garden, Rhymer's Haugh Woodland Garden, Loch and parkland to visit.

An evening guided walk (meeting in the Walled Garden) round the Gardens with the Head Gardener. Learn about the collection of Scottish fruits and their cultivation, and the exciting projects for the future.

BOOKING ESSENTIAL - Contact 01651 891363 or email gthomson@nts.org.uk for more information.

The evening will end with a 3 course dinner and a glass of wine in the Victorian Tea Room which will include produce from the Kitchen garden.

Route: Off A947 8m SE of Turriff and 25m NW of Aberdeen.

ABERDEENSHIRE

Admission: £25.00 - Includes Guided Walk with 3 Course Dinner and Glass of Wine
FRIDAY 27 AUGUST 7:00pm - 10:00pm
Web Site: www.nts.org.uk
Telephone: 01651 891363 or 01651 891266 Email Address: gthomson@nts.org.uk
Donation to SGS Beneficiaries
✿ Daily Plant and Produce Stand ♿ 🐕 ☕ Castle Tea Room (Same Opening Hours as Castle)

11. GRANDHOME Aberdeen AB22 8AR

Mr and Mrs D R Paton
18th century walled garden, incorporating rose garden; policies with daffodils, rhododendrons, azaleas, mature trees and shrubs. At its best in April through June, and in October.
Route: From north end of North Anderson Drive, continue on A90 over Persley Bridge, turning left at Tesco roundabout. 1¾miles on left.
Admission: £4.00 Concessions £2.50
BY ARRANGEMENT ON REQUEST
Telephone: 01224 722202 Email Address: davidpaton@btconnect.com
Children's 1st receives 40%, the net remaining to SGS Beneficiaries.
♿ Fruit and Vegetables Available at Times   ☕ If Requested in Advance

12. GREENRIDGE Craigton Road, Cults AB15 9PS

BP Exploration
Large secluded garden surrounding 1840 Archibald Simpson house. For many years winner of Britain in Bloom 'Best Hidden Garden'. Mature specimen trees and shrubs. Sloping walled rose garden and terraces. Kitchen garden.
Route: Directions with booking.
Admission: £3.50
BY ARRANGEMENT 01 JULY - 31 AUGUST
Telephone: 01224 860200 or Fax 01224 860210
Cancer Research Scotland receives 40%, the net remaining to SGS Beneficiaries.
♿ Partly 🐕 ☕

13. GREGELLEN HOUSE Banchory-Devenick AB12 5XP

Mr & Mrs W McGregor
Former Victorian Manse set in 1½ acres of garden. Herbaceous borders, lawns and rockeries with a wide and varied range of interesting plants which include azaleas, meconopsis, peonies and rhododendrons, making a colourful display.
Route: Approximately 1¾ miles from Bridge of Dee off the B9077 South Deeside Road
Admission: £4.00
BY ARRANGEMENT 10 MAY - 13 JUNE 2:00pm - 5:00pm

Telephone: 01224 861090 Email Address: wahmcgregor@aol.com
Marie Curie Cancer Care receives 40%, the net remaining to SGS Beneficiaries.
♿ 🐕 ☙ Homemade

14. HADDO HOUSE Methlick, Ellon AB41 7EQ

The National Trust for Scotland
Terrace garden with geometric rosebeds and fountain, a lavish herbaceous border and
secluded glades and knolls. A magnificent avenue of lime trees leads to adjacent
Haddo country park with its lakes, monuments, walks and wildlife.
Guided Garden Walks at 12:00pm, 2:00pm and 4:00pm - £4.00
Route: Off B999 near Tarves, at 'Raxton' crossroads, 19m north of Aberdeen, 4m north
of Pitmedden and 10m NW of Ellon. Cycle: 1m from NCN 1 Bus: Stagecoach Bluebird
from Aberdeen bus station (01224) 212666, c. 4m walk
Admission: Charge for Guided Walks Only
SUNDAY 16 MAY 10:00am - 5:00pm
Web Site: www.nts.org.uk
Telephone: 0844 493 2179 Email Address: haddo@nts.org.uk
Donation to SGS Beneficiaries
♺ ♿ Limited   🐕 ☙ Cream Light Refreshments

15. HATTON CASTLE Turriff AB53 8ED

Mr and Mrs James Duff
Two acre walled garden featuring mixed borders and shrub roses with yew and box
hedges and alleys of pleached hornbeam. Kitchen garden and fan trained fruit trees.
Lake and woodland walks.
Route: On A947, 2 miles south of Turriff.
Admission: £4.50 Children Free
BY ARRANGEMENT ON REQUEST
Telephone: 01888 562279
Email Address: jjdgardens@btinternet.com
Juvenile Diabetes Research Foundation receives 40%, the net remaining to SGS Beneficiaries.
♿ With Help   ☙ Teas and Lunch Parties by Arrangement

16. HILLOCKHEAD Glendeskry, Strathdon AB36 8XL

Stephen Campbell and Sue Macintosh
This garden is set against the stunning backdrop of Morven, at an altitude of 1300 feet,
where wilderness meets cultivation. Wildflower areas, herbaceous borders, and organic
fruit and vegetables are punctuated by numerous sit-ooteries and quiet corners, and
probably the world's smallest grouse-moor!
Route: From Deeside, head north on A97 for 9 miles, turn sharp left at crossroads
shortly after Boultinstone. After ½ mile take first left signposted 'Ardgeith Fishings'.
Hillockhead is 2 miles along road on right. Grass verge parking on single track road.

ABERDEENSHIRE

<u>Admission:</u> £3.00 Concessions £2.50

SATURDAY 03 JULY 2:00pm - 5:00pm

RNLI receives 40%, the net remaining to SGS Beneficiaries.

✿ ⠿ With Help - No Disabled Toilets 🐕 ☕ Homemade

17. HOWEMILL Craigievar AB33 8JD

Mr D Atkinson

Increasingly mature garden with a wide range of unusual shrubs, herbaceous plants and trees. Long mixed borders, wild areas and more intimate spaces.

<u>Route:</u> From Alford take A980 Alford/Lumphanan road

<u>Admission:</u> £4.00 Children Under 12 Free

BY ARRANGEMENT ON REQUEST

Telephone: 01975 581278

Email Address: davidmatkinson@tiscali.co.uk

Cancer Relief Macmillan Fund receives 40%, the net remaining to SGS Beneficiaries.

18. KILDRUMMY CASTLE GARDENS Alford AB33 8RA

Kildrummy Garden Trust

April shows the gold of the lysichitons in the water garden and the small bulbs naturalised beside the copy of the 14th century Brig o' Balgownie. Rhododendrons and azaleas from April (frost permitting). September/October brings colchicums and brilliant colour with acers, fothergillas and viburnums.

<u>Route:</u> On A97, 10 miles from Alford, 17 miles from Huntly. Car park free inside hotel main entrance. Coaches park up at hotel delivery entrance.

<u>Admission:</u> £4.00 Senior Citizens £3.00 Children Free

SUNDAY 06 JUNE 10:00am - 5:00pm

APRIL - OCTOBER FOR GROUPS 10:00am - 5:00pm

Web Site: www.kildrummy-castle-gardens.co.uk

Telephone: 01975 571203

Aberdeen Branch Multiple Sclerosis Society receives 40%, the net remaining to SGS Beneficiaries.

✿ ⠿ With Help Play Area ☕

19. LEITH HALL Huntly AB54 4NQ

The National Trust for Scotland

A Series of Evening Guided Tours with the Head Gardener Toby Loveday.

This attractive old country house, the earliest part of which dates from 1650, was the home of the Leith and Leith-Hay families for more than three centuries. The west garden was made by Mr and The Hon Mrs Charles Leith-Hay around the beginning of the twentieth century. The property was given to the Trust in 1945. The rock garden has been enhanced by the Scottish Rock Garden Club. In summer the magnificent zigzag herbaceous border and serpentine catmint border provide a dazzling display.

<u>Route:</u> On B9002 1 mile west of Kennethmont. **Meet at the car park 7pm**

Admission: £5.00 (Includes Tea and Cake) Booking Essential
THURSDAY 27 MAY 7:00pm
THURSDAY 24 JUNE 7:00pm
THURSDAY 29 JULY 7:00pm
Web Site: www.nts.org.uk
Telephone: 01464 831148 Email Address: tloveday@nts.org.uk
Donation to SGS Beneficiaries
♿ ☕

20. LOCHAN HOUSE Blackchambers, Nr. Blackburn AB32 7BU

Mrs M Jones
Maturing country garden of one and a half acres. Includes ponds and waterfowl collection, herbaceous plantings, formal courtyard and ornamental grass garden. Adjoining new native woodland with walks and fine views to Bennachie.
Route: A96, 2 miles south of Kinellar roundabout, follow signs for Millbuie.
Admission: £4.00
BY ARRANGEMENT ON REQUEST
Telephone: 01224 791753 Email Address: mo@moragjones.demon.co.uk
All proceeds to SGS Beneficiaries
❀ ☕ Homemade

21. MANSEFIELD Alford AB33 8NL

Diane and Derek Neilson
Developing three-acre country garden. Woodland and burnside walks together with a more formal walled garden
Route: On A980 Alford/Lumphanan road, adjacent to Alford West Church
Admission: £4.00 Concessions £3.00 Children Under 12 Free
SUNDAY 04 JULY 2:00pm - 5:00pm
ALSO BY ARRANGEMENT ON REQUEST
Telephone: 019755 63086
Email Address: manse.field@virgin.net
Parkinson's Disease Society receives 40%, the net remaining to SGS Beneficiaries.
♿ With Help ☕ Homemade

22. PITMEDDEN GARDEN Ellon AB41 7PD

The National Trust for Scotland
Garden created by Sir Alexander Seton in 1675. Elaborate floral designs in parterres of box edging, inspired by the garden at the Palace of Holyroodhouse, have been re-created by the Trust. Fountains and sundials make fine centrepieces to the garden, filled in summer with 40,000 annual flowers. Also herb garden, herbaceous borders, trained fruit, plant sales, museum of farming life, visitor centre, nature hut, woodland walk and wildlife garden.

ABERDEENSHIRE

Behind the scenes tours at 1:30pm and 3:00pm
Route: On A920, 1 mile west of Pitmedden village and 14 miles north of Aberdeen.
Admission: £5.50, Concessions £4.50, Family £15.00, NTS/NT Members Free
SUNDAY 22 AUGUST 10:00am - 5:30pm
01 MAY - 30 SEPTEMBER DAILY 10:00am - 5:30pm (LAST ADMISSION 5:00pm)
Web Site: www.nts.org.uk
Telephone: 0844 493 2177 Email Address: sburgess@nts.org.uk
Donation to SGS Beneficiaries
✿ ♿ 🐕 Not in the Walled Garden ☕ Light Refreshments Tearoom

23. PLOUGHMAN'S HALL Old Rayne AB52 6SD
Mr and Mrs A Gardner
One acre garden. Rock, herbaceous, kitchen, herb and woodland gardens.
Route: Off A96, 9 miles north of Inverurie. Turn off at Pitmachie.
Admission: £3.00
SUNDAY 27 JUNE 1:30pm - 6:00pm
ALSO BY ARRANGEMENT ON REQUEST
Telephone: 01464 851253 Email Address: tony@ploughmanshall.co.uk
Wycliffe Bible Translators receives 40%, the net remaining to SGS Beneficiaries.
✿ ♿ ☕ Light Refreshments Homemade Biscuits and Fresh Lemonade

24. TILLYPRONIE Tarland AB34 4XX
The Hon Philip Astor
Late Victorian house for which Queen Victoria laid a foundation stone. Herbaceous borders, terraced garden, heather beds, water garden and new rockery. New Golden Jubilee garden still being laid out. Shrubs and ornamental trees, including pinetum with rare specimens. Fruit garden and greenhouses. Superb views. In June there is a wonderful show of azaleas and spring heathers.
Route: Off A97 between Ballater and Strathdon.
Admission: £5.00 Children £2.00
SUNDAY 06 JUNE 2:00pm - 5:00pm
SUNDAY 29 AUGUST 2:00pm - 5:00pm
ALSO BY ARRANGEMENT ON REQUEST
Telephone: 01339 881529
All proceeds to SGS Beneficiaries
✿ June Opening Only ♿ 🐕 ☕ June Opening: Homemade Teas, August Opening: Cream Teas

Angus

'Gardens of Scotland' 2010 is sponsored by **Rensburg Sheppards Investment Management**

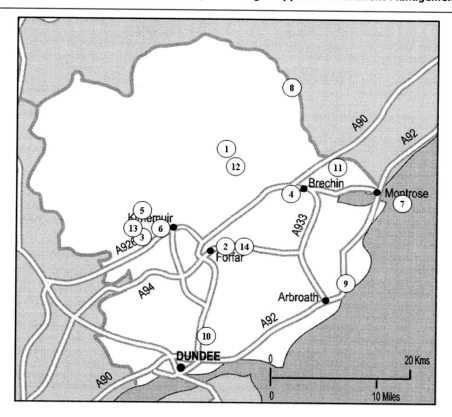

District Organiser: **Mrs T Dobson** Logie House, Kirriemuir DD8

Area Organisers: **Miss R Dundas** Caddam, Kinnordy, Kirriemuir DD8 4LP

Mrs J Henderson Mains of Panmuir, By Carnoustie DD7

Mrs R Porter West Scryne, By Carnoustie DD7 6LL

Mrs Nici Rymer Nether Finlarg, Forfar DD8 1XQ

Mrs C Smoor Gagie House, Tealing DD4 0PR

Mrs G Stewart Ramsay Street, Edzell, Brechin DD9 7TT

Mrs A Stormonth Darling Lednathie, Glen Prosen, Kirriemuir DD8

Treasurer: **Col R H B Learoyd** Wedderburn, 9b The Glebe, Edzell DD9 7SZ

ANGUS

Gardens Open On a Specific Date

3 Balfour Cottages, Menmuir	Sunday 25 April	1:00pm - 4:00pm
Brechin Castle, Brechin	Sunday 09 May	2:00pm - 5:00pm
Dunninald, Montrose	Sunday 16 May	2:00pm - 5:00pm
Dalfruin, Kirriemuir	Sunday 23 May	2:00pm - 5:00pm
Cortachy Castle, Cortachy	Sunday 06 June	2:00pm - 6:00pm
Ethie Castle, By Arbroath	Sunday 13 June	2:00pm - 5:00pm
Edzell Village, Edzell	Sunday 27 June	2:00pm - 5:00pm
6 Strathview, Forfar	Saturday 03 July	10:00am - 5:00pm
6 Strathview, Forfar	Sunday 04 July	10:00am - 5:00pm
Gallery, Montrose	Sunday 11 July	2:00pm - 5:00pm
Airlie Castle, By Kirriemuir	Sunday 08 August	2:00pm - 6:00pm
Cortachy Castle, Cortachy	Sunday 10 October	2:00pm - 5:00pm

Gardens Open By Arrangement
When organising a visit to a garden open by arrangement, please enquire if there are facilities and catering available

6 Strathview, Forfar	On request	Tel: 01307 469090
Kirkside of Lochty, Menmuir	On request	Tel: 01356 660431

Gardens Open Regularly

Gagie House, Duntrune	13 Feb. - 14 March	10:00am - 5:00pm
Pitmuies Gardens, Guthrie	01 - 14 March	10:00am - 5:00pm
	21 March - 31 Oct.	10:00am - 5:00pm
Gagie House, Duntrune	15 March - 31 May	10:00am - 5:00pm
Melgam House, Lintrathen	April - October	9:00am - 9:00pm
Dunninald, Montrose	01 July - 01 August	12:30pm - 5:00pm

1. 3 BALFOUR COTTAGES Menmuir DD9 7RN

Dr Alison Goldie and Mark A Hutson

Small cottage garden with rare and unusual plants. It comprises various 'rooms', containing a myriad of plants from potted herbs, spring bulbs and alpines in a raised bed, to a 'jungle' with a range of bamboos. Many other interesting plants include Primula, Hosta, Meconopsis, Fritillaria, Trillium, Allium, a large display of bonsai and an Auricula theatre.

Route: Leave the A90 two miles south of Brechin and take the road to Menmuir (3.5miles). At the T-junction turn right and it is in the first group of cottages on your left (175yards).

Admission: £3.00 Children Free

SUNDAY 25 APRIL 1:00pm - 4:00pm

Web Site: www.angusplants.co.uk

Telephone: 01356 660280
Email Address: alisongoldie@btinternet.com
R.N.L.I. receives 40%, the net remaining to SGS Beneficiaries.
✿ 🐕 ☕ Homemade

2. 6 STRATHVIEW Forfar DD8 1XA NEW

Martin & Eleanor Gledhill
Over 1½ acres, overlooking the Valley of Strathmore. Mainly herbaceous beds with ponds and willow hedge. Grass tennis court, small woodland and meadow. Sunken drinking hole, small orchard, Classical garden with a small Knot garden.
Route: Take the southmost entrance to Forfar from the A90. Turn right at the 'Welcome to Forfar' sign.
Admission: £4.00
SATURDAY 03 JULY 10:00am - 5:00pm
SUNDAY 04 JULY 10:00am - 5:00pm
ALSO BY ARRANGEMENT ON REQUEST
Telephone: 01307 469090 Email Address: craichie@aol.com
Christina Noble Children's Foundation receives 40%, the net remaining to SGS Beneficiaries.
✿ ☕ Homemade

3. AIRLIE CASTLE Airlie, By Kirriemuir DD8 5NG NEW

Lord and Lady Ogilvy
An 18th century walled garden with topiary and herbaceous borders, laburnum arch and river walk.
Route: Take B951 out of Kirriemuir signposted Glen Isla. Pass Kinnordy Loch and then take left turn off signposted Airlie and Alyth. Keep on this road for 3.5 miles, pass Mains of Airlie farm on left hand side and entrance to castle is just beyond on right hand side.
Admission: £4.00
SUNDAY 08 AUGUST 2:00pm - 6:00pm
Web Site: www.airlieestates.com
Email Address: office@airlieestates.com
Maggie's Centre receives 40%, the net remaining to SGS Beneficiaries.
🐕 Stalls etc.   ☕ Homemade

4. BRECHIN CASTLE Brechin DD9 6SG

The Earl and Countess of Dalhousie
Ancient fortress of Scottish kings on cliff overlooking River South Esk. Rebuilt by Alexander Edward - completed in 1711. Extensive walled garden 300 yards from Castle with ancient and new plantings and mown lawn approach. Rhododendrons, azaleas, bulbs, interesting trees, wild garden.

ANGUS

Route: A90, Brechin 1 mile
Admission: £4.00 OAPs £3.00 Children under 12 free
SUNDAY 09 MAY 2:00pm - 5:00pm
Web Site: www.dalhousieestates.co.uk
Telephone: 01356 624566
Email Address: mandyferries@dalhousieestates.co.uk
Dalhousie Day Centre receives 20%, Unicorn Preservation Society receives 20%, the net remaining to SGS Beneficiaries.
🐕 ☕

5. CORTACHY CASTLE Cortachy, By Kirriemuir DD8 4LX

The Earl and Countess of Airlie
16th century castellated house. Additions in 1872 by David Bryce. Spring garden and wild pond garden with a mass of azaleas, primroses and rhododendrons. Garden of fine American species trees and river walk along South Esk.
Spectacular autumn colours.
Castle is not open for October opening.
Route: B955 Kirriemuir 5 miles.
Admission: 06 June: £5.00. 10 October: £4.00
SUNDAY 06 JUNE 2:00pm - 6:00pm
SUNDAY 10 OCTOBER 2:00pm - 5:00pm
Web Site: www.airlieestates.com
Telephone: 01575 570108
Email Address: office@airlieestates.com
Charity to be announced and will receives 40%, the net remaining to SGS Beneficiaries.
❀ Both Openings 🐕 Both Openings The Macallan Fine Oak Highland Single Malt Whisky Promotion, Pipe Band, Tombola and Ice Cream on 6 June ☕ Homemade on 6 June only and can be taken in the Castle Ballroom & Dining Room

6. DALFRUIN Kirktonhill Road, Kirriemuir DD8 4HU

Mr and Mrs James A Welsh
A well-stocked mature garden of almost one-third of an acre situated at end of cul-de-sac. Unusual plants, dactylorhiza, tree peonies, meconopsis, trilliums. Stream added in autumn 2000 (Common newts first seen autumn 2003, also frogs galore!).
Route: From centre of Kirriemuir turn left up Roods (immediately after the pedestrian crossing); Kirktonhill Road is on left near top of hill just before the school 20mph zone. Please park on Roods or at St Mary's Church. Disabled parking only in Kirktonhill Road.
Admission: £3.00 Accompanied Children Free
SUNDAY 23 MAY 2:00pm - 5:00pm
St Mary's Episcopal Church receives 40%, the net remaining to SGS Beneficiaries.
❀ Should Include Trilliums, Meconopsis and Tree Peonies ♿ With Assistance - Grass Paths ☕ Teas at St Mary's Church

7. DUNNINALD Montrose DD10 9TD

The Stansfeld Family

Traditional walled garden with mixed borders, vegetables, fruit trees and greenhouse. Extensive grounds with drifts of bluebells and beech avenue. Castle built in 1823 by James Gillespie Graham.

Route: 2 miles south of Montrose, signposted off A92 off Arbroath/Montrose road.

Admission: £3.00 Children Under 12 Free

SUNDAY 16 MAY 2:00pm - 5:00pm

01 JULY - 01 AUGUST HOUSE & GARDEN 12:30pm - 5:00pm

Web Site: www.dunninald.com

Telephone: 01674 672031

Email Address: estateoffice@dunninald.com

Marie Curie Cancer Care receives 40%, the net remaining to SGS Beneficiaries.

❁ ☕

8. EDZELL VILLAGE Edzell DD9 7TT

The Gardeners of Edzell & Historic Scotland

Walk round several gardens in Edzell village including those of Edzell Castle. Tickets are on sale in the village and a plan is issued with the tickets.

Route: On B966

Admission: £4.00

SUNDAY 27 JUNE 2:00pm - 5:00pm

Stracathro Cancer Care Fund UK receives 40%, the net remaining to SGS Beneficiaries.

☕

9. ETHIE CASTLE By Arbroath DD11 5SP

Adrian & Kirstin de Morgan

Formal garden with mixed herbaceous borders, parterre, pool and fountain. Working walled garden with restored 19th century glass houses and raised vegetable beds.

Route: From Arbroath: A92 to Montrose - As you leave Arbroath pass Shell petrol Station on right and turn right to Auchmithie - T junction turn left and continue for approximately 3 miles - Glass BT telephone box on left - enter by gates immediately in front signed Ethie Barns/Private.

Admission: £4.00 Children under 12 free

SUNDAY 13 JUNE 2:00pm - 5:00pm

Telephone: 01241 830434

Breakthrough Breast Cancer receives 40%, the net remaining to SGS Beneficiaries.

❁ ☕ Homemade

ANGUS

10. GAGIE HOUSE Duntrune, by Dundee DD4 0PR

France and Clare Smoor

A one-mile springtime woodland walk in a delightful secluded den along the Sweet Burn and its artesian ponds. Semi-wild pond garden in the policies of early 17th century Gagie House. Naturalised and more recent plantations of snowdrops, followed by daffodils, bluebells, primroses and candelabra primulas.

Route: From A90, about 2 miles north of Dundee, take turning to east sign-posted MURROES. Continue for 2 miles, wood on left, sharp right bend ahead; turn in to left along far side of wood, signpost GAGIE; follow this road, then through stone gateposts at end (marked Private Road). Car park sign-posted immediately to right.

Admission: £4.00

13 FEBRUARY - 14 MARCH FOR SNOWDROP FESTIVAL 10:00am - 5:00pm
15 MARCH - 31 MAY 10:00am - 5:00pm

Web Site: www.gagie.com
Telephone: 01382 380207
Email Address: smoor@gagie.com
Donation to SGS Beneficiaries
❀ Snowdrops/Snowflakes in the Green 🐕 ☕ ☕ Rustic Do-It-Yourself Tea Facilities in Farm Building

11. GALLERY Montrose DD10 9LA

Mr John Simson

Redesign and replanting of this historic garden have preserved and extended its traditional framework of holly, privet and box. A grassed central alley, embellished with circles, links interesting theme gardens and lawns. Noteable among these is a fine collection of old roses in their own space, the yellow and blue floral borders of the entrance garden and the fountain and pond at the centre of the formal white garden. A short walk through the external woodland garden, home to rare breed sheep, enhanced in 2008 by an extensive border of mixed heathers, leads to the raised bank of the river North Esk with views towards the Howe of the Mearns. From that point rough paths lead west and east along the bank.

Route: From A90 immediately south of Northwater Bridge take exit to 'Hillside' and next left to 'Gallery & Marykirk'. Or from A937 immediately west of rail underpass follow signs to 'Gallery & Northwater Bridge'.

Admission: £4.00 Children 50p

SUNDAY 11 JULY 2:00pm - 5:00pm

Email Address: galleryhomefarm@btinternet.com
Practical Action receives 40%, the net remaining to SGS Beneficiaries.
☕

12. KIRKSIDE OF LOCHTY Menmuir, by Brechin DD9 6RY

James & Irene Mackie

The garden contains a large collection of plants, several rare and unusual, also many different varieties of ferns. It is approached by a strip of woodland and expands into various compartments in an overall area of two acres, part of which is cultivated as a flowering meadow.

Route: Leave the A90 two miles south of Brechin and take the road to Menmuir. After a further two miles pass a wood on the left and a long beech hedge in front of the house.

Admission: £3.50 Children Free

BY ARRANGEMENT ON REQUEST

Telephone: 01356 660431

All proceeds to SGS Beneficiaries

13. MELGAM HOUSE Lintrathen DD8 5JH

Mr and Mrs M Anstice

A mid 18th century restored manse garden of approximately two and a half acres beside Lintrathen Loch. The grounds include a terraced walled garden that descends to the river Melgam. Elsewhere are climbing roses, herbaceous borders and shrubs. There are also some impressive trees. The garden includes a riverside walk and a magnificent waterfall that can be viewed from above or visited by the more agile. There are also many bulbs in the spring. Small vegetable garden.

Route: B951 from Kirriemuir to Glenilsa, turn left to Lintrathen and first left to church. B954 from Alyth and 2 miles from Peel Farm.

Admission: £3.00

APRIL - OCTOBER 9:00am - 9:00pm

Telephone: 01575 560269

Hope & Homes for Children receives 40%, the net remaining to SGS Beneficiaries.

14. PITMUIES GARDENS House of Pitmuies, Guthrie, By Forfar DD8 2SN

Mrs Farquhar Ogilvie

Two semi-formal wall gardens adjoin 18th century house and shelter long borders of herbaceous perennials, superb delphiniums, old fashioned roses and pavings with violas and dianthus. Spacious lawns, river and lochside walks beneath fine trees. A wide variety of shrubs with good autumn colours. Interesting picturesque turreted doocot and 'Gothick' wash-house. Myriad spring bulbs include carpets of crocus following the massed snowdrops.

Route: A932. Friockheim 1½ miles.

Admission: £3.50 Children Free

01 - 14 MARCH FOR SNOWDROP FESTIVAL 10:00am - 5:00pm
21 MARCH - 31 OCTOBER 10:00am - 5:00pm

Donation to SGS Beneficiaries

Argyllshire

'Gardens of Scotland' 2010 is sponsored by **Rensburg Sheppards Investment Management**

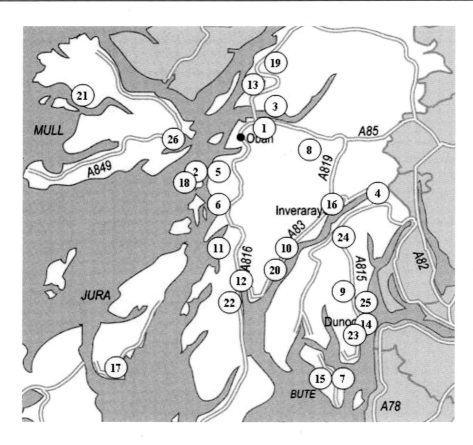

District Organiser: **Minette Struthers** Ardmaddy Castle, Balvicar, By Oban PA34 4QY
Area Organisers: **Mrs G Cadzow** Duachy, Kilninver, Oban PA34 4RH
Mrs E B Ingleby Braighbhaille, Crarae, Inveraray PA32 8YA
Mrs P McArthur Bute Cottage, Newton, Strachlachan PA27 8DB
Mrs C Shaw Kilbrandon House, Balvicar, Oban PA34 4RA
Treasurer: **Minette Struthers** Ardmaddy Castle, Balvicar, By Oban PA34 4QY

Gardens Open On a Specific Date

Benmore Bot. Garden, Dunoon	Sunday 25 April	10:00am - 6:00pm
Drim na Vullin, Lochgilphead	Saturday 01 May	2:00pm - 5:30pm
Strachur House Flower &	Saturday 01 May	1:00pm - 5:00pm
Woodland Gardens, Strachur		

68

Drim na Vullin, Lochgilphead	Sunday 02 May	2:00pm - 5:30pm
Strachur House Flower & Woodland Gardens, Strachur	Sunday 02 May	1:00pm - 5:00pm
Knock Cottage, Lochgair	Saturday 08 May	12:00pm - 5:00pm
Arduaine, Kilmelford,	Sunday 09 May	9:30am - 6:00pm
Knock Cottage, Lochgair	Sunday 09 May	12:00pm - 5:00pm
Knock Cottage, Lochgair	Saturday 15 May	12:00pm - 5:00pm
Crarae Garden, Inveraray	Sunday 16 May	10:00am - 5:00pm
Knock Cottage, Lochgair	Sunday 16 May	12:00pm - 5:00pm
Strachur House Flower & Woodland Gardens, Strachur	Saturday 05 June	1:00pm - 5:00pm
Strachur House Flower & Woodland Gardens, Strachur	Sunday 06 June	1:00pm - 5:00pm
Lip Na Cloiche Garden & Nursery, Isle of Mull	Saturday 12 June	11:00am - 5:00pm
Lip Na Cloiche Garden & Nursery, Isle of Mull	Sunday 13 June	11:00am - 5:00pm
Crarae Garden, Inveraray	Saturday 19 June	9:00am - 5:00pm
Seafield, Dunoon	Saturday 19 June	2:00pm - 5:00pm
Seafield, Dunoon	Sunday 20 June	2:00pm - 5:00pm
The Shore Villages, by Dunoon	Saturday 26 June	1:00pm - 5:00pm
The Shore Villages, by Dunoon	Sunday 27 June	1:00pm - 5:00pm
Glecknabae, Rothesay	Sunday 15 August	1:00pm - 4:30pm

Gardens Open By Arrangement

When organising a visit to a garden open by arrangement, please enquire if there are facilities and catering available

Fairwinds, Dunoon	Spring - Autumn	Tel: 01369 702666
Kilbrandon, Balvicar	April - October	Tel: 01852 300400
Kinlochlaich House Gardens, Appin	Christmas and New Year	Tel: 01631 730342
Knock Cottage, Lochgair	Mid April - Mid June	Tel: 01546 886 331

Gardens Open Regularly

Ardkinglas Woodland Garden, Cairndow	All Year	Daylight Hours
Ardmaddy Castle, By Oban	All Year	9.00am till Sunset
Barguillean's "Angus Garden", Taynuilt	All Year	9:00am - 6:00pm
Jura House, Ardfin, Isle of Jura	All Year	9:00am - 5:00pm
Torosay Castle & Gardens, Craignure, Isle of Mull	All Year	9:00am - 7:00pm (or dusk)
Benmore Botanic Garden	March & October	10:00am - 5:00pm

ARGYLLSHIRE

Achnacloich, Connel, Oban	31 March - 31 Oct.	10:00am - 6:00pm
Druimneil House, Port Appin	April - October	Dawn - Dusk
Kinlochlaich House Gardens, Appin	April - September (Mons - Sats)	9:00am - 5:30pm
	April - September (Sundays)	10:30am - 5:30pm
	October - March (Mons - Sats)	9:00am - 5:00pm (or Dusk)
An Cala, Ellenabeich, Isle of Seil	01 April - 31 Oct.	10:00am - 6:00pm
Ardchattan Priory, North Connel	01 April - 31 Oct.	9:30am - 5:30pm
Ascog Hall, Ascog, Isle of Bute	Easter – October (ex. Mons & Tues)	10:00am - 5:00pm
Crinan Hotel Garden, Crinan	01 May - 31 August	Dawn - Dusk
Oakbank, Ardrishaig	01 May - 31 August	10:00am - 5:00pm
Inveraray Castle Gardens, Inveraray	16 May - 12 June	10:00am - 5:45pm

1. ACHNACLOICH Connel, Oban PA37 1PR

Mrs T E Nelson

Scottish baronial house by John Starforth of Glasgow. Succession of wonderful bulbs, flowering shrubs, rhododendrons, azaleas, magnolias and primulas. Woodland garden with ponds above Loch Etive. Good autumn colours.

Route: On A85 3 miles east of Connel

Admission: £3.50 OAP £3.00 Children Free

31 MARCH - 31 OCTOBER 10:00am - 6:00pm

Telephone: 01631 710796 Email: jyn@btinternet.com and charlie_milne@msn.com

Donation to SGS Beneficiaries

♿ Partial 🐕 Toilet

2. AN CALA Ellenabeich, Isle of Seil PA34 4RF

Mrs Thomas Downie

A wonderful example of a 1930s designed garden, An Cala sits snugly in its horseshoe shelter of surrounding cliffs. A spectacular and very pretty garden with streams, waterfall, ponds, many herbaceous plants as well as azaleas, rhododendrons and cherry trees in spring. Archive material of Mawson's design found recently.

Route: Proceed south from Oban on Campbeltown road for 8 miles, turn right at Easdale sign, a further 8 miles on B844; garden between school and village.

Admission: £3.00

01 APRIL - 31 OCTOBER 10:00am - 6:00pm

Telephone: 01852 300237

Cancer Research U.K. receives 40%, the net remaining to SGS Beneficiaries.

♿ Partial 🐕

3. ARDCHATTAN PRIORY North Connel PA37 1RQ

Mrs Sarah Troughton

Beautifully situated on the north side of Loch Etive. In front of the house there is a rockery, extensive herbaceous and rose borders, with excellent views over the loch. To the west of the house there are shrub borders and a wild garden, numerous roses and over 30 different varieties of sorbus providing excellent autumn colour. The Priory, founded in 1230, is now a private house. The ruins of the chapel and graveyard, with fine early stones, are in the care of Historic Scotland and open with the garden.
Route: Oban 10 miles. From north, turn left off A828 at Barcaldine on to B845 for 6 miles. From Oban or the east on A85, cross Connel Bridge and turn first right, proceed east on Bonawe Road. Well signed.
Admission: £3.50
01 APRIL - 31 OCTOBER 9:30am - 5:30pm
Web Site: www.gardens-of-argyll.co.uk Telephone: 01796 481355
Donation to SGS Beneficiaries
  80% - Can be limited in Wet Weather Garden Fete on 25 July

4. ARDKINGLAS WOODLAND GARDEN Cairndow PA26 8BH

Ardkinglas Estate

In peaceful setting overlooking Loch Fyne the garden contains one of the finest collections of rhododendrons and conifers in Britain. This includes the mightiest conifer in Europe and one of Britain's tallest trees as well as many other champion trees. Gazebo with unique "Scriptorium" based around a collection of literary quotes. Woodland lochan, ancient mill ruins and many woodland walks. VisitScotland 3* garden.
Route: Entrance through Cairndow village off A83 Loch Lomond/Inveraray road.
Admission: £3.50 Children Under 16 Free
ALL YEAR - DAYLIGHT HOURS
Web Site: www.ardkinglas.com
Telephone: 01499 600261
Donation to SGS Beneficiaries
  Partial Gift Sales, Picnic Facilities, Toilets, Nearby Tree Shop offers Take-away Food

5. ARDMADDY CASTLE By Oban PA34 4QY

Mr and Mrs Charles Struthers

Ardmaddy Castle gardens, set in a most spectacular position, are shielded to the north by mature woodlands, carpeted with bluebells and daffodils, and protected from the atlantic winds by the elevated Castle. The Walled Garden is full of magnificent rhododendrons, some huge, an increasing collection of rare and unusual shrubs and plants, the 'Clock Garden' with its cutting flowers, fruit and vegetables grown with labour saving formality, all set within dwarf box hedging. Beyond, a woodland walk, with its amazing hydrangea climbing to 60', leads to the water gardens - in early summer a riot of candelabra primulas, irises, rodgersias and other damp loving plants and grasses. Lovely autumn colour. A garden for all seasons.

ARGYLLSHIRE

<u>Route:</u> Take A816 south of Oban for 8 miles. Turn right B844 to Seil Island/Easdale. 4 miles on, take Ardmaddy road for further 2 miles.
<u>Admission:</u> £3.00 Children Free
ALL YEAR - 9.00AM TILL SUNSET
Web Site: www.gardens-of-argyll.co.uk
Telephone: 01852 300353 Email Address: ardmaddycastle@btinternet.com
Donation to SGS Beneficiaries
✿ ♿ Mostly 🐕 [B&B] Five Self Catering Cottages Toilet Suitable for Disabled

6. ARDUAINE Kilmelford, PA34 4XQ

The National Trust for Scotland
An outstanding 20 acre coastal garden on the Sound of Jura. Begun more than 100 years ago on the south facing slope of a promontory separating Asknish Bay from Loch Melfort. This remarkable hidden paradise, protected by tall shelterbelts and influenced favourably by the North Atlantic Drift, grows a wide variety of plants from the four corners of the globe. Internationally known for the rhododendron species collection, the garden also features magnolias, camellias, azaleas and many other wonderful trees and shrubs, many of which are tender and not often seen. A broad selection of perennials, bulbs, ferns and water plants ensure a year-long season of interest. Walks with head gardener at 11:00am and 2:30pm.
<u>Route:</u> Off A816 Oban-Lochgilphead, sharing an entrance with the Loch Melfort Hotel.
<u>Admission:</u> £5.00
SUNDAY 09 MAY 9:30am - 6:00pm
Web Site: www.nts.org.uk
Telephone: 0844 493 2216 Email Address: mwilkins@nts.org.uk
Donation to SGS Beneficiaries
♿ Most of Garden Accessible With Assistance ☕ Available in Local Hotel

7. ASCOG HALL Ascog, Isle of Bute PA20 9EU

Mrs Susannah Alcorn
This appealing 3 acre garden is continuing to develop and mature with an abundance of choice plants and shrubs which delight the eye from spring to autumn. It includes a small formal rose garden with a profusion of fragrant old shrub roses. Through a rustic ivy-clad stone arch which in bygone years led to the tennis court, there is now a large gravel garden with sun-loving plants and grasses. Undoubtedly, however, the most outstanding feature is our acclaimed Victorian fernery. This rare and beautiful structure houses subtropical and temperate fern species, including an ancient Todea barbara - the only survivor from the original collection and said to be around 1,000 years old.
<u>Route:</u> EITHER 30 mins on ferry from Wemyss Bay - 3 miles south of Rothesay on A844 OR 5 mins on ferry from Colintraive and 11 miles south on A844
<u>Admission:</u> £4.00 Season ticket £10.00
EASTER - OCTOBER (EX. MONDAYS & TUESDAYS) 10:00am - 5:00pm
Donation to SGS Beneficiaries
✿ ♿ Partial

8. BARGUILLEAN'S "ANGUS GARDEN" Taynuilt, Argyll PA35 1HY

Mr Robin Marshall

Nine acre woodland garden around an eleven acre loch set in the Glen Lonan hills. Spring flowering shrubs and bulbs, extensive collection of rhododendron hybrids, deciduous azaleas, conifers and unusual trees. The garden contains a large collection of North American rhododendron hybrids from famous contemporary plant breeders. Some paths can be steep. Three marked walks from thirty minutes to one and a half hours.
Route: 3 miles south off A85 Glasgow/Oban road at Taynuilt; road marked Glen Lonan; 3 miles up single track road; turn right at sign.
Admission: £3.00 Children Free
ALL YEAR 9:00am - 6:00pm
Web Site: www.barguillean.co.uk
Telephone: 01866 822 333 Email Address: info@barguillean.co.uk
Donation to SGS Beneficiaries
B&B Self -Catering Accommodation Coach Tours by Arrangement - Contact Sean Honeyman Tel 01866 822 335

9. BENMORE BOTANIC GARDEN Benmore, Dunoon PA23 8QU

Regional Garden of the Royal Botanic Garden Edinburgh

World famous for its magnificent conifers and its extensive range of flowering trees and shrubs, including over 250 species of rhododendron. From a spectacular avenue of Giant Redwoods numerous marked walks lead the visitor via a formal garden and pond through hillside woodlands to a dramatic viewpoint overlooking the Eachaig valley and the Holy Loch. Visit the newly restored Benmore Fernery now open daily from 11am, closing an hour before the Garden closes. Guided tours of the Garden every Tuesday, Wednesday, Thursday & Sunday at 2.00pm.
Route: 7 miles north of Dunoon or 22 miles south from Glen Kinglass below Rest and be Thankful pass; on A815.
Admission: Adults £5.00 Concessions £4.00 Children £1.00 Families (2 adults and up to 4 children) £10.00
SUNDAY 25 APRIL 10:00am - 6:00pm
MARCH & OCTOBER 10:00am - 5:00pm
Web Site: www.rbge.org.uk Telephone: 01369 706261
Donation to SGS Beneficiaries
🌸 ♿ Partial ☕ Benmore Cafe

10. CRARAE GARDEN Inveraray PA32 8YA

The National Trust for Scotland

A spectacular 50 acre garden in a dramatic setting. Crarae has a wonderful collection of woody plants centered on the Crarae Burn, which is spanned by several bridges and tumbles through a rocky gorge in a series of cascades. A wide variety of shrubs and trees chosen for spring flowering and autumn colour grow in the shelter of towering conifers. The lush naturalistic planting and rushing water gives the garden the feel of a valley in the Himalayas. Sturdy shoes advised.

Route: On A83 10 miles south of Inveraray

Admission: £5.50 Concessions £4.50

SUNDAY 16 MAY 10:00am - 5:00pm

SATURDAY 19 JUNE 9:00am - 5:00pm

Web Site: www.nts.org.uk

Telephone: 0844 493 2210 Email Address: nprice@nts.org.uk

Donation to SGS Beneficiaries

❀ ♿ To Lower Garden Only   NCCPG Nothofagus   ☕ Light Refreshments

11. CRINAN HOTEL GARDEN Crinan PA31 8SR

Mr and Mrs N Ryan

Small rock garden with azaleas and rhododendrons created into a steep hillside over a century ago with steps leading to a sheltered, secluded garden with sloping lawns, herbaceous beds and spectacular views of the canal and Crinan Loch

Route: Lochgilphead A83, then A816 to Oban, then A841 Cairnbaan to Crinan

Admission: Donation Box

01 MAY - 31 AUGUST DAWN - DUSK

Web Site: www.crinanhotel.com

Telephone: 015456 830261 Email Address: nryan@crinanhotel.com

Feedback Madagascar receives 40%, the net remaining to SGS Beneficiaries.

🐕 B&B Crinan Hotel - Prices on Request   Raffle of Flower Painting by Frances Macdonald (Ryan) - Tickets available at Coffee Shop   ☕ Homemade   Coffee Shop, Art Gallery by Crinan Canal Basin and in Hotel

12. DRIM NA VULLIN Blarbuie Road, Lochgilphead PA31 8LE

Mr and Mrs Robin Campbell Byatt

Drim na Vullin, originally a mill, and its woodland garden has been owned by the one family since 1829 but the major part of the development of the garden as seen today was landscaped and planted in the 1950s by Sybil Campbell OBE, Britain's first woman professional magistrate, with the help of Percy Cane the garden designer. The garden lies along a cleft formed by the Cuilarstitch Burn with a spectacular waterfall at the top. Mature species and hybrid rhododendrons, magnolias, azaleas and other shrubs are under a canopy of mostly native trees. The present owners' planting brings the developed area to about 5 acres. Some uphill walking. Waterproof shoes are recommended.

Route: A83 to Lochgilphead. At the top of the main street in front of the parish church, turn right up Manse Brae. The garden is a third of a mile up the hill on the left. Beyond the houses on the left a high fence leads to the Drim na Vullin entrance. Please park on the road and walk in.

Admission: £3.00 Children Free

SATURDAY 01 MAY 2:00pm - 5:30pm

SUNDAY 02 MAY 2:00pm - 5:30pm

Telephone: 01546 602615
Wildlife & Wetlands Trust receives 20%, the net remaining to SGS Beneficiaries.
🐕 ☕ Homemade

13. DRUIMNEIL HOUSE Port Appin PA38 4DQ

Mrs J Glaisher (Gardener - Mr Andrew Ritchie)
Ten acre garden overlooking Loch Linnhe with many fine varieties of mature trees and rhododendrons and other woodland shrubs.
Route: Turn in for Appin off A828 (Connel/Fort William road). 2 miles, sharp left at Airds Hotel, second house on right.
Admission: By Donation
APRIL - OCTOBER DAWN - DUSK
Telephone: 01631 730228
All proceeds to SGS Beneficiaries
♻ ☕ Homemade   Lunches by Prior Arrangement

14. FAIRWINDS 14 George Street, Hunter's Quay, Dunoon PA23 8JU

Mrs Carol Stewart
This mature medium size garden is situated in George Street, a minute's drive up the hill from Western Ferries. Originally created from a simple plot in the late fifties, the present owner has inherited a charming garden which can be seen at its best from late May to early July. Daffodils, rhododendrons and azaleas. Later the walls of the house are covered by clematis and passion flowers, fighting for space with jasmine and honeysuckle. Trees range from a young but beautiful copper beech to a range of conifers, acers, a large silver birch and embothrium. Over the last 34 years the aim has been to create colour and interest for all seasons and to this end sorbus, bottlebrush, a palm tree and a magnificent pampas grass have been added among many other plants of interest. The long winding drive provides wheelchair access so that all the garden can be viewed.
Route: Situated on Cowal Peninsula Hunter's Quay on A815. Approaching Dunoon on loch side road, turn right up Cammesreinach Brae just before the Royal Marine Hotel opposite Western Ferries terminal. The Brae becomes George Street, Fairwinds is on left.
Admission: £2.50 Children Free
BY ARRANGEMENT SPRING - AUTUMN
Telephone: 01369 702666 Email Address: Carol.argyll@talk21.com
The Cowal Hospice receives 40%, the net remaining to SGS Beneficiaries.
♿ Limited   🐕 ☕ On Request

15. GLECKNABAE Rothesay PA20 0QX

John and Marianne McGhee
A south facing hillside garden in the least known part of the island of Bute with magnificent views to the mountains of Arran. A collection of formal courtyard gardens, all different, shrubs and trees. New pond gardens and rockery and herbaceous border.

ARGYLLSHIRE

This unusual garden is welcoming and inspirational.

Sunday 15 August - Music in the garden day: Bring your own picnic and enjoy music by The Tim Saul Modern Jazz Trio. Activities for children. Teas and home baking. Under cover if wet.

Route: A844 to Ettrick Bay, signposted off the coast road between Rhubodach and Rothesay; continue to end of "made up" road - approximately 5 miles.

Admission: £4.00 (Under 16 and Over 60 £2.00)

SUNDAY 15 AUGUST 1:00pm - 4:30pm

Telephone: 01700 504742 (gardener) Email Address: glecknabae@btinternet.com

Achievement Bute receives 40%, the net remaining to SGS Beneficiaries.

🐕 🍵 Homemade

16. INVERARAY CASTLE GARDENS Inveraray Castle PA32 8XT   NEW

The Duke & Duchess of Argyll

The climate in Argyll, with its yearly average rainfall of 230cms (90 inches), is ideally suited to Rhododendrons and Azaleas, which flower in the gardens from April until June. Conifers also grow well in the poor acidic soil of a high rainfall area, as can be seen by the fine specimens such as Cedrus Deodars, Sequoiadendron Wellingtonia, Cryptomeria Japonica and Taxus Baccata.

The borders on each side of the main drive, beyond the lawns, are known as the 'Flag-Borders' - the paths having been laid out in the shape of Scotland's National flag, the St. Andrew's Cross. These borders, outstanding in the spring with beautiful Prunus 'Ukon' and Prunus subhirtella, are underplanted with an interesting mixture of Rhododendrons, Eucrypyias, various shrubs and herbaceous plants, giving interest all year round.

Route: Inveraray nestles on the banks of Loch Fyne approximately 60 miles North of Glasgow and is well serviced by road links North and South.

By Car

From the South, exit the M74 at junction 4 and follow signs for Glasgow City centre (M8) then head for the Erskine Toll Bridge and join the A82 to Dumbarton and Loch Lomond. At Tarbet, near the head of picturesque Loch Lomond, bear left onto the A83 signposted for Inveraray.

By Bus

Scottish Citylink provide a regular bus service to Inveraray from Glasgow: Travel time 1hr 40 minutes

Travel Distances

Dalmally Railway Station: Approx 15 miles

Glasgow Airport: Approx 56 miles

Prestwick Airport: Approx 86 miles

Admission: £4.00

16 MAY - 12 JUNE 10:00am - 5:45pm

Web Site: www.inveraray-castle.com

Telephone: 01499 302203 Email Address: enquiries@inveraray-castle.com

Donation to SGS Beneficiaries

♿ 🐕 Guide Dogs Only 🍵Cream Wine Light Refreshments In Castle Tearoom during Castle Opening Times

17. JURA HOUSE Ardfin, Isle of Jura PA60 7XX

The Ardfin Trust

Organic walled garden with wide variety of unusual plants and shrubs including large Australasian collection. Also interesting woodland and cliff walk with spectacular views. Points of historical interest; abundant wildlife and flowers.

Route: 5 miles east from ferry terminal on A846. Ferries to Islay from Kennacraig by Tarbert.

Admission: £3.00 Children Under 16 £1.00

ALL YEAR 9:00am - 5:00pm

Donation to SGS Beneficiaries

✿ ♿ With Assistance   🐕   Toilet   Ⓡ Homemade June, July and August Only

18. KILBRANDON Balvicar PA34 4RA

The Hon. Michael Shaw

The designed landscape affording a pleasant seaside outlook for a regency house was largely the work of Lord and Lady Kilbrandon between 1951 and 1991. The associated garden and woodlands feature numerous rhododendrons and azaleas with a variety of other trees and shrubs running almost to the water's edge. The regency walled garden is almost entirely decorative preserving the original herbaceous borders and capitalising on a largely frost-free environment. There are some interesting specimens and the overall effect is much enhanced by a remarkable natural setting.

Route: Take A816 south from Oban, 8 miles. Turn right on B844 (signed Easdale) 7 miles. At Balvicar take B8003 (signed Cuan) 1 mile, entrance on left at Kilbrandon Church. 1 mile of private road - not suitable for coaches.

Admission: £3.00

BY ARRANGEMENT APRIL - OCTOBER

Telephone: 01852 300400

All proceeds to SGS Beneficiaries

♿ Limited   🐕

19. KINLOCHLAICH HOUSE GARDENS Appin PA38 4BD

Mr & Mrs D E Hutchison and Miss F M M Hutchison

Walled garden incorporating the Western Highlands' largest Nursery Garden Centre. Amazing variety of plants growing and for sale! Extensive grounds with Woodland Walk; Spring Garden: Vegetable Gardens and Fruit Polyhouse and Formal Garden. Fantastic display of rhododendrons, azaleas, shrubs and herbaceous, including many unusuals - Embothrium, Davidia, Magnolia, Eucryphia, Tropaeolum.

Route: A828. Oban 18 miles, Fort William 27 miles. Look out for the Police Station, entrance is next to it.

Admission: £3.00 Accompanied Children Free

APRIL - SEPTEMBER (MONDAYS - SATURDAYS) 9:00am - 5:30pm

APRIL - SEPTEMBER (SUNDAYS) 10:30am - 5:30pm

OCTOBER - MARCH (MONDAYS TO SATURDAYS) 9:00am - 5:00pm or dusk

ALSO BY ARRANGEMENT CHRISTMAS AND NEW YEAR

Web Site: www.kinlochlaichgardencentre.co.uk

ARGYLLSHIRE

Telephone: 01631 730342 Email Address: gardens@kinlochlaich-house.co.uk
Appin Village Hall receives 40%, the net remaining to SGS Beneficiaries.
✿ ♿ Gravel Paths, Rear Car Park Available   B&B Self-catering

20. KNOCK COTTAGE Lochgair PA31 8RZ

Mr David Sillar
A 5 acre woodland and water garden centred round a small loch and a lily pond. Shrubs and trees were planted around the house in the late 1960s but the present garden began with the creation of the lochan in 1989 and the plantings of the 1990s. Development continues. Camelias, rhododendrons, azaleas and other shrub species are sheltered by mixed conifer, eucalyptus, birch, rowan, alder and beech. Several of the 50 different rhododendrons are scented including Rh. Fragrantissimum and some early flowering varieties. The garden is quite level but access is by grassed paths so waterproof footwear is recommended
Route: A83 ½ mile south of Lochgair Hotel on west side of the road between two sharp bends. **Very limited parking**
Admission: £3.00
SATURDAY 08 MAY 12:00pm - 5:00pm
SUNDAY 09 MAY 12:00pm - 5:00pm
SATURDAY 15 MAY 12:00pm - 5:00pm
SUNDAY 16 MAY 12:00pm - 5:00pm
ALSO BY ARRANGEMENT MID APRIL - MID JUNE
Telephone: 01546 886 331
Marie Curie receives 40%, the net remaining to SGS Beneficiaries.
♿ Partly, Very Limited Access   ☕ Homemade In the Afternoon Only

21. LIP NA CLOICHE GARDEN & NURSERY Ballygown, Nr Ulva Ferry, Isle of Mull PA73 6LU

Lucy Mackenzie Panizzon
A fabulous small densely planted coastal garden with stunning views over Loch Tuath and the Isle of Ulva. A wide and eclectic range of plants for long season interest. Much use is made of beachcombed and re-claimed material to help integrate the garden with its surroundings.
Route: From Craignure or Fishnish ferry terminals take A849 north to Salen. Turn left at church onto B8035 and after 3 miles turn right onto B8073. Lip Na Cloiche is approximately 10 miles along, 2 miles after turn-off to Ulva Ferry
Admission: £3.00
SATURDAY 12 JUNE 11:00am - 5:00pm
SUNDAY 13 JUNE 11:00am - 5:00pm
Web Site: www.lipnacloiche.co.uk
Telephone: 01688 500257 Email Address: lipnacloiche@btinternet.com
Macmillan Nurses receives 40%, the net remaining to SGS Beneficiaries.
✿ B&B ☕ Homemade

22. OAKBANK Ardrishaig PA30 8EP NEW

Helga MacFarlane

An unusual and delightful garden which has recently been transformed by the removal of overgrown trees and scrub, which covered a hillside of 3 acres. Paths have now been created and they wind through a varied collection of trees, shrubs, bulbs and wild flowers. There are several small ponds, many wonderful wood carvings and a secret garden for children. A viewpoint looks over Loch Fyne to the Isle of Arran.
Route: Tarbert side of Ardrishaig, just beyond church.
Admission: £3.00
01 MAY - 31 AUGUST 10:00am - 5:00pm
Web Site: www.gardenatoakbank.blogspot.com Telephone: 01546 603405
Diabetes UK receives 40%, the net remaining to SGS Beneficiaries.

23. SEAFIELD 173 Marine Parade, Hunter's Quay, Dunoon PA23 8HJ

Scoular Anderson

Stunning seaside garden on a hillside with clever plantings, divided into separate smaller gardens including gravel garden, damp pond garden, heather garden, shady garden, herbaceous beds, shrubs, ferns and grasses.
Route: Situated on the Cowal Peninsula at Hunter's Quay on A815 a few hundred yards south (Dunoon Side) of the Western Ferries terminal. Parking on promenade.
Admission: £3.00 Children Free
SATURDAY 19 JUNE 2:00pm - 5:00pm
SUNDAY 20 JUNE 2:00pm - 5:00pm
Email Address: scoulara9@aol.com
CHAS receives 40%, the net remaining to SGS Beneficiaries.
✿ 🐕 ☕ Homemade

24. STRACHUR HOUSE FLOWER & WOODLAND GARDENS Strachur PA27 8BX

Sir Charles and Lady Maclean

Directly behind Strachur House, the flower garden is sheltered by magnificent beeches, limes, ancient yews and Japanese maples. There are herbaceous borders, a burnside rhododendron and azalea walk and a rockery. Old fashioned and species roses, lilies, tulips, spring bulbs and Himalayan poppies make a varied display in this informal haven of beauty and tranquility. The garden gives onto Strachur Park, laid out by General Campbell in 1782, which offers spectacular walks through natural woodland with 200-year-old trees, rare shrubs and a lochan rich in native wildlife.
Route: Turn off A815 at Strachur House Farm entrance; park in farm square.
Admission: £3.00
SATURDAY 01 MAY 1:00pm - 5:00pm
SUNDAY 02 MAY 1:00pm - 5:00pm
SATURDAY 05 JUNE 1:00pm - 5:00pm
SUNDAY 06 JUNE 1:00pm - 5:00pm
CLASP receives 40%, the net remaining to SGS Beneficiaries.
✿ ♿ ☕ Homemade

ARGYLLSHIRE

25. THE SHORE VILLAGES by Dunoon PA23 8SE

The Gardeners of The Shore Villages
Arboretum Lodge, Kilmun (Mrs L Clough)
19-20 Graham's Point, Kilmun (Mr and Mrs A McClintock)
Fountain Villa, Kilmun (Miss J Valentine)
Dunclutha, Strone (Mr and Mrs R Aldam)
Duncreggan View, Blairmore (Mr and Mrs J Lynn)
Belhaven, Blairmore (Mr and Mrs J Hampson)
4 Swedish Houses, Ardentinny (Miss E Connell)
5 Swedish Houses, Ardentinny (Mr and Mrs B Waldapfel)
Eight very different gardens on a seven mile stretch off the A880, overlooking the Holy
Loch, the Clyde and Loch Long. Gardening for wildlife, colour combinations and for low
maintenance, with terracing, sculpture, wildflower meadows and ponds, herbaceous
borders and trees from seed. Some gardens are on steep slopes with limited disabled
access.
Route: Approaching Dunoon from the north on the A815, take the left hand turning for
Kilmun and follow the yellow arrows.
Admission: £4.00 Accompanied Children Free (Tickets, with information sheet, can be
purchased at all gardens)
SATURDAY 26 JUNE 1:00pm - 5:00pm
SUNDAY 27 JUNE 1:00pm - 5:00pm
All proceeds to SGS Beneficiaries
❀ ♿ For Some Gardens ☕ Homemade Available at Blairmore Village Hall

26. TOROSAY CASTLE & GARDENS Craignure, Isle of Mull, PA65 6AY

Mr Christopher James
Torosay is a beautiful and welcoming family home completed in 1858 by David Bryce in
the Scottish Baronial style and is surrounded by 12 acres of spectacular contrasting
gardens which include formal terraces and an impressive Italian statue walk
surrounded by informal woodland and water gardens. Many rare and tender plants.
Snowdrop Festival from 1 February till 14 March - masses of snowdrops.
Route: 1½ miles from Craignure on A849 south. Regular daily ferry service from Oban
to Craignure, and by road or woodland paths to Castle
Admission: £5.50 Children £3.25 Concessions £4.50 Castle Extra. Out of Season:
Reduced rates & honesty box.
ALL YEAR 9:00am - 7:00pm or Dusk
Web Site: www.torosay.com
Telephone: 01680 812421
Email Address: torosay@aol.com
Donation to SGS Beneficiaries
❀ Sometimes ♿ Partial 🐕 🐾 Self Catering Cottages ☕ Homemade Light
Refreshments   Café Open April to October

Ayrshire

'Gardens of Scotland' 2010 is sponsored by **Rensburg Sheppards Investment Management**

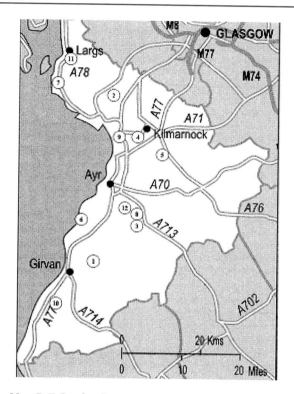

District Organiser: **Mrs R F Cuninghame** Caprington Castle, Kilmarnock KA2 9AA
Area Organisers: **Mrs Glen Collins** Grougarbank House, Kilmarnock KA3 6HP
                               Mrs Hywel Davies Peatland, Gatehead, Kilmarnock KA2 9AN
                               Mrs Michael Findlay Carnell, Hurlford, Kilmarnock KA1 5JS
                               Mrs John MacKay Pierhill, Annbank, Ayr KA6 5AW
Treasurer: **Brigadier A J Sandiford** Harrowhill Cottage, Kilmarnock KA3 6HX

Gardens Open On a Specific Date

Blair House, Dalry	Saturday 06 February	1:00pm - 4:00pm
Blair House, Dalry	Sunday 07 February	1:00pm - 4:00pm
Caprington Castle, Kilmarnock	Sunday 14 February	12:30pm - 4:00pm
Blairquhan, Straiton, Maybole	Sunday 21 February	12:00pm - 4:00pm
Kirkhill Castle, Colmonell	Sunday 16 May	2:00pm - 5:00pm
Blair House, Dalry	Sunday 23 May	2:00pm - 5:30pm

AYRSHIRE

Holmes Farm, Drybridge	Saturday 29 May	12:00pm - 5:00pm
Holmes Farm, Drybridge	Sunday 30 May	12:00pm - 5:00pm
Gardens of West Kilbride and Seamill	Saturday 19 June	1:00pm - 5:00pm
Gardens of West Kilbride and Seamill	Sunday 20 June	1:00pm - 5:00pm
Largs Gardening Club	Sunday 27 June	1:30pm - 5:00pm
Glenhaven, Kirkmichael	Sunday 04 July	2:00pm - 5:00pm
Barr Village Gardens, By Girvan	Saturday 10 July	1:00pm - 5:00pm
Barr Village Gardens, By Girvan	Sunday 11 July	1:00pm - 5:00pm
Carnell, Hurlford	Sunday 18 July	2:00pm - 5:00pm
Culzean, Maybole	Tuesday 20 July	10:30am - 5:00pm
Skeldon, Dalrymple	Sunday 01 August	2:00pm - 5:00pm

Gardens Open By Arrangement
When organising a visit to a garden open by arrangement, please enquire if there are facilities and catering available

Caprington Castle, Kilmarnock	February	Tel: 07748 280036

1. BARR VILLAGE GARDENS By Girvan KA26 9TU

Barr Village Gardeners

A large number of attractive gardens, mostly well established but some new, within this small beautiful conservation village. Included will be the garden of Barr Primary School, featuring the pupils' barrel garden.

Maps and tickets available at each open garden.

Route: Barr is on the B734. Girvan 8 miles, Ballantrae 17 miles, Ayr 24 miles.

Admission: £3.50 Children 50p

SATURDAY 10 JULY 1:00pm - 5:00pm
SUNDAY 11 JULY 1:00pm - 5:00pm

Children's Hospice Association Scotland receives 40%, the net remaining to SGS Beneficiaries.

✿ ♿ Partly 🐕 ☕ Homemade In Barr Community Hall

2. BLAIR HOUSE Dalry KA24 4ER

Mr and Mrs Luke Borwick

The extensive and fine-timbered policies surrounding this tower house of great antiquity are first mentioned by Pont in the early 17th century. The well laid out park is attributed to Captain William Fordyce Blair RN in the 1850s. Visitors are permitted to walk through these delightful historic grounds all the year round. Particularly spectacular are the spring and early summer gardens with continuous interest from the drifts of snowdrops and bluebells to the species rhododendrons and azaleas. Recent renovations to the private gardens are providing year round interest. For Scotland's Gardens Scheme the private gardens at Blair House and the Carriage House will be open.

Route: Enter by North Lodge. From A737 in Dalry follow signs to Railway Station. Continue on this road past farm on right. North Lodge entrance signposted.

Admission: **6 and 7 February:** Donations

Sunday 23 May: £4.00 Family Ticket £10.00 Chidren under 12 Free

SATURDAY 06 FEBRUARY FOR SNOWDROP FESTIVAL 1:00pm - 4:00pm

SUNDAY 07 FEBRUARY FOR SNOWDROP FESTIVAL 1:00pm - 4:00pm

SUNDAY 23 MAY 2:00pm - 5:30pm

Web Site: www.blairestate.com

North Ayrshire Guides Association receives 40% on 6th & 7th February Opening, CLIC Sargeant Charity, Prestwick receives 40% on 23 May Opening, the net remaining to SGS Beneficiaries.

✿ On 23 May Only ♿ Partly 🐕 ✿ [B&B] Also Self Catering Cottage Plant Stall, Cake Stall and Face Painting on 23 May ☕ Teas in the Guide Lodge 6 & 7 February for Snowdrop Festival, Homemade Teas 23 May at Blair

3. BLAIRQUHAN Straiton, Maybole KA19 7LZ

Sir Patrick and Lady Hunter Blair

Regency Castle built by William Burn, 1821 - 1824 for Sir David Hunter Blair 3rd Bart. Sixty-foot high saloon with gallery. The kitchen courtyard is formed with stones and sculpture from an earlier castle. 3 mile private drive along the River Girvan. Walled garden, pinetum and Regency glasshouse. The castle is surrounded by an extensive park including an arboretum. There is a tree trail and a shop.

Route: From Ayr A77 south. Take B7045 to Kirkmichael. At village centre take Straiton road. After ½ mile signpost Entry over bridge on right

Admission: £6.00 Children £3.00 Concessions £4.00 (includes access to main reception rooms and tea)

SUNDAY 21 FEBRUARY FOR SNOWDROP FESTIVAL 12:00pm - 4:00pm

Ayrshire Rivers Trust receives 40%, the net remaining to SGS Beneficiaries.

✿ ♿ Partly 🐕 ✿ Snowdrop and Tree Trail ☕ Homemade in the Castle (First Cup & Home Baking included in admission charge)

4. CAPRINGTON CASTLE Kilmarnock KA2 9AA

Captain and Mrs Robert Cuninghame and Mr William Cuninghame

Caprington stands in a landscape bordered by the River Irvine, close to Kilmarnock. The mixed woodland policies are well carpeted with snowdrops and there is a walled garden with fruit trees, vegetables and flowers in season. New Stump garden. Strong waterproof footwear recommended

Route: From M77 take the A71 to Irvine and go off at first roundabout to Troon, Dundonald and Gatehead. In Gatehead go over railway line and river bridge and take first left at Old Rome Farmhouse. The twin lodges are about ½ mile on.

Admission: £3.50 Children Under 12 Free

SUNDAY 14 FEBRUARY FOR SNOWDROP FESTIVAL 12:30pm - 4:00pm

ALSO BY ARRANGEMENT FEBRUARY

Telephone: 07748 280036

✿ ♿ Partly 🐕 ✿ Fun for Children ☕ Homemade

AYRSHIRE

5. CARNELL Hurlford KA1 5JS

Mr & Mrs J R Findlay and Mr & Mrs Michael Findlay

The 16th century Peel Tower looks down over a 10 acre garden which has featured in the "Beechgrove Garden", "Country Life", The "Good Gardens Guide" as well as Suki Urquhart's book "The Scottish Gardener". Carnell has a traditional walled garden with a 100 yard long herbaceous border, as well as a rock and water garden, Gazebo with Burmese statues, lawns and many other features of interest. Herbaceous, rose and phlox borders are in full bloom during July. The Scottish Delphinium Society have show beds within the walled garden with information and sales stall.

Route: From A77 (Glasgow/Kilmarnock) Take A76 (Mauchline/Dumfries) then right on to the A719 to Ayr for 1½ miles.

Admission: £4.00 School Children Free

SUNDAY 18 JULY 2:00pm - 5:00pm

Web Site: www.carnellestates@com

Telephone: 01563 884236 Email Address: carnellestates@aol.com

Craigie Parish Church receives 10%, Craigie Village Hall receives 10%, British Red Cross Society receives 10%, SSPCA receives 10%, the net remaining to SGS Beneficiaries.

❀ ♿ Partial 🐕 Silver Band on Lawn, Various Stalls and Children's Activities

☕ Homemade Light Refreshments

6. CULZEAN Maybole KA19 8LE

The National Trust for Scotland

One of Scotland's major attractions – a perfect day out for all the family. Robert Adam's romantic 18th-century masterpiece is perched on a cliff high above the Firth of Clyde. The Fountain Garden lies in front of the castle with terraces and herbaceous borders reflecting its Georgian elegance.

The extensive country park offers beaches and rockpools, parklands, gardens, woodland walks and adventure playground. It contains fascinating restored buildings contemporary with the castle.

Guided Walk with the Head Gardener at 2:00pm

Route: OS Ref: NS232103

Road: On A719, 12m S of Ayr, 4m W of Maybole

Cycle: NCN 7

Bus: Stagecoach, Ayr to Girvan via Maidens (No 60). Bus stops at entrance. NB 1m walk downhill from bus stop to Castle/Visitor Centre

Rail: Maybole station, 4m

Admission: £12.00 Concessions £8.00

TUESDAY 20 JULY 10:30am - 5:00pm

Web Site: www.nts.org.uk

Telephone: 0844 493 2148 Email Address: culzean@nts.org.uk

Donation to SGS Beneficiaries

❀ Visitor Centre, Exhibitions, Guided Tours of Castle, Guided Walk, Shops, Ranger Service Events ☕ Homemade Wine Light Refreshments Licensed Restaurant

7. GARDENS OF WEST KILBRIDE AND SEAMILL KA23

The Gardeners of West Kilbride and Seamill

A selection of varied gardens, some new this year, close to the sea in Scotland's Craft Town. Signposted for parking and entrance map.

Route: Heading from Dalry take B781 for 7 miles. Alternatively take the A78 south for 8 miles from Largs or the A78 north for 7 miles from Kilwinning.

Admission: £4.00 Children Free

SATURDAY 19 JUNE 1:00pm - 5:00pm
SUNDAY 20 JUNE 1:00pm - 5:00pm

North Ayrshire Cancer Care receives 20%, Medicines sans Frontieres receives 20%, the net remaining to SGS Beneficiaries.

♿ & Partly as Advised on Map Given on Admission   🐕 See Map given on admission
☕ Homemade Teas in Village Hall

8. GLENHAVEN Kirkmichael KA19 7PR NEW

Mr & Mrs Stewart Selbie

The garden at Glenhaven has been planted in the past five years in a peaceful, woodland setting. There are distinct planting areas including a formal courtyard, herbaceous border, mixed planting and a small vegetable garden.

Route: From Ayr, take A77 south, then B7045 to Kirkmichael. At village centre take Straiton road and follow yellow signs. Park appropriately. **Please No Parking in Kirkmichael Estate grounds.**

Admission: £3.50 Children Under 12 Free

SUNDAY 04 JULY 2:00pm - 5:00pm

Help For Heroes receives 40%, the net remaining to SGS Beneficiaries.

& Partial   Cookery Demonstration with Seasonal Tips, Wine Tasting   ☕ Homemade

9. HOLMES FARM Drybridge, near Irvine KA115BS

Mr Brian A Young

Farmhouse garden created with extensive collections of many interesting herbaceous plants by a confirmed plantaholic. Predominant herbaceous plantings mix with conifers and shrubs to provide interest throughout the year. The garden is opening with Scotland's Gardens Scheme to coincide with the peak bloom of some of the 300 irises contained within the garden. **No dogs please.**

Route: Holmes is the only farm between Drybridge and Dreghorn on B730

Admission: £4.00 Children Free

SATURDAY 29 MAY 12:00pm - 5:00pm
SUNDAY 30 MAY 12:00pm - 5:00pm

Web Site: www.yungi.co.uk Tel: 01294 311210 Email: yungi@fsmail.net

Ayrshire Hospice receives 40%, the net remaining to SGS Beneficiaries.

♿ The Macallan Fine Oak Highland Single Malt Whisky Promotion, Arts and Crafts Gallery, Various Stalls   ☕ Homemade

AYRSHIRE

10. KIRKHILL CASTLE Colmonell KA26 0SB

Mr and Mrs Paul Gibbons

8½ acre garden with rhododendrons, magnolias and camellias. Azalea walk rose garden, and woodland walkways, with newly restored Vine House and Peach House.

No Dogs Please

Route: Kirkhill Castle is in Colmonell Village next to the village hall

Admission: £3.50 Children Free

SUNDAY 16 MAY 2:00pm - 5:00pm

St. Colmon Church receives 40%, the net remaining to SGS Beneficiaries.

♿ Partial   Pipe Band on the Lawn   ☕ Homemade

11. LARGS GARDENING CLUB KA30 8BY   NEW

Largs Gardening Club

Two Town gardens and three Glen gardens. A very pretty cottage garden full of colour, planted with traditional plants and climbers; a surprising front garden with a rill running down to a pond with lots of plants shrubs and grasses. A trio of Glen gardens, one to encourage the wildlife with a pond, specimen trees and shrubs and a mini orchard; a peacefull and sensual garden with perfumed and tactile plants adjacent to the burn; by minibus travel to the third garden which is packed with different layers of plants, shrubs and trees, created over the years by its plantswoman owner.

Route: A 78 south from Greenock and north from Irvine to Tickets and Map point at the Monastery on Mackerston Place, Largs, KA30 8BY (opposite the Putting Green) signposted car park at rear.

Admission: £4.00 Children Free

SUNDAY 27 JUNE 1:30pm - 5:00pm

Telephone: 01475 673194 Email Address: heidistone@btinternet.com

Guide Dogs receives 20%, St. Columba's Church receives 20%, the net remaining to SGS Beneficiaries.

♿ Partly as Advised on Map Given on Admission   🐕 ☕ Refreshments in Tearooms on the Seafront

12 SKELDON Dalrymple KA6 6AT

Mr S E Brodie QC

One and a half acres of formal garden with herbaceous borders and arched pathways. Large Victorian glasshouse with a substantial collection of plants. Four acres of woodland garden within a unique setting on the banks of the River Doon.

Route: From Dalrymple take B7034 Dalrymple/Hollybush Road

Admission: £4.00 Children Free

SUNDAY 01 AUGUST 2:00pm - 5:00pm

Princess Royal Trust for Carers receives 40%, the net remaining to SGS Beneficiaries.

✿ ♿ Partial   Silver Band on Lawn   ☕ Homemade

Berwickshire

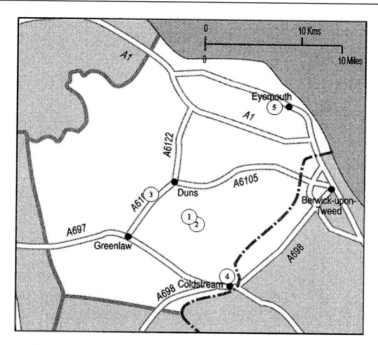

District Organiser: **Mrs F Wills** Antons Hill, Coldstream TD12 4JD
Treasurer: **Mr F Wills**   Antons Hill, Coldstream TD12 4JD

Gardens Open On a Specific Date

Charterhall, Duns	Sunday 02 May	1:00pm - 5:00pm
Lennel Bank, Coldstream	Sunday 23 May	10:30am - 5:00pm
Anton's Hill and Walled Garden, Leitholm	Sunday 27 June	2:00pm - 5:30pm
Netherbyres, Eyemouth	Sunday 04 July	2:00pm - 5:30pm

Gardens Open By Arrangement

When organising a visit to a garden open by arrangement, please enquire if there are facilities and catering available

Anton's Hill and Walled Garden	On request	Tel: 01890 840203
Lennel Bank, Coldstream	On request	Tel: 01890 228897
Netherbyres, Eyemouth	May – September	Tel: 018907 50337
	(Groups of 10 or more)	

Gardens Open Regularly

Bughtrig, Near Leitholm   01 June - 01 September 11:00am - 5:00pm

1. ANTON'S HILL AND WALLED GARDEN Leitholm, Coldstream TD12 4JD

Mr & Mrs Wills, Alec West & Pat Watson

Well treed mature garden which has been improved and added to since 1999. There are woodland walks including a stumpery and a large well planted pond, shrubberies and herbaceous borders. Topiary Elephant family of yew and a new woodland pond. A restored organic walled garden and greenhouse with an apple and pear orchard containing a growing collection of over 230 varieties. Model Railway

Route: Signed off B6461 west of Leitholm

Admission: £3.50 Children £1.50

SUNDAY 27 JUNE 2:00pm - 5:30pm

ALSO BY ARRANGEMENT ON REQUEST

Telephone: 01890 840203

Email Address: cillwills@antonshill.co.uk

Friends of Oakfield - Home for People with Special Needs receives 40%, the net remaining to SGS Beneficiaries.

✿ ⌖ 🐕 ☕ Homemade

2. BUGHTRIG Near Leitholm, Coldsteam TD12 4JP

Major General C and The Hon Mrs Ramsay

A traditional hedged Scottish family garden with an interesting combination of herbaceous plants, shrubs, annuals and fruit. It is surrounded by fine specimen trees which provide remarkable shelter.

Route: Quarter mile east of Leitholm on B6461

Admission: Adults £3.00 Children under 18 £1.00

01 JUNE - 01 SEPTEMBER 11:00am - 5:00pm

Telephone: 01890 840678

Email Address: ramsay@bughtrig.co.uk

Donation to SGS Beneficiaries

⌖ Mostly   Special Arrangements Including House Visit Possible for Bona Fide Groups, Small Picnic Area

3. CHARTERHALL Duns TD11 3RE

Major and Mrs A Trotter

Mature and young rhododendrons and azaleas and shrubs in an old woodland garden surrounding a lovely family home with an outstanding view. Flower garden with fine collection of roses, bulbs and perennial plants. Also a new addition of a greenhouse and vegetable garden.

Route: On B6460, 6 miles south west of Duns and 3 miles east of Greenlaw

Admission: £4.00 Children £1.50

SUNDAY 02 MAY 1:00pm - 5:00pm

Christ Church Duns receives 40%, the net remaining to SGS Beneficiaries.

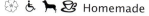 Homemade

4. LENNEL BANK Coldstream TD12 4EX NEW

Mrs Honor Brown

Lennel Bank is a terraced garden overlooking the River Tweed, consisting of wide borders packed with shrubs and perennial planting, some unusual. The water garden, built in 2008, is surrounded by a rockery and utilises the slope ending in a pond. There is a small kitchen garden with raised beds in unusual shapes. Different growing conditions throughout the garden from dry, wet, shady and sun lends itself to a variety of plants, which hopefully enhances the garden's interest.

Route: On A6112 Coldstream to Duns Road. 1 mile from Coldstream.

Admission: £3.50

SUNDAY 23 MAY 10:30am - 5:00pm

ALSO BY ARRANGEMENT ON REQUEST

Telephone: 01890 228897

British Heart Foundation receives 40%, the net remaining to SGS Beneficiaries.

 Homemade

5. NETHERBYRES Eyemouth TD14 5SE

Col. S J Furness & Leonard Cheshire Disability

A unique 18th century elliptical walled garden. Annuals, roses, herbaceous borders, fruit and vegetables in summer.

Route: ½ mile south of Eyemouth on A1107 to Berwick

Admission: Adults £4.00, OAPs £3.00, Children Under 14 Free

SUNDAY 04 JULY 2:00pm - 5:30pm

ALSO BY ARRANGEMENT MAY - SEPTEMBER: FOR GROUPS OF 10 OR MORE

Telephone: 018907 50337

Friends of Netherbyres receives 40%, the net remaining to SGS Beneficiaries.

Wrap spring bulbs in a thin layer of steel wool. It does not harm the bulbs but will help prevent animals from digging up and eating them.

Caithness, Sutherland & Orkney

'Gardens of Scotland' 2010 is sponsored by **Rensburg Sheppards Investment Management**

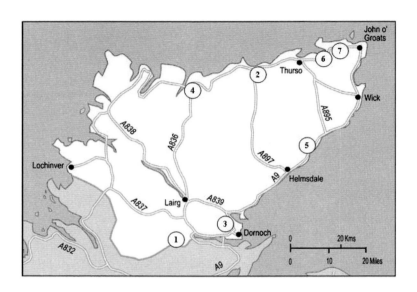

District Organiser: Mrs Judith Middlemas 22 Miller Place, Scrabster, Thurso KW14 7UH

Area Organiser: **Mrs Jonny Shaw** Amat, Ardgay, Sutherland IV24 3BS

Treasurer: **Mr Chris Hobson** Braeside, Dunnet, Caithness KW14 8YD

Gardens Open On a Specific Date

Amat, Ardgay	Saturday 05 June	2:00pm - 5:00pm
Amat, Ardgay	Sunday 06 June	2:00pm - 5:00pm
Pentland Firth Gardens, Dunnet	Sunday 13 June	1:00pm - 5:00pm
Bumblebee Cottage, Dornoch	Sunday 27 June	2:00pm - 5:00pm
The Castle & Gardens of Mey	Wednesday 07 July	10:00am - 5:00pm
The Castle & Gardens of Mey	Thursday 15 July	10:00am - 5:00pm
House of Tongue, Tongue	Saturday 31 July	2:00pm - 6:00pm
Langwell, Berriedale	Sunday 08 August	2:00pm - 5:00pm
The Castle & Gardens of Mey	Saturday 14 August	10:00am - 5:00pm
Langwell, Berriedale	Sunday 15 August	2:00pm - 5:00pm
Bighouse Lodge, By Melvich	Saturday 28 August	2:30pm - 5:30pm

Gardens Open By Arrangement

When organising a visit to a garden open by arrangement, please enquire if there are facilities and catering available

Langwell, Berriedale	On request	Tel: 01593 751278/751237

Gardens Open Regularly

The Castle & Gardens of Mey	02 April - 05 April	10:00am - 5:00pm
	01 May - 29 July	10:00am - 5:00pm
	10 Aug. - 30 Sept.	10:00am - 5:00pm

1. AMAT Ardgay IV24 3BS

Jonny and Sara Shaw

Riverside garden set in Amat forest. Old and new rhododendrons. Woodland and river walk.

Route: Take road from Ardgay to Croick 9 miles. Turn left at red phone box. 400 yards on left

Admission: £4.00

SATURDAY 05 JUNE 2:00pm - 5:00pm

SUNDAY 06 JUNE 2:00pm - 5:00pm

Croick Church receives 20%, Mercy Ships receives 20%, the net remaining to SGS Beneficiaries.

✿ ♿ Partial 🐕 ☕ Homemade £2.50

2. BIGHOUSE LODGE By Melvich KW14 8YJ NEW

Bighouse Estate

Bighouse Lodge is situated on the north coast of Sutherland at the mouth of the River Halladale. The 2 acre walled garden, originally laid out in 1715, consists of a central axis leading to a charming bothy with lawn, herbaceous borders, a sunken garden and four separate conceptual gardens behind the hedgerows. Each garden contains a sculpture to reflect the aspects of the Bighouse Estate namely the River, the Forest, the Strath and the Hill. The garden has recently been restored and is now a most interesting place to visit.

Route: Off A836 ½ mile East of Melvich

Admission: £4.00. Children Under 12 £0.50p

SATURDAY 28 AUGUST 2:30pm - 5:30pm

RNLI receives 40%, the net remaining to SGS Beneficiaries.

♿ Partial ☕ Homemade

3. BUMBLEBEE COTTAGE Embo Street, Dornoch IV25 3PW NEW

Mr and Mrs Steve and Esther Farquharson

A mixed garden containing a cottage garden, a secret garden, wooded area, small orchard & herbaceous border. Also a varied kitchen garden complete with 2 polytunnels and a greenhouse.

CAITHNESS, SUTHERLAND & ORKNEY

<u>Route:</u> From Dornoch Square take road signposted Embo. After 1½ miles turn left to Embo Street. Garden on left in 500 yards signed Bumblebee Cottage.

<u>Admission:</u> £3.50

SUNDAY 27 JUNE 2:00pm - 5:00pm

Guide Dogs for the Blind receives 20%, Macmillan Nurses receives 20%, the net remaining to SGS Beneficiaries.

☕ Homemade

4. HOUSE OF TONGUE Tongue, Lairg IV27 4XH

The Countess of Sutherland

17th century house on Kyle of Tongue. Walled garden, herbaceous borders, old fashioned roses, vegetables, soft fruit and small orchard.

<u>Route:</u> Tongue half a mile. House just off main road approaching causeway.

<u>Admission:</u> £4.00, OAPs £3.00, Children (under 12) 50p

SATURDAY 31 JULY 2:00pm - 6:00pm

Email Address: ginrik@btopenworld.com

Children First receives 40%, the net remaining to SGS Beneficiaries.

♿ Partial 🐕 ☕ Homemade

5. LANGWELL Berriedale KW7 6HD

Welbeck Estates

A beautiful and spectacular old walled-in garden with spectacular borders situated in the secluded Langwell Strath. Charming access drive with a chance to see deer.

<u>Route:</u> A9 Berriedale 2 miles

<u>Admission:</u> £4.00 OAPs £3.00 Children Under 12 Free

SUNDAY 08 AUGUST 2:00pm - 5:00pm
SUNDAY 15 AUGUST 2:00pm - 5:00pm
ALSO BY ARRANGEMENT ON REQUEST

Telephone: 01593 751278/751237

Email Address: macanson@hotmail.com

RNLI receives 40%, the net remaining to SGS Beneficiaries.

♿ Partial 🐕 ☕ Homemade Teas Under Cover

6. PENTLAND FIRTH GARDENS Dunnet KW14 8YD NEW

The Pentland Firth Gardeners

With panoramic views of the Pentland Firth and Ham Harbour, these gardens show what is possible when gardening on the Northern coast of Scotland. Three varied gardens, one with a sea shore walk with cairns and the chance to see swans and other water and sea birds. All gardens have a good variety of hardy plants and shrubs to enjoy. Transport required in order to visit all gardens.

<u>Route:</u> Start at Britannia Hall, Dunnet KW14 8YD where a map of all gardens will be available on payment of admission fee.

Admission: £4.00 Concessions £3.00 Children Under 12 Free
SUNDAY 13 JUNE 1:00pm - 5:00pm
Telephone: 01847 851757
Dunnet Forest Trust receives 40%, the net remaining to SGS Beneficiaries.
❀ ♿ Partial   🐕   Toilets Available at Britannia Hall   ☕ Homemade Available at Britannia Hall

7. THE CASTLE & GARDENS OF MEY Mey KW14 8XH

The Queen Elizabeth Castle of Mey Trust
Originally a Z plan castle bought by the Queen Mother in 1952 and then restored and improved. The walled garden and the East Garden were also created by the Queen Mother. An Animal Centre has been created over the last 2 years and is proving very popular with all ages.
Route: On A836 between Thurso and John O'Groats, 1½ miles from Mey.
Admission: **Gardens and Animal Centre:** £4.00
Castle, Gardens and Animal Centre: £9.50, Concessions £8.50, Children £4.00.
Family ticket £23.00 (2 adults and up to 4 children)
WEDNESDAY 07 JULY 10:00am - 5:00pm
THURSDAY 15 JULY 10:00am - 5:00pm
SATURDAY 14 AUGUST 10:00am - 5:00pm
02 APRIL - 05 APRIL 10:00am - 5:00pm
01 MAY - 29 JULY 10:00am - 5:00pm
10 AUGUST - 30 SEPTEMBER 10:00am - 5:00pm
Web Site: www.castleofmey.org.uk
Telephone: 01847 851473
Email Address: castleofmey@totalise.co.uk
Marie Curie receives 40%, the net remaining to SGS Beneficiaries.
♿ Limited   🐕   Visitor & Animal Centres, Shop   ☕ Cream Wine Light Refreshments   Restaurant

To deter cats add rose thorns onto your flowerbeds as cats hate them, dogs can be deterred by spray perfume or aftershave in your garden. To deter slugs spread egg shells as they will not crawl over them because of the sharpness.

Dumfriesshire

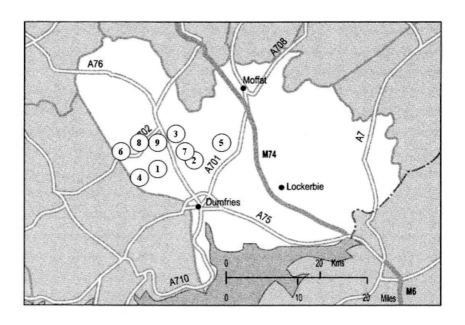

District Organiser: **Mrs Sarah Landale** Dalswinton House, Dalswinton, Auldgirth DG2 0XZ

Area Organiser: **Mrs Fiona Bell-Irving** Bankside, Kettleholm, Lockerbie DG11 1BY

Treasurer: **Mr J C Smith** Kirkmichael Old Manse, Parkgate, Dumfries DG1 3LY

Gardens Open On a Specific Date

Portrack House, Holywood	Sunday 02 May	12:00pm - 5:00pm
Dalswinton House, Dalswinton	Sunday 16 May	2:00pm - 5:00pm
Cowhill Tower, Holywood	Sunday 30 May	2:00pm - 5:00pm
Glenae, Amisfield	Sunday 06 June	2:00pm - 5:00pm
Dunesslin, Dunscore	Sunday 13 June	2:00pm - 5:00pm
The Garth, Tynron, Thornhill	Sunday 27 June	2:00pm - 5:00pm
Woodend Cottage, Closeburn	Sunday 11 July	2:00pm - 5:00pm
Berscar House, Closeburn	Sunday 25 July	2:00pm - 5:00pm

Gardens Open By Arrangement

When organising a visit to a garden open by arrangement, please enquire if there are facilities and catering available

Peilton, Moniaive   April and May   Tel: 01848 200363

1. BERSCAR HOUSE Closeburn DG3 5JJ

Toni Cunningham Cade and Phillip Cade

Late 18th century house set in 5 acres of garden. Replanted in 1960s and now under restoration by present owners. Oustanding location with exceptional views; interesting combination of a sheltered and well-established sunken walled garden, woodland walks and a terraced garden.

Route: 2 miles North of Auldgirth on the A76. Entrance is an awkward turning on the left.

Admission: £4.00 Children 50p

SUNDAY 25 JULY 2:00pm - 5:00pm

Closeburn Church receives 40%, the net remaining to SGS Beneficiaries.

❀ ♿ Very Limited ☕ Homemade

2. COWHILL TOWER Holywood DG2 0RL

Mr and Mrs P Weatherall

Interesting walled garden; topiary animals, birds and figures. Woodland walk. Splendid views from lawn down the Nith valley. Variety of statues from the Far East.

Route: Holywood 1½ miles off A76, 5 miles north of Dumfries.

Admission: £4.00 Children 50p

SUNDAY 30 MAY 2:00pm - 5:00pm

Telephone: 01387 720304

Maggie's Cancer Caring Centres receives 40%, the net remaining to SGS Beneficiaries.

❀ ♿ 🐕 ☕ Homemade

3. DALSWINTON HOUSE Dalswinton DG2 0XZ

Mr and Mrs Peter Landale

Late 18th century house sits on top of a hill surrounded by herbaceous beds and well established shrubs, including rhododendrons and azaleas overlooking the loch. Attractive walks through woods and around the loch. It was here that the first steamboat in Britain made its maiden voyage in 1788 and there is a life-size model beside the water to commemorate this. A recently established plant centre is now in the old walled garden.

Route: Seven miles North of Dumfries off A76.

Admission: £4.00 Children Free

SUNDAY 16 MAY 2:00pm - 5:00pm

Telephone: 01387 740220

Kirkmahoe Parish Church receives 40%, the net remaining to SGS Beneficiaries.

☕ Homemade

DUMFRIESSHIRE

4. DUNESSLIN Dunscore DG2 0UR

Iain and Zara Milligan

Set in Dumfriesshire hills with good views. Principal garden consists of a series of connecting rooms filled with herbaceous plants. Woodland walk and Andy Goldsworthy sculptures.

Route: From Dunscore, follow road to Corsock. Approx 1½ miles on, turn right at post box, still on road to Corsock and at small crossroads ½ mile on, turn left.

Admission: £4.00

SUNDAY 13 JUNE 2:00pm - 5:00pm

Telephone: 01387 820345

Altzheimers Dumfries receives 40%, the net remaining to SGS Beneficiaries.

✿ ☕ Homemade

5. GLENAE Amisfield DG1 3NZ

Mr and Mrs Sebastian Morley

A beautiful walled garden, well stocked with interesting plants, 4 small lawns surrounded by colourful herbaceous borders, a woodland garden and a restored Victorian glass-house.

Route: 1½ miles north of Amisfield on A701. Turn left to Duncow and Auldgirth and 1 mile on right.

Admission: £3.00 Children 50p

SUNDAY 06 JUNE 2:00pm - 5:00pm

Telephone: 01387 710236

South West Scotland R and R receives 40%, the net remaining to SGS Beneficiaries.

✿ ♿ Limited 🐕 ☕ Homemade

6. PEILTON Moniaive DG3 4HE

Mrs Alison Graham

Very attractive and interesting small woodland garden with rhododendrons, shrubs and flowering trees.

Route: Off A702 between Kirkland of Glencairn and Moniaive

Admission: £3.00

BY ARRANGEMENT APRIL AND MAY

Telephone: 01848 200363

Cancer Active receives 40%, the net remaining to SGS Beneficiaries.

7. PORTRACK HOUSE Holywood DG2 0RW

Charles Jencks

Original 18th century manor house with Victorian addition; octagonal folly-library. Twisted undulating landforms and terraces designed by Charles Jencks as "The Garden of Cosmic Speculation"; lakes designed by Maggie Keswick; rhododendrons, large new greenhouse in a geometric Kitchen Garden of the Six Senses; Glengower Hill plantation and view; woodland walks with Nonsense Building (architect: James Stirling); Universe cascade and rail garden of the Scottish Worthies; interesting sculpture including that of DNA and newly completed Comet Bridge.

Route: Holywood 1½ miles off A76, five miles north of Dumfries.

Admission: £6.00

SUNDAY 02 MAY 12:00pm - 5:00pm

Web Site: www.charlesjencks.com

Maggie's Cancer Caring Centres receives 40%, the net remaining to SGS Beneficiaries.

Local Pipe Band ☕

8. THE GARTH Tynron, Thornhill DG3 4JY

Mimi and Christopher Craig

Old Manse, established 1750 with additions. Two acre garden - woodland, waterside and walled.

Route: Off A702 between Penpont and Moniaive.

Admission: £3.50 Children 50p

SUNDAY 27 JUNE 2:00pm - 5:00pm

Telephone: 01848 200364

Village Hall Fund receives 40%, the net remaining to SGS Beneficiaries.

♿ With Gravel ☕ In Village Hall Nearby

9. WOODEND COTTAGE Closeburn DG3 5JD NEW

Mr and Mrs Martin McGrail

Mature Garden under renovation with vegetable plot. Collection of trees and shrubs. Water feature.

Route: Off A76 at Closeburn Village on Dumfries to Thornhill road.

Admission: £3.00

SUNDAY 11 JULY 2:00pm - 5:00pm

Telephone: 01848 331426

Email Address: martin.mcgrail101@btinternet.com

Guide Dogs for the Blind receives 40%, the net remaining to SGS Beneficiaries.

✿ 🐕 ☕ Homemade Light Refreshments £2.00

Adding Brillo pads or old rusty nails will improve limey soil.

Dunbartonshire

'Gardens of Scotland' 2010 is sponsored by **Rensburg Sheppards Investment Management**

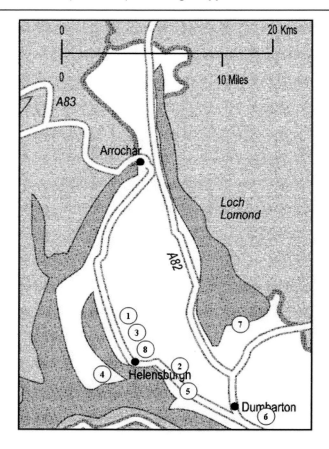

District Organiser: **Mrs K Murray** 7 The Birches, Shandon, Helensburgh G84 8HN

Area Organisers: **Mrs M Greenwell** Avalon, Shore Road, Mambeg, Garelochead G84 0EN

Mrs R Lang Ardchapel, Shandon, Helensburgh G84 8NP

Mrs R Macaulay Denehard, Garelochhead G84 0EL

Mrs S Miller 8 Laggary Park, Rhu G84 8LY

Mrs J Theaker 19 Blackhill Drive Helensburgh, G84 9AF

Mrs H Wands Lindowan, Rhu G84 8NH

Treasurer: **Mrs S Miller** 8 Laggary Park, Rhu G84 8LY

Gardens Open On a Specific Date

Kilarden, Rosneath	Sunday 18 April	2:00pm - 5:00pm
Ardchapel and Seven The Birches, Shandon	Sunday 09 May	2:00pm - 5:00pm
Geilston Garden, Cardross	Sunday 16 May	1:00pm - 5:00pm
Ross Priory, Gartocharn	Sunday 23 May	2:00pm - 5:30pm
Milton House, Milton, Dunbarton	Sunday 30 May	2:00pm - 5:00pm
Kirkton Cottage, Cardross	Sunday 20 June	2:00pm - 5:00pm
The Hill House, Helensburgh	Sunday 05 Sept.	11:00am - 4:00pm

Gardens Open Regularly

Glenarn, Glenarn Road, Rhu	21 March - 21 Sept.	Dawn - Dusk

Plant Sales

The Hill House Plant Sale, Helensburgh	Sunday 05 Sept.	11:00am - 4:00pm

1. ARDCHAPEL AND SEVEN THE BIRCHES Shandon, Helensburgh G84 8HN

ARDCHAPEL Mr and Mrs J S Lang

Well established garden with mature interesting trees overlooking the Gareloch in three and a half acres of ground. Woodland walks with burn, rhododendrons, azaleas and camellias. Flower and vegetable garden. Herbaceous border sheltered by high wall on north side.

SEVEN THE BIRCHES: Mr and Mrs R. Murray

Small, intensively planted garden which has been developed over the past 12 years. Borders filled with perennials, shrubs, roses, ferns and spring flowering bulbs. Colourful containers. Alpine bed

Route: Three and three quarter miles north of Helensburgh on A814. Parking on service road below houses.

Admission: £4.00 Children under 12 Free

SUNDAY 09 MAY 2:00pm - 5:00pm

Sight Savers receives 40%, the net remaining to SGS Beneficiaries.

With Shortbread at Ardchapel

2. GEILSTON GARDEN Main Road, Cardross G82 5HD

The National Trust for Scotland

The present design of Geilston Garden was laid out over 200 years ago to enhance Geilston House, which dates back to the late 17th century. The garden has many attractive features including the walled garden wherein a notable specimen of Sequioadendron giganteum dominates the lawn and the herbaceous border provides summer colour on a grand scale. In addition a wide range of fruit, vegetables and cut flowers is still cultivated in the kitchen garden. The Geilston Burn winds its way through enchanting woodland walks which provide spring displays of bluebells and azaleas.

Route: A814, Cardross 1 mile

DUNBARTONSHIRE

Admission: £4.00 Children Under 12 Free

SUNDAY 16 MAY 1:00pm - 5:00pm

Web Site: www.nts.org.uk

Telephone: 0844 493 2219

Email Address: jgough@nts.org.uk

Donation to SGS Beneficiaries

✿ ♿ ☕ Homemade

3. GLENARN Glenarn Road, Rhu, Helensburgh G84 8LL

Michael & Sue Thornley

Sheltered woodland garden overlooking the Gareloch, famous for its collection of rare and tender rhododendrons, together with fine magnolias and other interesting trees and shrubs. Beneath are snowdrops, crocus, daffodils, erythroniums and primulas in abundance. We have a new potting shed and cold frames and the drystone wallers are continuing their work. There are beehives near the vegetable patch.

Route: On A814, two miles north of Helensburgh. Cars to be left at gate unless passengers are infirm

Admission: £4.00 No charge for Accompanied Children Under 16

21 MARCH - 21 SEPTEMBER DAWN - DUSK

Web Site: www.gardens-of-argyll.co.uk

Telephone: 01436 820493

Email Address: masthome@dsl.pipex.com

Donation to SGS Beneficiaries

✿ ♿ Limited 🐕 Honey for Sale at Times Catering for Groups by Prior Arrangement

4. KILARDEN Rosneath G84 0PU

Mr & Mrs J.E. Rowe

Sheltered hilly 10 acre woodland with notable collection of species and hybrid rhododendrons gathered over a period of 50 years by the late Neil and Joyce Rutherford as seen on "Beechgrove Garden". Paths may be muddy

Route: ¼ mile from Rosneath off B833

Admission: £2.50

SUNDAY 18 APRIL 2:00pm - 5:00pm

Friends of St Modan's receives 40%, the net remaining to SGS Beneficiaries.

✿ ♿ In Restricted Part Only 🐕 Rosneath Peninsula Pipe Band, Church Open - Organ Music ☕ Homemade

5. KIRKTON COTTAGE Cardross, Dumbarton G82 5EZ

Mr & Mrs T. Duggan

A garden of just under one acre on a south facing slope with a burn running through, which provides a variety of growing conditions. Mixed borders, fruit, vegetables, herbs and bog garden.

Route: ½ mile up Darleith Road at west end of Cardross off A814.

Admission: £3.00 Children Free

SUNDAY 20 JUNE 2:00pm - 5:00pm

Smile Train receives 20%, Alzheimer Scotland, Helensburgh & District Branch receives 20%, the net remaining to SGS Beneficiaries.

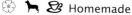 Homemade at Nearby Kirkton House

6. MILTON HOUSE Milton, Dunbarton G82 2TU

Mr. & Mrs. Charles Villiers

Beautiful rhododendron garden: many mature species and old hybrids as well as new plantings over the past decade. Fine extensive views out high above the Clyde estuary. Large lawn sweeps down in front of late 18th century house which is sheltered by extensive arboretum of mature trees. Large variety of interesting shrubs including azaleas, camellias, magnolia wilsonii, stewartia. Herbaceous borders with tree and herbaceous peonies, alliums, agapanthus and many more plants. Rich carpet of Spring bulbs in themed colours; box parterre and some topiary; island beds with meconopsis, roses and perennials. Folly and bluebell woodland garden. Glen and lochan not open to the public.

Route: On the north side of the Clyde, off the A82 at Milton; west of Dunglass Roundabout turn right at Esso Service Station; east of Dumbarton/Loch Lomond junction turn left before BP service station. Entrance is on left up Milton Brae. Parking as directed.

Admission: £4.00 Children Under 16 Free

SUNDAY 30 MAY 2:00pm - 5:00pm

Hope and Homes for Children receives 40%, the net remaining to SGS Beneficiaries.

Homemade

7. ROSS PRIORY Gartocharn G83 8NL

University of Strathclyde

1812 Gothic addition by James Gillespie Graham to house of 1693 overlooking Loch Lomond. Rhododendrons, azaleas, selected shrubs and trees. Walled garden with glasshouses, pergola, ornamental plantings. Family burial ground. Nature and garden trails. House not open to view.

Route: Gartocharn 1½ miles off A811. Bus: Balloch to Gartocharn leaves Balloch at 1pm and 3pm

Admission: £4.00 Children Free

SUNDAY 23 MAY 2:00pm - 5:30pm

CHAS receives 40%, the net remaining to SGS Beneficiaries.

Putting Green   Homemade In House

DUNBARTONSHIRE

8. THE HILL HOUSE Helensburgh G84 9AJ

The National Trust for Scotland

The Hill House has fine views over the Clyde estuary and is considered Charles Rennie Mackintosh's domestic masterpiece. The gardens continue to be restored to the patron's planting scheme with many features that reflect Mackintosh's design.

Route: Follow signs to The Hill House

Admission: Free: Donations to Scotland's Gardens Scheme welcome.

House open 1.30pm - 5.30pm (normal entrance charges apply)

SUNDAY 05 SEPTEMBER 11:00am - 4:00pm

Web Site: www.nts.org.uk

Telephone: 01436 673900

Email Address: gsmith@nts.org.uk

All proceeds, except teas, to SGS Beneficiaries

 ♿ ☕ Served in House from 11.00am

PLANT SALES

8. THE HILL HOUSE PLANT SALE Helensburgh G84 9AJ

The National Trust for Scotland

Scotland's Gardens Scheme's Plant Sale is held in the garden of The Hill House. The sale includes nursery grown perennials and locally grown trees, shrubs, herbaceous, alpines and house plants. See Dunbartonshire garden entry no. 8 for details of the garden

Route: Follow signs to The Hill House

Admission: Free: Donations to Scotland's Gardens Scheme welcome.

House open 1.30pm - 5.30pm (normal entrance charges apply)

SUNDAY 05 SEPTEMBER 11:00am - 4:00pm

Web Site: www.nts.org.uk

Telephone: 01436 673900

Email Address: gsmith@nts.org.uk

All proceeds, except teas to SGS Beneficiaries

 ♿ ☕ Served in House from 11.00am

Soap can be used to stop squirrels eating your bulbs, just grate some soap into holes where you are planting.

East Lothian

'Gardens of Scotland' 2010 is sponsored by **Rensburg Sheppards Investment Management**

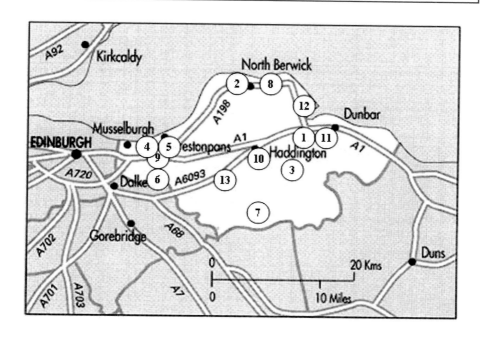

District Organiser:	**Mr W Alder** Granary House, Kippielaw, Haddington EH41 4PY
Area Organisers:	**Mr P Atkins** Mizzentop, Westerdunes Park, North Berwick EH39 5HJ
	Mrs C Gwyn The Walled Garden, Tyninghame, Dunbar EH42 1XY
	Mr T W Jackson Highbury, Whim Road, Gullane EH31 2BD
	Mrs J Lindsay Kirkland, Whittinghame EH41 4QA
	Mrs N Parker Steading Cottage, Stevenson, Haddington EH41 4PU
Area Plant Sales Organiser:	**The Hon Michael Dalrymple** Oxenfoord Castle, Oxenfoord, Pathhead EH22 2PF
Treasurer:	**Mr S M Edington** Meadowside Cottage, Strathearn Road, North Berwick EH39 5BZ

Gardens Open On a Specific Date

Shepherd House, Inveresk	Sunday 21 February	12:00pm - 3:00pm
Winton House, Pencaitland	Sunday 11 April	12:00pm - 4:30pm
Shepherd House, Inveresk	Sunday 25 April	2:00pm - 5:00pm
Tyninghame House, Dunbar	Sunday 16 May	1:00pm - 5:00pm
Stenton Village, East Lothian	Sunday 30 May	2:00pm - 5:30pm
St Mary's Pleasance, Haddington	Saturday 05 June	2:00pm - 5:00pm
Inveresk Village, Musselburgh	Sunday 06 June	2:00pm - 5:00pm
Shepherd House, Inveresk	Sunday 06 June	2:00pm - 5:00pm
Dirleton Village, North Berwick	Saturday 12 June	2:00pm - 5:00pm
Dirleton Village, North Berwick	Sunday 13 June	2:00pm - 5:00pm
Inveresk Lodge Garden, Inveresk Village	Sunday 20 June	10:00am - 6:00pm
Tyninghame House, Dunbar	Sunday 20 June	1:00pm - 5:00pm
North Berwick Coastal Gardens	Saturday 26 June	2:00pm - 5:00pm
Clint, Stenton, Nr. Dunbar	Sunday 27 June	2:00pm - 5:30pm
Gifford Village, Gifford	Sunday 04 July	2:00pm - 6:00pm
Inwood, Carberry	Sunday 11 July	2:00pm - 5:00pm
Johnstounburn House, Humbie	Sunday 22 August	2:00pm - 5:30pm

Gardens Open By Arrangement
When organising a visit to a garden open by arrangement, please enquire if there are facilities and catering available

Inwood, Carberry	Groups Welcome	Tel: 0131 665 4550
Shepherd House, Inveresk	Groups Welcome	Tel: 0131 665 2570

Gardens Open Regularly

Shepherd House, Inveresk	09 February - 04 March and 01 April - 29 June Tuesdays & Thursdays	2:00pm - 4:00pm
Inwood, Carberry, Musselburgh	1 April to 30 September Tues, Thurs & Sats	2:00pm - 5:00pm
St Mary's Pleasance, 28 Sidegate, Haddington	Summer Winter	9:00am - 5:00pm 9:00am – 3:30pm

Plant Sales

SGS Plant Sale, Oxenfoord Mains	Saturday 09 October	9:30am - 1:30pm

1. CLINT Stenton, Nr. Dunbar EH42 1TQ
Mr and Mrs John W Blair
Burnside garden with assortment of primulae, good herbaceous borders, woodland

walks. All in a wonderful setting.

Route: East Linton 3 miles, Stenton ½ mile. South on the A1 turn right at East Linton follow sign to Stenton, after 2 miles turn right B6370 to Gifford. Drive entrance on left, Exit through fields.

Admission: £4.00 Children Under 12 Free

SUNDAY 27 JUNE 2:00pm - 5:30pm

Save the Children receives 40%, the net remaining to SGS Beneficiaries.

✿ ♿ Reasonable ⚘ Ice-cream ☕ Homemade

2. DIRLETON VILLAGE North Berwick EH39 5EH

The Gardeners of Dirleton & Historic Scotland

Dirleton is a beautiful conservation village with a large Green, historic church and castle. Gardens of various sizes and types are open throughout the village, including the famous castle gardens. Parking, tickets and maps are available at the Green and teas are served in the Church Hall.

Route: Dirleton Village is 2 miles west of North Berwick

Admission: £4.00 Children Free

SATURDAY 12 JUNE 2:00pm - 5:00pm

SUNDAY 13 JUNE 2:00pm - 5:00pm

RNLI receives 40%, the net remaining to SGS Beneficiaries.

♿ To Most Gardens ⚘ Flower Festival in Dirleton Kirk ☕ Teas in Church Hall

3. GIFFORD VILLAGE Gifford EH41 4QY

The Gardeners of Gifford

Various gardens from small patio to quite large, up to ¾ acre.

Route: The village is signposted from Haddington.

Admission: £4.00

SUNDAY 04 JULY 2:00pm - 6:00pm

Gifford Horticultural Society receives 40%, the net remaining to SGS Beneficiaries.

⚘ ☕

4. INVERESK LODGE GARDEN 24 Inveresk Village, Musselburgh EH21 7TE

The National Trust for Scotland

A must visit destination for all keen gardeners. A delightful hillside garden just awaiting discovery, tucked away within its stone boundary walls. Discover many unusual plants and familiar friends growing within mixed beds and borders. You'll also be drawn to the beautiful restored Victorian conservatory which is also home to an aviary. The garden is a true treat for the senses with scented plants and birdsong. Below the garden lies the meadow and pond, a haven for wildlife waiting to be spotted.

Route: OS Ref: NT348716

Road: A6124, S of Musselburgh, 6m E of Edinburgh

Cycle: 1m from NCN 1

Bus: Lothian Region Transport from Edinburgh city centre

EAST LOTHIAN

Admission: £3.00

SUNDAY 20 JUNE 10:00am - 6:00pm

Web Site: www.nts.org.uk

Telephone: 0844 493 2126

Email Address: inveresk@nts.org.uk

Donation to SGS Beneficiaries

♿ Partial   NCCPG   Pond Dipping Platform, Scented Plants

5. INVERESK VILLAGE Musselburgh EH21

The Gardeners of Inveresk

A collection of walled gardens in an elegant and historic village. Each has its own individual character displaying a wide variety of interesting and unusual trees, shrubs and plants.

Route: South side of Musselburgh, Inveresk Village Road - A6124

Admission: £5.00 Children Free

SUNDAY 06 JUNE 2:00pm - 5:00pm

Victim Support Scotland receives 40%, the net remaining to SGS Beneficiaries.

⚚ ♿ Not all Gardens   Homemade

6. INWOOD Carberry, Musselburgh EH21 8PZ

Mr and Mrs I Morrison

With the backdrop of mature woodland the garden at Inwood sits snugly around the house of which a fine Cornus contraversa variagata forms the centrepiece. Springtime includes masses of tulips and rhododendrons whilst rambling roses romp through the trees in high summer and hydrangeas, dahlias and perennials bring the season to a close. A fine display of begonias and streptocarpus awaits the visitor in the glasshouse and the depths of the pond can be explored for newts and frogs.

RHS Recommended Garden.

Route: 1 mile south of Whitecraig on A6124

Admission: £3.00 Accompanied Children Free

SUNDAY 11 JULY 2:00pm - 5:00pm

1 APRIL TO 30 SEPTEMBER TUESDAY, THURSDAY & SATURDAYS 2:00pm - 5:00pm

ALSO BY ARRANGEMENT GROUPS WELCOME

Web Site: www.inwoodgarden.com

Telephone: 0131 665 4550

Email Address: lindsay@inwoodgarden.com

All proceeds to SGS Beneficiaries

⚚ ♿ With Help

7. JOHNSTOUNBURN HOUSE Humbie EH36 5PL

Mr & Mrs Charles Plowden

Formal Scottish walled garden newly restored with contemporary and traditional planting schemes. Policies include a doocot, gazebo, mature specimen trees and delightful parkland setting. Large potager with fruit, vegetables and flowers, restored Victorian glasshouse, fountain and pergola. Ornamental terraces, sunken French garden, large lawns, ancient yew hedges, double herbaceous border, nut walk, orchard and rose garden. New plantings for 2010.

Route: Halfway between Humbie and Fala (A68) on the B6368. If travelling from Fala turn right off the B6457. From Humbie go past the junction to Fala. The gate arch is on the left.

Admission: £4.00. Children under 12 free

SUNDAY 22 AUGUST 2:00pm - 5:30pm

The Lamp of Lothian Trust receives 40%, the net remaining to SGS Beneficiaries.

 Other Stalls ☕ Cream

8. NORTH BERWICK COASTAL GARDENS North Berwick EH39

North Berwick Coastal Gardeners

Two neighbouring walled gardens overlooking golf course and Firth of Forth, within walking distance of North Berwick centre and station. Good herbaceous borders, hedges and topiary.

Route: Proceed to Cromwell Road & Fidra Road. Signed from main road.

Admission: £4.00

SATURDAY 26 JUNE 2:00pm - 5:00pm

Maggie's Cancer Caring Centres receives 40%, the net remaining to SGS Beneficiaries.

& Limited from Golf Course Only 🐕 ☕ Cream

9. SHEPHERD HOUSE Inveresk, Musselburgh EH21 7TH

Sir Charles and Lady Fraser

Shepherd House and its one-acre garden form a walled triangle in the middle of the 18th century village of Inveresk The main garden is to the rear of the house where the formality of the front garden is continued with a herb parterre and two symmetrical potagers. A formal rill runs the length of the garden, beneath a series of rose, clematis and wisteria pergolas and arches and connects the two ponds. The formality is balanced by the romance of the planting. Ann Fraser is an artist and the garden provides much of her inspiration.

Route: Near Musselburgh. From A1 take A6094 exit signed Wallyford and Dalkeith and follow signs to Inveresk.

Admission: £3.50 Children Free. Honesty Box Tuesdays and Thursdays £5.00 on Sunday 6 June (includes Shepherd House and Inveresk Village Gardens)

SUNDAY 21 FEBRUARY 12:00pm - 3:00pm
SUNDAY 25 APRIL 2:00pm - 5:00pm
SUNDAY 06 JUNE (IN CONJUNCTION WITH INVERESK VILLAGE) 2:00pm - 5:00pm
09 FEBRUARY - 04 MARCH TUESDAYS & THURSDAYS 2:00pm - 4:00pm
01 APRIL - 29 JUNE TUESDAYS & THURSDAYS 2:00pm - 4:00pm

ALSO BY ARRANGEMENT GROUPS WELCOME
Web Site: www.shepherdhousegarden.co.uk
Telephone: 0131 665 2570
Email Address: annfraser@talktalk.net
Victim Support Scotland receives 40%, the net remaining to SGS Beneficiaries.
❀ Sunday Openings Only 🐕 ⚘ ☕ Homemade 25 April, 21 February:
Homemade Soup and Roll (£2.50)

10. ST MARY'S PLEASANCE 28 Sidegate, Haddington EH41 4BO
Haddington Garden Trust
The secluded 1.6 acre garden lies behind Haddington House which dates from 1648. It
was designed in the 1970s with trees and plants known to have been in cultivation in
Scotland in the 17th Century. The garden includes a range of features common at the
time. These include a walkway of pleached Laburnums that are in full flower at the
beginning of June. The restoration of the garden by the Trust is now well under way
with the rose beds having been recently replanted. The garden opening is one of the
events of the final day of the annual Haddington Festival.
Route: From the centre of Haddington take the B6368 for Gifford. The gated entrance
to the garden is beside Haddington House. It adjoins St Mary's Churchyard
Admission: By donation (suggested £3.50)
SATURDAY 05 JUNE 2:00pm - 5:00pm
WINTER - DAILY 9:00am - 3:30pm   SUMMER - DAILY 9:00am - 5:00pm
Haddington Garden Trust receives 40%, the net remaining to SGS Beneficiaries.
❀ 5 June Only ♿ 5 June Only - Conducted Tours of the Garden & Various Stalls
5 June Only

11. STENTON VILLAGE East Lothian EH42
The Gardeners of Stenton Village
Stenton is a lovely conservation village at the edge of the Lammermuir hills with a
great variety of gardens.
Route: Follow signs from A199/A1
Admission: £4.00 Children Free
SUNDAY 30 MAY 2:00pm - 5:30pm
Parish of Traprain Organ Fund receives 40%, the net remaining to SGS Beneficiaries.
❀ ♿ partly 🐕 ☕ Homemade

12. TYNINGHAME HOUSE Dunbar EH42 1XW
Tyninghame Gardens Ltd
Splendid 17th century pink sandstone Scottish baronial house, remodelled in 1829 by
William Burn, rises out of a sea of plants. Herbaceous border, formal rose garden, Lady
Haddington's secret garden with old fashioned roses, formal walled garden with
sculpture and yew hedges. The "wilderness" spring garden with magnificent
rhododendrons, azaleas, flowering trees and bulbs. Grounds include one mile beech

avenue to sea, famous "apple walk", Romanesque ruin of St Baldred's Church, views across parkland to Tyne estuary and Lammermuir Hills.

Route: Gates on A198 at Tyninghame Village

Admission: £4.00

SUNDAY 16 MAY 1:00pm - 5:00pm

SUNDAY 20 JUNE 1:00pm - 5:00pm

Edinburgh Cyrenians receives 40% May 16th opening, Abbeyfield Society for Scotland (East Lothian) receives 40% June 20th opening, the net remaining to SGS Beneficiaries.

✿ 16 May Only ♿ 🐕 ☕

13. WINTON HOUSE Pencaitland EH34 5AT

Sir Francis Ogilvy Winton Trust

The gardens continue to develop and improve, in addition to the natural areas around Sir David's loch and the Dell, extensive mixed borders are planned for the terrace borders and walled garden. In spring a glorious covering of daffodils make way for cherry and apple blossoms. Enjoy an informative tour of this historic house and walk off delicious lunches and home baking around the estate.

Route: Entrance off B6355 Tranent/Pencaitland road.

Admission: Estate Entrance £5.00 per Car

Guided House Tours £5.00/£3.00 Children Under 10 Free

SUNDAY 11 APRIL 12:00pm - 4:30pm

Web Site: www.wintonhouse.co.uk

Telephone: 01875 340222

Princess Royal Trust for Carers receives 40% of Entrance Fee, the net remaining to SGS Beneficiaries.

♿ 🐕 ☕ Homemade Wine Light Refreshments

PLANT SALES

14. SGS PLANT SALE Oxenfoord Mains, Near Pathhead EH22 2PF

Held under cover

Excellent selection of garden and house plants donated from private gardens.

Contact telephone number: Mrs Parker 01620 824788 or Hon Michael Dalrymple 01875 320844 (office hours)

Route: On A6093 signed off A68 4 miles south of Dalkeith.

Admission: Free - Donations to Scotland's Gardens Scheme welcome.

SATURDAY 09 OCTOBER 9:30am - 1:30pm

Cancer Research receives 40%, the net remaining to SGS Beneficiaries.

♿ 🐕 Compost Making, Vegetables and Homemade Jams ☕ Light Refreshments Soup and Rolls Homebaking

Edinburgh & West Lothian

'Gardens of Scotland' 2010 is sponsored by **Rensburg Sheppards Investment Management**

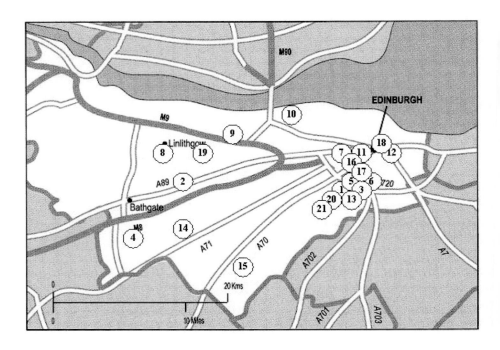

District Organisers: Mrs Victoria Reid Thomas Riccarton Mains Farmhouse, Currie
EH14 4AR

Mrs Charles Welwood Kirknewton House, Kirknewton EH27 8DA

Treasurer: **Mrs Charles Welwood** Kirknewton House, Kirknewton EH27 8DA

Gardens Open On a Specific Date

Dalmeny Park, South Queensferry	To be Advised	
61 Fountainhall Road, Edinburgh	Sunday 04 April	2:00pm - 5:00pm
61 Fountainhall Road, Edinburgh	Sunday 11 April	2:00pm - 5:00pm
Moray Place & Bank Gardens, Edinburgh	Sunday 25 April	2:00pm - 5:00pm
Redhall Walled Garden, Edinburgh	Sunday 25 April	12:00pm - 5:00pm
Roscullen, Edinburgh	Saturday 08 May	2:00pm - 5:30pm
Roscullen, Edinburgh	Sunday 09 May	2:00pm - 5:30pm

61 Fountainhall Road, Edinburgh	Sunday 16 May	2:00pm - 5:00pm
Hunter's Tryst, Edinburgh	Sunday 16 May	2:00pm - 5:00pm
61 Fountainhall Road, Edinburgh	Sunday 23 May	2:00pm - 5:00pm
Dean Gardens, Edinburgh	Sunday 11 April	2:00pm - 4:00pm
101 Greenbank Cresent, Edinburgh	Saturday 05 June	2:00pm - 5:00pm
9 Osborne Terrace, Edinburgh	Saturday 19 June	2:00pm - 5:00pm
61 Fountainhall Road, Edinburgh	Sunday 20 June	6:00pm - 9:30pm
Malleny Garden, Balerno	Thursday 24 June	7:00pm - 9:00pm
61 Fountainhall Road, Edinburgh	Sunday 27 June	2:00pm - 5:00pm
Merchiston Cottage, Edinburgh	Sunday 27 June	2:00pm - 5:00pm
Midmar Allotments Association, Edinburgh	Sunday 27 June	2:00pm - 5:00pm
Hunter's Tryst, Edinburgh	Sunday 18 July	2:00pm - 5:00pm
9 Braid Farm Road, Edinburgh	Saturday 24 July	2:00pm - 5:00pm
9 Braid Farm Road, Edinburgh	Sunday 25 July	2:00pm - 5:00pm
Annet House Garden, Linlithgow	Sunday 25 July	11:00am - 5:00pm
2 Houstoun Gardens, Uphall	Saturday 31 July	1:00pm - 4:30pm
45 Northfield Crescent, Longridge	Saturday 31 July	1:00pm - 5:00pm
Dr Neil's Garden, Duddingston Village	Saturday 31 July	2:00pm - 5:00pm
2 Houstoun Gardens, Uphall	Sunday 01 August	1:00pm - 4:30pm
45 Northfield Crescent, Longridge	Sunday 01 August	1:00pm - 5:00pm
Dr Neil's Garden, Duddingston Village	Sunday 01 August	2:00pm - 5:00pm
61 Fountainhall Road, Edinburgh	Sunday 05 September	2:00pm - 5:00pm
61 Fountainhall Road, Edinburgh	Sunday 12 September	2:00pm - 5:00pm
61 Fountainhall Road, Edinburgh	Sunday 03 October	2:00pm - 5:00pm

Gardens Open By Arrangement
When organising a visit to a garden open by arrangement, please enquire if there are facilities and catering available

36 Morningside Drive, Edinburgh	12 - 20 June and 14 - 22 August	Tel: 0131 447 9487
Newliston, Kirkliston	1 May - 4 June Weds to Sats	Tel: 0131 333 3231

Gardens Open Regularly

'Avant - Gardens Festival' at New Hopetoun Gardens	May - October	10:00am - 5:30pm
Kirknewton House, Kirknewton	June - Tues &Thurs	11:00am - 4:00pm

EDINBURGH & WEST LOTHIAN

1. 101 GREENBANK CRESENT Edinburgh EH10 5TA NEW
Mr and Mrs Jerry and Christine Gregson

Interesting terraced garden with water feature, various flowering shrubs. Marvellous views over hills and neighbouring park.

Route: From Edinburgh centre, Turn right at Greenbank Church crossing. Nos 16 and 5 buses.

Admission: £3.00

SATURDAY 05 JUNE 2:00pm - 5:00pm

Telephone: 0131 447 6492

Email Address: jerry_gregson@yahoo.co.uk

Macmillan Cancer Support receives 40%, the net remaining to SGS Beneficiaries.

✿ ☕ Homemade

2. 2 HOUSTOUN GARDENS Uphall, West Lothian EH52 5PX
John & Isabel Macdonald

A detached 1980s bungalow garden. Large variety of shrubs and plants. Fruit & vegetables are also grown. An outstanding feature of this garden is its summer bedding with over 120 baskets and containers

Route: Leave A89 at the B8046 junction towards Uphall. Travel 80 yards & turn right into Stankards Road, take 2nd left into Houstoun Gardens. From Uphall village travel west along Main Street, turn left at mini roundabout onto B8046, travel 150 yards then turn left into Stankards Road and then onto Houstoun Gardens

Admission: £4.00 - Tea Included

SATURDAY 31 JULY 1:00pm - 4:30pm

SUNDAY 01 AUGUST 1:00pm - 4:30pm

Teenage Cancer Trust, East of Scotland receives 40%, the net remaining to SGS Beneficiaries.

Tombola Stall   ☕ Homemade

3. 36 MORNINGSIDE DRIVE Edinburgh EH10 5LZ
Mrs Elizabeth Casciani

Private Victorian walled garden (85ft x 45ft). Owner aims for year-round colour with attractive shrubs, roses and herbaceous plantings. There are fruit trees, fruit bushes and tubs of various vegetables.

Route: On bus routes 11, 15, 16, 41, 5, 23.

Admission: £3.00

BY ARRANGEMENT 12 - 20 JUNE AND 14 - 22 AUGUST 2.00pm - 5.00pm

Telephone: 0131 447 9487 Email Address: liz.casciani@blueyonder.co.uk

Sightsavers International receives 20%, Water Aid receives 20%, the net remaining to SGS Beneficiaries.

✿ ☕

4. 45 NORTHFIELD CRESCENT Longridge, Bathgate EH47 8AL

Mr and Mrs Jamie Robertson

A delightful new garden. A wide variety of shrubs and herbaceous plants. Large pond with a small waterfall and a colourful decked area with an attractive selection of bedding plants.
Route: From the A71 turn right after Breith at the traffic lights, drive down about a mile and turn right into the Crescent.

From Whitburn head up the A706 Longridge Road to Longridge, take last left into Crescent.

Admission: £4.00 - Includes Teas

SATURDAY 31 JULY 1:00pm - 5:00pm
SUNDAY 01 AUGUST 1:00pm - 5:00pm

Telephone: 01501771092 Email Address: luvinlife1988@hotmail.co.uk
World Cancer Research Fund receives 40%, the net remaining to SGS Beneficiaries.
❀ ☕

5. 61 FOUNTAINHALL ROAD Edinburgh EH9 2LH

Dr J A and Mrs A Hammond

Large walled town garden in which trees and shrubs form an architectural backdrop to a wide variety of flowering plants. The growing collection of hellebores and trilliums and a large variety of late blooming flowers provide interest from early March to late October. In addition there are now several alpine beds which include a large collection of Sempervivums. Three ponds, with and without fish, have attracted a lively population of frogs.
Route: See "Contact Details" on Website
Admission: £4.00

SUNDAYS 04 & 11 APRIL 2:00pm - 5:00pm
SUNDAYS 16 & 23 MAY 2:00pm - 5:00pm
SUNDAYS 20 & 27 JUNE 6:00pm - 9:30pm
SUNDAYS 05 & 12 SEPTEMBER 2:00pm - 5:00pm
SUNDAY 03 OCTOBER 2:00pm - 5:00pm

Web Site: www.froglady.pwp.blueyonder.co.uk
Telephone: 0131 667 6146 Email Address: froglady@blueyonder.co.uk
Froglife receives 40%, the net remaining to SGS Beneficiaries.
❀ ♿ 🐕 ☕ Wine Light Refreshments   Coffee, Chocolate, Juice, Springwater

6. 9 BRAID FARM ROAD Edinburgh EH10 6LG

Mr and Mrs R Paul

A fabulous medium sized town garden of different styles. Cottage garden with pond. Mediterranean courtyard and colourful decked area with water feature and exotic plants. Mosaics and unusual features throughout.
Route: Near Braid Hills Hotel, on the 11 and 15 bus routes.
Admission: £4.00

SATURDAY 24 JULY 2:00pm - 5:00pm

EDINBURGH & WEST LOTHIAN

SUNDAY 25 JULY 2:00pm - 5:00pm
Telephone: 0131 447 3482 Email Address: raymondpaul@btinternet.com
CHAS receives 40%, the net remaining to SGS Beneficiaries.
❀ ♿ Limited   ☕ Homemade

7. 9 OSBORNE TERRACE Edinburgh EH12 5HG
Mrs Christine Glover
Walled town garden with a good herbaceous border.
Route: Nos. 12, 26 and 31 buses stop at Donaldsons at Osborne Terrace, coming from
Princes Street. House is just 30 yards from stop.
Admission: £3.00
SATURDAY 19 JUNE 2:00pm - 5:00pm
Migraine Action Association receives 40%, the net remaining to SGS Beneficiaries.
 ❀ ♿ 🐕 ☕ Homemade

8. ANNET HOUSE GARDEN 143 High Street, Linlithgow EH49 7EJ
Linlithgow Heritage Trust
Restored terraced garden, situated to the rear and an integral part of Linlithgow's
Museum, has a wide range of flowers, fruit, vegetables and herbs, which were grown in
the past to meet the culinary, medicinal and household needs of those who stayed in
the house. Also see the unique life-size statue of Mary Queen of Scots.
Route: Turn off M9 Stirling/Edinburgh from North exit 4, from South exit 3. From M8
take junction 4 and follow signs to Linlithgow. Located in High Street close to Palace
and west of Cross. Bus & Train services operate from Edinburgh & Glasgow.
Admission: £3.00 Concessions £2.00 Children Free (Includes Entry to Museum)
SUNDAY 25 JULY 11:00am - 5:00pm
Telephone: 01506 670677 Email Address: Enquiries@linlithgowstory.fsnet.co.uk
All proceeds to SGS Beneficiaries
Historical Re-enactments   ☕ Light Refreshments

9. 'AVANT - GARDENS FESTIVAL' AT NEW HOPETOUN GARDENS Newton Village EH52 6QZ
Dougal Philip & Lesley Watson
The six winning designs in the ' Avant - Gardens ' Festival design competition are
created at New Hopetoun Gardens and are on view from May to October.
New Hopetoun Gardens contains 18 themed demonstration gardens and is open daily.
An unusual garden centre with The Orangery Tearoom
Route: Find us on the A904 three miles west of the Forth Road Bridge roundabout
heading towards Linlithgow in West Lothian.
Admission: Free entry - Donations welcome at 'Avant - Gardens'
MAY - OCTOBER DAILY 10:00am - 5:30pm
Web Site: www.newhopetoungardens.co.uk
Telephone: 01506 834433 Email Address: info@newhopetoungardens.co.uk

'Perennial' Gardeners Royal Benevolent Fund receives 40%, the net remaining to SGS Beneficiaries.

♿ ☕ Homemade Light Refreshments   Orangery Tearoom for Coffee, Tea, Homebaking and Light Lunches, Daily 10:00am - 4:30pm

10. DALMENY PARK South Queensferry EH30 9TQ

The Earl & Countess of Rosebery

Acres of superb snowdrops on Mons Hill. Paths can be slippy so please wear sensible footwear with good grip.

Route: South Queensferry off A90 road to B924. Pedestrians and cars enter by Leuchold Gate and exit by Chapel Gate.

Admission: £3.00

TO BE ADVISED

Web Site: www.dalmeny.co.uk

Columbia's Hospice receives 40%, the net remaining to SGS Beneficiaries.

✦ ☕

11. DEAN GARDENS Edinburgh EH4

Dean Gardens Management Committee

Privately owned town gardens on north bank of the Water of Leith.13.5 acres of spring bulbs, daffodils and shrubs with lovely views over the Dean Valley. The Victorian Pavilion has been reinstated and there is seating throughout the garden.

Route: Entrance at Ann Street or Eton Terrace.

Admission: £4.00

SUNDAY 11 APRIL 2:00pm - 4:00pm

All proceeds to SGS Beneficiaries

♿ Limited   🐕   Please Note No Refreshments Available

12. DR NEIL'S GARDEN Duddingston Village EH15 7DG

Dr Neil's Garden Trust

Landscaped garden on the lower slopes of Arthur's Seat using conifers, heathers, alpines and herbaceous borders.

Route: Kirk car park on Duddingston Road West. Then follow signposts

Admission: £3.00

SATURDAY 31 JULY 2:00pm - 5:00pm

SUNDAY 01 AUGUST 2:00pm - 5:00pm

Web Site: www.drneilsgarden.co.uk

Email Address: info@drneilsgarden.co.uk

Dr Neil's Garden Trust receives 40%, the net remaining to SGS Beneficiaries.

⚘ ♿ ☕ Homemade

EDINBURGH & WEST LOTHIAN

13. HUNTER'S TRYST 95 Oxgangs Road, Edinburgh EH10 7BA **NEW**

Jean Knox

Well stocked mature town garden comprising herbaceous/shrub beds,lawn, vegetables and fruit. Seating areas and trees

Route: From Fairmilehead crosshead down Oxgangs Road to Hunter's Tryst roundabout, last house on the left. Bus No 4,16,18,27. Bus Stop at Hunter's Tryst. Garden opposite Hunter's Tryst.

Admission: £3.00

SUNDAY 16 MAY 2:00pm - 5:00pm

SUNDAY 18 JULY 2:00pm - 5:00pm

Telephone: 0131 477 2919

Email Address: jean.knox@blueyonder.co.uk

Lothian Cat Rescue receives 40%, the net remaining to SGS Beneficiaries.

✿ ♿ Partial ☕ Homemade Tea/Coffee/Soft Drinks and Homebaking £2.00

14. KIRKNEWTON HOUSE Kirknewton EH27 8DA

Mr & Mrs Charles Welwood

Old landscaped gardens, surrounded by mature trees, shrubs and rhododendrons. Spring and herbaceous borders.

Route: Either A70 or A71 onto B7031

Admission: £4.00

TUESDAYS & THURSDAYS JUNE 11:00am - 4:00pm

Web Site: www.Kirknewtonestate.co.uk

Telephone: 01506 881 235

Email Address: cwelwood@kirknewtonestate.co.uk

Children's Hospice Scotland receives 40%, the net remaining to SGS Beneficiaries.

✿ ♿

15. MALLENY GARDEN Balerno EH14 7AF

National Trust for Scotland

A rare opportunity to savour the scents of Malleny with an evening stroll through this beautiful garden on midsummer's eve.

Route: In Balerno off A70 Lanark Road. Bus: LRT No. 44 First No. 44

Admission: £6.00 (Includes Glass of Wine or Fruit Juice)

THURSDAY 24 JUNE 7:00pm - 9:00pm (LAST ADMISSION 8:15pm)

Web Site: www.nts.org.uk

Telephone: 0844 493 2123

Email Address: pdeacon@nts.org.uk

Donation to SGS Beneficiaries

♿ Entrance beside Malleny House NCCPG 19th Century Shrub Roses ☕ Wine

16. MERCHISTON COTTAGE 16 Colinton Road, Edinburgh EH10 5EL

Esther Mendelssohn

Small, walled, urban wildlife friendly, organic, bee keeper's garden. Open for the fourth time, this eco friendly tapestry of wildlife habitats encourages birds, insects and frogs as pest control. In addition the bees not only provide honey, but also act as pollinators for the many fruit trees including blueberries and mulberries. When possible the bees can be seen at close quarters in an observation hive.

Route: Near Holy Corner, opposite Watson's College School. Bus nos. 11 and 16
Admission: £3.00 Children Free

SUNDAY 27 JUNE 2:00pm - 5:00pm

Edinburgh Hebrew Congregation receives 40%, the net remaining to SGS Beneficiaries.
⬕ ♿ Most Areas ☕ Homemade

17. MIDMAR ALLOTMENTS ASSOCIATION Midmar Drive, Edinburgh EH10 6BU

Midmar Allotments Association

A group of 140 allotments growing a splendid variety of vegetables, fruit and flowers. Scandinavian Log Cabin on Communal Plot. Several Raised Beds.

Route: Midmar Drive, off Cluny gardens, (½ mile from Morningside Clock) under Blackford Hill.
Admission: £3.00

SUNDAY 27 JUNE 2:00pm - 5:00pm

Hermitage of Braid; Doocot & Walled Restoration Fund receives 40%, the net remaining to SGS Beneficiaries.
🐕 ☕ Homemade Available at The Log Cabin

18. MORAY PLACE & BANK GARDENS Edinburgh EH3 6BX

The Gardeners of Moray Place and Bank Gardens

Moray Place: Private garden of 3½ acres in Georgian New Town recently benefited from five-year programme of replanting. Shrubs, trees and beds offering atmosphere of tranquility in the city centre.
Bank Gardens: Nearly six acres of secluded wild gardens with lawns, trees and shrubs with banks of bulbs down to the Water of Leith. Stunning vistas across Firth of Forth.
Route: **Moray Place:** Enter by north gate in Moray Place.
Bank Gardens: Enter by gate at top of Doune Terrace
Admission: £3.00

SUNDAY 25 APRIL 2:00pm - 5:00pm

Maggie's Centre receives 40%, the net remaining to SGS Beneficiaries.
🐕 ☕ Homemade

19. NEWLISTON Kirkliston EH29 9EB

Mr and Mrs R C Maclachlan

18th century designed landscape. Rhododendrons and azaleas. The house, designed by Robert Adam, is open. On Sundays there is a ride-on steam model railway from 2-5pm

Route: Four miles from Forth Road Bridge, entrance off B800.

Admission: £3.00 OAPs and Children £2.00

BY ARRANGEMENT 1 MAY - 4 JUNE WEDNESDAY TO SATURDAY 2:00pm - 6:00pm

Telephone: 0131 333 3231

Email Address: mac@newliston.fsnet.co.uk

Children's Hospice Association receives 40%, the net remaining to SGS Beneficiaries.

♿ Please Note there are No Catering Facilities

20. REDHALL WALLED GARDEN 97 Lanark Road, Edinburgh EH14 2LZ

Scottish Association for Mental Health

C18th walled garden working to organic principles featuring Zen garden, sunken garden, beech garden, round house, sensory garden vegetable, fruit, herbaceous and shrubs. Since last opening for SGS in 2004 the garden has changed and now includes a pond and wildlife garden and woodland walk.

Route: No. 44 LRT bus. There is disabled parking available at the garden, for other cars parking would be on the main street.

Admission: £4.00 Concessions £2.50 Children Free

SUNDAY 25 APRIL 12:00pm - 5:00pm

Telephone: 0131 443 0946

Email Address: redhall@samhservices.org.uk

Redhall Walled Garden SAMH receives 40% and 100% of Plant Sales, the net remaining to SGS Beneficiaries.

❀ ♿ Disabled Parking 🐕 Children's Activities ☕ Cream

21. ROSCULLEN 1 Bonaly Road, Edinburgh EH13 0EA **NEW**

Mrs Anne Duncan

Fabulous spring garden with numerous varieties of tulips. Also rhododendrons and azaleas.

Route: From city take left fork at traffic lights at top of Colinton village. Bonaly road is 3rd road along on the left. Parking best on Grant Avenue. Bus Route No 10.

Admission: £3.00

SATURDAY 08 MAY 2:00pm - 5:30pm

SUNDAY 09 MAY 2:00pm - 5:30pm

Telephone: 0131 441 2905

Brooke Hospital for Animals receives 40%, the net remaining to SGS Beneficiaries.

🐕

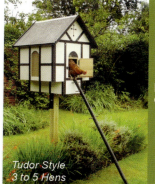

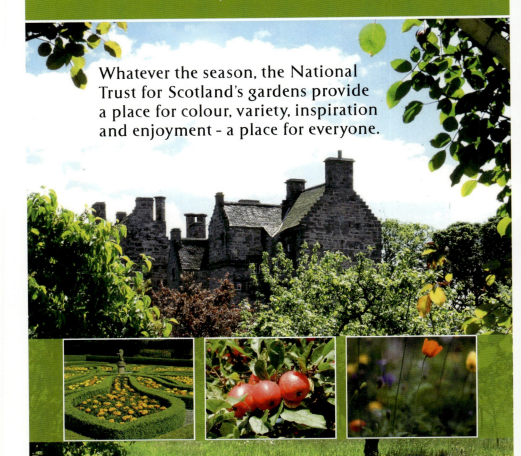

Scotland's Gardens Scheme

Gardens open for charity

Gardens of North West Scotland

Kerrachar

We are delighted to organise another exclusive garden tour in association with Scotland's Gardens Scheme. This will not only raise more funds for the deserving causes they support but also give us the chance to visit some wonderful private gardens in the north west of Scotland, most of which are not normally open on a regular basis.

Our short break will be based in the Dundonnell Hotel, spectacularly set among the dramatic mountains, lochs and forests of Wester Ross and the perfect base for our tour.

The magnificent gardens at Inverewe are of course justly famous, and while we have of course included a visit here this most scenic area is also home to a wealth of beautiful gardens that are perhaps not so well known. All gardens that we visit are open at certain times under the wing of the SGS; however on our tour we have arranged wherever possible for a private viewing to enable a degree of intimacy normally only enjoyed by the owners.

En route to the far north west we will stop for lunch at Aigas House and Field Centre, a unique facility near Beauly with a splendid arboretum.

There are more fine specimen trees at Leckmelm, near Ullapool, and we are delighted to get special viewing of the very remote Kerrachar Gardens - only reached by boat.

Dundonnell House and the House of Gruinard are beautiful gardens in stunning mountain locations, and the House and gardens at Attadale overlooking Loch Carron make for a wonderful conclusion to this splendid garden tour.

Departs

28 June 2010
4 days from £425pp

Departure points
Glasgow, Edinburgh, Dunfermline, Kinross, Perth, Dundee, Inverness

Supplements per person

> Single room £30.00
> Insurance

What's Included

> 3 nights dinner, bed and full breakfast, plus a sherry reception, at the Dundonnell Hotel, Dundonnell
> Lunch at House of Aigas
> Comfortable coaching throughout. Rail/air connections into Inverness and out of Glasgow or Edinburgh. Overnight accommodation before or after the tour is available on request
> Visits to the gardens of House of Aigas; Leckmelm; Kerrachar; Dundonnell House; House of Gruinard; Inverewe and Attadale House and Gardens
> An evening presentation by Scotland's Garden Scheme
> Service of a Brightwater Holidays guide

Photo: Ray Cox

AUSTRALIA'S OPEN GARDEN SCHEME

Australia's
Open Garden Scheme

Around 700 inspiring private gardens drawn from every Australian state and territory feature in our annual program.

Included are tropical gardens in the Northern Territory and Queensland, awe-inspiring arid zone gardens, traditional gardens in the temperate south, gardens which feature Australia's unique flora, and gardens designed by many of Australia's contemporary designers.

Our full colour guide is published each August by Hardie Grant Magazines and every entry includes a full description, map references and directions, opening details and amenities.

State-by-state calendars make it easy to plan a personal itinerary, and a special index identifies gardens with a particular plant collection or area of interest.

Also included are comprehensive listings of regularly open gardens around the country.

President: Mrs Malcolm Fraser
Chief Executive Officer: Neil Robertson

PO Box 187, New Gisborne, Victoria 3438
Tel +61 3 5428 4557 Fax +61 3 5428 4558
email: national@opengarden.org.au
website: www.opengarden.org.au
Australia's Open Garden Scheme
ABN 60 057 467 553

hardie grant magazines

THE GARDEN CONSERVANCY'S OPEN DAYS PROGRAM

Stone Palms, Austin, Texas
Photo: Casey Dunn, caseydunn.net

www.opendaysprogram.org

The Garden Conservancy has been opening America's very best, rarely seen, private gardens to the public through its Open Days program since 1995. Visit us online at **opendaysprogram.org** for more information.

The Open Days program is a project of The Garden Conservancy, a nonprofit organization dedicated to preserving America's gardening heritage.

New Gardens

Farleyer Field House, Perth & Kinross

Bumblebee Cottage, Caithness, Orkney & Sutherland

Drumelzier Place, Peeblesshire

Achnacloich, Perth & Kinross

New Gardens

Cousland Village Allotments, Midlothian

Lowwood House Garden, Ettrick & Lauderdale

Lennel Bank, Berwickshire

Applecross Walled Garden, Ross, Cromarty, Skye & Inverness

New Gardens

Pitcurran House, Perth & Kinross

Armadale Castle Gardens, Ross, Cromarty, Skye & Inverness

The Waterhouse Gardens at Stockarton, Kirkcudbrightshire

Westfield Road Gardens, Fife

All photography that is not credited was supplied by the individual garden owners

Town Gardens

Kevock Garden, Midlothian © Andrea Jones

9 Braid Farm Road, Edinburgh & West Lothian © Andrea Jones

Cruickshank Botanic Gardens, Aberdeenshire

Blackmill, Kilsyth Gardens, Glasgow & District

Town Gardens

Parkhead House, Perth & Kinross

Ingadi Enhle, Glasgow & District

Drim Na Vullin, Argyllshire

Bents Green, Moray & Nairn

All photography that is not credited was supplied by the individual garden owners

Topiary

Several gardens have creative and interesting topiary.

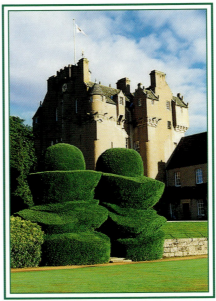

Crathes Castle, Kincardine & Deeside © Andrea Jones

Anton's Hill & Walled Garden, Berwickshire

Biggar Park, Lanarkshire

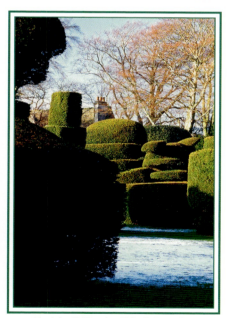

Earlshall Castle, Fife © Ray Cox

Drummond Castle Gardens, Perth & Kinross

All photography that is not credited was supplied by the individual garden owners

Discover a world of plants

Royal Botanic Garden Edinburgh
Inverleith Row, Edinburgh EH3 5LR
Tel 0131 552 7171
Open daily
✳NEW JOHN HOPE GATEWAY OPEN✳

Benmore Botanic Garden
Nr Dunoon, Argyll PA23 8QU
Tel 01369 706 261

Open daily 1 Mar - 31 Oct
✳VISIT THE NEWLY RESTORED
VICTORIAN FERNERY✳

Dawyck Botanic Garden
Stobo, Scottish Borders EH45 9JU
Tel 01721 760 254

Open daily 1 Feb - 30 Nov
✳SCOTLAND'S FIRST 5 STAR GARDEN✳

Logan Botanic Garden
Port Logan,
Dumfries & Galloway DG9 9ND
Tel 01776 860 231

Open daily 15 Mar - 31 Oct

www.rbge.org.uk

Royal
Botanic Garden
Edinburgh

Johnstons

Since 1797

&

SCOTLAND'S GARDENS SCHEME

Will be holding a

Gardeners Question Time

at Johnstons, Newmill, Elgin

Thursday 1st April

Doors Open 6.00pm   Event starts 6.30pm

Frieda Morrison - Chairman

Panel

Carole Baxter of *"Beechgrove Garden" & "Beechgrove Potting Shed"*
Donald McBean of *"Beechgrove Potting Shed"*
Donald Davidson of Abriachan Garden Nursery
Julie Edmonstone of Duntreath Castle

In aid of: Help for Heroes, Maggie's Centres, Queen's Nursing Institute
Scotland & The Gardens Fund of The National Trust of Scotland

Tickets £10.00 (includes wine & canapes)
Available from Kenneth MacRae   Tel: 01343 554094
E-mail: k.macrae@johnstonscashmere.com

DOUGLAS HOME & CO
Chartered Accountants

"OF COURSE IT WAS NECESSARY TO BRING HER — SHE'S EATEN THE BOOKS!!"

47/49 The Square, Kelso TD5 7HW – Tel: 01573 225082
Fax: 01573 226442 – Email: mail@douglashomeandco.co.uk
www.douglashomeandco.co.uk

Munro Greenhouses & Garden Buildings

10 Alexandra Drive Alloa FK10 2DQ

01259 222 811
07785 343 130

info@munrogreenhouses.co.uk
www.munrogreenhouses.co.uk

supply : erection : maintenance : repair : removal : relocation : all accessories

ngs gardens open for charity

OVER 3,600 GARDENS OPEN FOR CHARITY IN ENGLAND AND WALES

For more information telephone 01483 211535
or visit our website **www.ngs.org.uk**

The National Gardens Scheme registered charity number 1112664

Ettrick & Lauderdale

'Gardens of Scotland' 2010 is sponsored by **Rensburg Sheppards Investment Management**

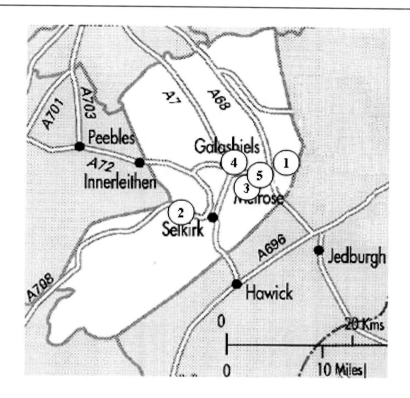

District Organiser:	**Mrs D Muir** Torquhan House, Stow TD1 2RX
Area Organiser:	**Mrs M Kostoris** Wester Housebyres, Melrose TD6 9BW
Treasurer:	**Mr Miller** 18 Craigpark Gardens, Galashiels TD1 3HZ

Gardens Open On a Specific Date

Bowhill Country Park, Selkirk	Saturday 20 February	2:00pm - 4:00pm
Bemersyde, Melrose	Sunday 18 April	2:00pm - 5:00pm
Priorwood Gardens, Melrose	Sunday 27 June	1:00pm - 4:00pm
Harmony Garden, Melrose	Sunday 27 June	1:00pm - 4:00pm
Lowwood House Garden, Melrose	Sunday 04 July	2:00pm - 6:00pm

ETTRICK & LAUDERDALE

1. BEMERSYDE Melrose TD6 9DP
The Earl Haig

16th century peel tower reconstructed in the 17th century with added mansion house. Garden laid out by Field Marshal Earl Haig. Views of Eildon Hills. Woodland garden and river walks. Good show of daffodils. Admission to garden only

Route: B6356 St Boswells via Clintmains or Melrose via Leaderfoot Bridge

Admission: £4.50

SUNDAY 18 APRIL 2:00pm - 5:00pm

Lady Haig's Poppy Factory receives 40%, the net remaining to SGS Beneficiaries.

2. BOWHILL COUNTRY PARK Selkirk TD7 5ET
Buccleuch Estates

Bowhill Country Park is at the centre of an extensive estate of hills and valleys where history and landscape combine to provide a unique experience. Extensive snowdrops and special snowdrop walk led by the Head Gardener

Route: 3 miles west of Selkirk on A708

Admission: £5.00 Children £4.00 (Includes Cup of Tea)

SATURDAY 20 FEBRUARY 2:00pm - 4:00pm

Donation to SGS Beneficiaries

Snowdrop Walk with Ranger, Children's Activities

3. HARMONY GARDEN (JOINT OPENING WITH PRIORWOOD GARDENS)
St. Mary's Road, Melrose TD6 9LJ
The National Trust for Scotland

Wander through this tranquil garden's wonderful herbaceous borders, lawns and fruit and vegetable plots, and enjoy fine views of the Abbey and Eildon Hills.

Route: OS Ref: NT547342

Road: Off A6091, in Melrose, opposite the Abbey.

Cycle: NCN1

Bus: First Edinburgh from Edinburgh and Peebles.

Admission: £5.00 for both Harmony and Priorwood Gardens

SUNDAY 27 JUNE 1:00pm - 4:00pm

Web Site: www.nts.org.uk

Telephone: 0844 493 2251

Email Address: paulgibson@nts.org.uk

Donation to SGS Beneficiaries

Bottle Stall, Dried Flower Demonstrations, Music in the Orchard, Jewellery Stall

4. LOWWOOD HOUSE GARDEN Melrose TD6 9BJ NEW

Alexander Hamilton

Entry beside Lowwood Bridge, past a tiny lodge, half mile drive through a small wood and park. Lowwood House sits on the south bank of the Tweed, and was at one time used by the factor for Abbotsford although it has been added to over the years in somewhat haphazard fashion. South of the house is a large garden with some nice shrubs, trees and a lot of roses, including climbing and rambling roses. Features are a sunken garden, woodland walk, a walk through the park by the lochan, a river walk, a secret garden and a walled garden mainly used as a kitchen garden.

Route: Entrance from the B6374 at the south end of the single lane Lowwood Bridge leading from Melrose to Gattonside.

Admission: £4.00

SUNDAY 04 JULY 2:00pm - 6:00pm

Scottish Motor Neurone receives 40%, the net remaining to SGS Beneficiaries.

  Homemade Served in the Old Stable Courtyard

5. PRIORWOOD GARDENS (JOINT OPENING WITH HARMONY GARDENS) Melrose TD6 9PX

The National Trust for Scotland

In Melrose, overlooked by the Abbey ruins, this unique garden produces plants for a superb variety of dried flower arrangements, made and sold here. The orchard contains many historic apple varieties.

Route: OS Ref: NT548341.

Road: A68 Jedburgh Road, signposted for Melrose. Off A6091, in Melrose, adjacent to Abbey.

Cycle: NCN1

Bus: First Edinburgh from Edinburgh and Peebles

Admission: £ 5.00 for Both Priorwood and Harmony Gardens

SUNDAY 27 JUNE 1:00pm - 4:00pm

Web Site: www.nts.org.uk

Telephone: 01896 822493

Email Address: paulgibson@nts.org.uk

Donation to SGS Beneficiaries

Bottle Stall, Dried Flower Demonstrations, Music in the Orchard, Jewellery Stall

---

To keep compost warm use some bubble wrap to line pots and containers

---

Fife

'Gardens of Scotland' 2010 is sponsored by **Rensburg Sheppards Investment Management**

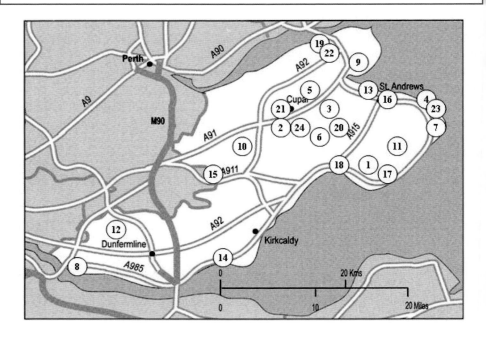

District Organiser: **Lady Erskine** Cambo House, Kingsbarns KY16 8QD

Area Organisers: **Mrs Jeni Auchinleck** 2 Castle Street, Crail KY10 3SQ
Mrs Evelyn Crombie West Hall, Cupar, KY15 4NA
Mrs Nora Gardner Inverie, 36 West End, St Monans KY10 2BX
Mrs Gill Hart Kirklands House, Saline KY12 9TS
Mr Sandy Mitchell Kirkland House, 43 Main Street, Ceres KY15 5NA
Mrs Lindsay Murray Craigfoodie, Dairsie KY15 4RU
Ms Louise Roger Chesterhill, Boarhills, St Andrews KY16 8PP
Mrs April Simpson The Cottage, Boarhills, St Andrews KY16 8PP
Mrs Fay Smith 37 Ninian Field, Pittenweem, Anstruther KY10 2QU

Treasurer: **Mrs Sally Lorimore** Willowhill, Forgan, Newport-on-Tay DD6 8RA

Gardens Open On a Specific Date

St. Andrews Botanic Garden, Canongate	Friday 07 May	6:30pm - 8:30pm
Craigrothie Village Gardens	Sunday 09 May	12:00pm - 5:00pm
Tayfield, Forgan	Sunday 16 May	2:00pm - 5:00pm
Willowhill, Forgan	Sunday 16 May	2:00pm - 5:00pm
Kirklands, Saline	Sunday 23 May	2:00pm - 5:30pm
Strathairly House, Upper Largo	Sunday 23 May	2:00pm - 5:00pm
Earlshall Castle, Leuchars	Sunday 30 May	2:00pm - 5:00pm
St. Monans Village Gardens	Sunday 30 May	2:00pm - 5:00pm
Kellie Castle, Pittenweem	Saturday 05 June	12:00pm - 5:00pm
Westfield Road Gardens, Cupar	Sunday 06 June	12:00pm - 5:00pm
Culross Palace, Culross	Sunday 13 June	10:00am - 5:00pm
Blebo Craigs Village Gardens, Cupar	Saturday 19 June	12:00pm - 5:00pm
Blebo Craigs Village Gardens, Cupar	Sunday 20 June	12:00pm - 5:00pm
Scotlandwell Community Allotments, Young's Moss	Sunday 20 June	10:00am - 4:00pm
Balcarres, Colinsburgh	Saturday 26 June	2:00pm - 5:30pm
Earlshall Castle, Leuchars	Sunday 27 June	2:00pm - 5:00pm
Craigfoodie, Dairsie	Sunday 04 July	2:00pm - 5:00pm
Wormistoune House, Crail	Sunday 11 July	12:00pm - 5:00pm
Scotlandwell Community Allotments, Young's Moss	Sunday 18 July	10:00am - 4:00pm
Crail: Small Gardens in the Burgh	Saturday 24 July	1:00pm - 5:30pm
Crail: Small Gardens in the Burgh	Sunday 25 July	1:00pm - 5:30pm
Ladies Lake, The Scores	Sunday 01 August	2:00pm - 5:00pm
Falkland's Small Gardens	Saturday 14 August	11:00am - 5:00pm
Falkland's Small Gardens	Sunday 15 August	1:00pm - 5:00pm
Scotlandwell Community Allotments, Young's Moss	Sunday 15 August	10:00am - 4:00pm
Willowhill, Forgan	Monday 16 August	2:00pm - 5:00pm
Willowhill, Forgan	Tuesday 17 August	2:00pm - 5:00pm
Willowhill, Forgan	Wednesday 18 August	2:00pm - 5:00pm
Willowhill, Forgan	Thursday 19 August	2:00pm - 5:00pm
Willowhill, Forgan	Friday 20 August	2:00pm - 5:00pm
Kirklands, Saline	Sunday 22 August	2:00pm - 5:30pm
Tayfield, Forgan	Sunday 12 September	2:00pm - 5:00pm
Willowhill, Forgan	Sunday 12 September	2:00pm - 5:00pm
Hill of Tarvit, Cupar	Sunday 03 October	10:30am - 4:00pm
Cambo House, Kingsbarns	Sunday 17 October	12:00pm - 4:00pm

FIFE

Gardens Open By Arrangement

When organising a visit to a garden open by arrangement, please enquire if there are facilities and catering available

Barham, Bow of Fife	24 February - 29 Sept. Wednesdays	Tel: 01337 810227
Micklegarth, Aberdour	01 May - 31 July	Tel: 01383 860796
Teasses Gardens, Nr. Ceres	All Year: Individuals or Groups	Tel: 01334 828048

Plant Sales

Hill of Tarvit Annual SGS Plant Sale and Fair, Cupar	Sunday 03 October	10:30am - 4:00pm

1. BALCARRES Colinsburgh KY9 1HN

The Earl and Countess of Crawford and Balcarres

Superb 19th century formal and extensive woodland gardens; wide variety of plants.

Route: ½ mile north of Colinsburgh off A942.

Admission: £4.50 Accompanied Children Free

SATURDAY 26 JUNE 2:00pm - 5:30pm

Colinsburgh Village Hall receives 40%, the net remaining to SGS Beneficiaries.

❀ ♿ ☕ Homemade

2. BARHAM Bow of Fife KY15 5RG

Sir Robert & Lady Spencer-Nairn

A small woodland garden with snowdrops, spring bulbs, trilliums, rhododendrons and ferns. Also a summer garden with rambler roses, herbaceous borders and island beds.

Route: A91 4 miles west of Cupar

Admission: £3.00 OAPs £2.50 Children Free

BY ARRANGEMENT 24 FEBRUARY - 29 SEPTEMBER WEDNESDAYS

Telephone: 01337 810227

Pain Association Scotland receives 40%, the net remaining to SGS Beneficiaries.

❀

3. BLEBO CRAIGS VILLAGE GARDENS Cupar KY15 5UF

The Gardeners of Blebo Craigs

A wide variety of gardens, including some new ones, will be open in this beautifully situated former quarry and farm village with stunning views over the Fife countryside.

Route: From St Andrews: B939 for 4 miles (2 miles after Strathkinnes crossroads). Small sign on left pointing to right hand turn. From Cupar: B940 and take left at Pitscottie then after 2 miles left at sign onto B939

Admission: £4.50

SATURDAY 19 JUNE 12:00pm - 5:00pm
SUNDAY 20 JUNE 12:00pm - 5:00pm
Village Hall Fund receives 40%, the net remaining to SGS Beneficiaries.
♻ ♿ Partial 🐕 Children's Activities ☕ Homemade

4. CAMBO HOUSE Kingsbarns KY16 8QD

Sir Peter and Lady Erskine

Renowned for snowdrops (mail order in February), this traditional walled garden with some of Scotland's best herbaceous displays is constantly evolving. Head Gardener, Elliott Forsyth, has created irresistible planting combinations with drifts of bold perennials and grasses in the style originally devised by Piet Oudolf and an outrageous annual potager garden. Outside the main garden, a winter garden and North American prairie are developing. Woodland walks to the sea. Featured in 'Gardens Illustrated' and 'The Beechgrove Garden'

Octoberfest: Make traditional corn dollies, halloween lanterns and apple pigs. Listen to Sylvia Troon and friends' traditional story telling. Press apples for juice and feed them to the pigs. Enjoy seasonal baking and home made jams. Buy clumps of plants. Garden ablaze with late flowering perennials and autumn colours

Route: A917
Admission: £4.00 Children Free
SUNDAY 17 OCTOBER 12:00pm - 4:00pm
Web Site: www.camboestate.com
Telephone: 01333 450313 Email Address: cambo@camboestate.com
All proceeds to SGS Beneficiaries
♻ ♿ 🐕 NCCPG B&B ☕ Homemade Soup and Rolls

5. CRAIGFOODIE Dairsie KY15 4RU

Mr and Mrs James Murray

Recently restored formal walled garden adjoining 17th century house with extensive range of plants and enjoying fine aspect. Parterre, clock lawn, mixed/herbaceous borders, terraces with exotic plantings and fruit and vegetable gardens. Also newly created woodland garden.

Route: On A91 from Cupar to St Andrews turn left at Dairsie School then follow signs.
Admission: £4.50 Children Free
SUNDAY 04 JULY 2:00pm - 5:00pm
Association for International Cancer Research (AICR) receives 40%, the net remaining to SGS Beneficiaries.
♿ Partial ☕

6. CRAIGROTHIE VILLAGE GARDENS KY15 5QA NEW

The Gardeners of Craigrothie Village

Picture a triangle on a hillside and this is Craigrothie. The village features an exciting mixture of mainly walled gardens opening for Scotland's Gardens Scheme for the first time.

FIFE

Route: On the A916 between Kennoway and Cupar situated at the junction to Ceres on the B939

Admission: £4.50 Children Free (Tickets and Maps Available at some Gardens and the Village Hall)

SUNDAY 09 MAY 12:00pm - 5:00pm

Fife Folk Museum Trust receives 40%, the net remaining to SGS Beneficiaries.

✿ ☕ Homemade

7. CRAIL: SMALL GARDENS IN THE BURGH KY10 3SQ

The Gardeners of Crail

A number of small gardens in varied styles: cottage, historic, plantsman's, bedding.

Route: Approach Crail from either St Andrews or Anstruther by A917. Park in the Marketgate.

Admission: £4.50 Tickets and Maps Available from Mrs Auchinleck, 2 Castle Street and Mr and Mrs Robertson, The Old House, 9 Marketgate.

SATURDAY 24 JULY 1:00pm - 5:30pm
SUNDAY 25 JULY 1:00pm - 5:30pm

Crail British Legion Hall receives 20%, RNLI receives 20%, the net remaining to SGS Beneficiaries.

✿ ☕ Homemade in British Legion Hall

8. CULROSS PALACE Culross KY12 8JH

The National Trust for Scotland

Relive the domestic life of the 16th and 17th centuries amid the old buildings and cobbled streets of this Royal Burgh on the River Forth. A model 17th-century garden has been recreated behind Culross Palace to show the range of plants available and includes vegetables, culinary and medicinal herbs, soft fruits and ornamental shrubs.

Route: OS Ref: NS985859 Road: Off A985, 12m E of Kincardine Bridge, 6m W of Dunfermline, 15m W of Edinburgh city centre Cycle: 3m from NCN 76 Bus: Stagecoach Stirling to Dunfermline. First Edinburgh to Dunfermline. Rail: Falkirk station 12m; Dunfermline station 6m

Admission: £5.00 (Includes Tea/Coffee and Cakes)

SUNDAY 13 JUNE 10:00am - 5:00pm

Web Site: www.nts.org.uk

Telephone: 0844 493 2189 Email Address: mjeffery@nts.org.uk

Donation to SGS Beneficiaries

🐕 Guided Walks Around the Garden   ☕ Light Refreshments

9. EARLSHALL CASTLE Leuchars KY16 0DP

Paul & Josine Veenhuijzen

Garden designed by Sir Robert Lorimer. Topiary lawn, for which Earlshall is renowned, rose terrace, croquet lawn with herbaceous borders, shrub border, box garden, orchard, kitchen and herb garden.

Route: On Earlshall road ¾ of a mile east of Leuchars Village (off A919)

Admission: £5.00 Children Free

SUNDAY 30 MAY 2:00pm - 5:00pm

SUNDAY 27 JUNE 2:00pm - 5:00pm

Telephone: 01334 839205

RAF Benevolent Fund receives 40% 30 May Opening, St Athernase Church receives 40%
27 June Opening, the net remaining to SGS Beneficiaries.

❀ ♿ Difficult but Possible ☕ Homemade

10. FALKLAND'S SMALL GARDENS KY15

The Gardeners of Falkland

A wonderful selection of small, secret and private gardens in this interesting historic village.

Route: On A912 and B936

Admission: £4.50

SATURDAY 14 AUGUST 11:00am - 5:00pm

SUNDAY 15 AUGUST 1:00pm - 5:00pm

Alzheimer's Society receives 20%, British Heart Foundation receives 20%, the net
remaining to SGS Beneficiaries.

❀ ♿ Partly ☕ In Village Tearooms, Organic Cafe & Pubs

11. HILL OF TARVIT Cupar KY15 5PB

The National Trust for Scotland

A Robert Lorimer designed garden.

Route: 2 miles south of Cupar off A916

Admission: Adults £1.00 Children Free

SUNDAY 03 OCTOBER 10:30am - 4:00pm

Seasons of Ceres receives 40%, the net remaining to SGS Beneficiaries.

12. KELLIE CASTLE Pittenweem KY10 2RF

The National Trust for Scotland

This superb garden around 400 years old was sympathetically restored by the Lorimer family in the late 19th century. The Arts and Crafts style garden has a selection of old-fashioned roses and herbaceous plants, cultivated organically and hosts an amazing 30 varieties of rhubarb and 75 different types of apple.

Take a tour with the Head Gardener and learn about organic vegetable production.

Route: NO520052 Road: B9171, 3m NNW of Pittenweem Bus: Flexible from local villages by pre-booking

Admission: Garden: £3.00

SATURDAY 05 JUNE 12:00pm - 5:00pm

Web Site: www.nts.org.uk

Telephone: 0844 4932184

Email Address: marmour@nts.org.uk

FIFE

Donation to SGS Beneficiaries
✿ Fresh Garden Produce Available to Purchase Throughout the Summer ♿ 🐕
Organic Garden Tours

13. KIRKLANDS Saline KY12 9TS

Peter & Gill Hart

Kirklands has been developed and restored over the last 31 years, although the house dates from 1832 and is on the site of an earlier building. Herbaceous borders, bog garden, woodland garden and newly developed terraced walled garden. Recently planted woodland area. Saline Burn divides the garden from the ancient woodland and the woodland walk.

Route: Junction 4, M90, then B914. Parking in the centre of the village.

Admission: £4.00 Children Free

SUNDAY 23 MAY 2:00pm - 5:30pm
SUNDAY 22 AUGUST 2:00pm - 5:30pm

Web Site: www.kirklandshouseandgarden.co.uk
Telephone: 01383 852737
Email Address: stay@kirklandshouseandgarden.co.uk

Prospect Burma receives 40%, the net remaining to SGS Beneficiaries.

✿ All Plants Grown in Garden ♿ Partial 🐕 [B&B] 4 Star Vegetable Growing Advice - August Opening ☕ Cream

14. LADIES LAKE The Scores, St. Andrews KY16 9AR

Mr and Mrs Gordon T Senior

The garden is small, no more than half an acre. It occupies a saucer-shaped curve on the cliff adjacent to St. Andrews Castle. In essence the garden consists of two terraces, one of which is cantilevered over the sea. About 6,000 bedding plants are crammed into half a dozen beds.

Route: From North Street turn left into North Castle Street, left in front of castle and house is 150 yards on right.

Admission: £3.00

SUNDAY 01 AUGUST 2:00pm - 5:00pm

Telephone: 01334 477769
Email Address: ladieslake@btinternet.com

Hope Park Church receives 40%, the net remaining to SGS Beneficiaries.

♿ Partial ☕ Homemade

15. MICKLEGARTH Aberdour KY3 0SW

Mr and Mrs Gordon Maxwell

Tucked away in what was once the back-lands of half a dozen High Street properties in a historic coastal village this gently-sloping half-acre garden benefits from a southern exposure and well-drained soils that have been worked for at least five centuries. Its present appearance – an informal and densely planted blend of specimen trees and shrubs, herbaceous island-beds and roses, linked by winding grassy paths - goes back to 1972 when the present owners rescued it from a derelict state and began to create a garden which would provide pleasure, interest and a warm personal welcome all year round. See Micklegarth website for updates on horticultural highlights.

Route: Access off Woodside Hotel car-park on High Street, Aberdour. **Nearest car parking:** Aberdour railway station in High Street

Admission: £3.50

BY ARRANGEMENT 01 MAY - 31 JULY

Web Site: www.micklegarth.co.uk

Telephone: 01383 860796

Email Address: kathleen@micklegarth.co.uk

SSPCA receives 40%, the net remaining to SGS Beneficiaries.

♿ Restricted 🐕 ☕ By Prior Arrangement for Individuals or Groups

16. SCOTLANDWELL COMMUNITY ALLOTMENTS Young's Moss, The Causeway, Scotlandwell KY13 9JQ NEW

Bob McCormick

Allotment Gardens

Route: The Allotments can be found on the Causeway, south of the village of Scotlandwell. From the village, head south on the B920. 100yds after the village take a left turn onto the red blaze access road. Heading from the south, on the B920, drive past the farm shop and the Red House, The access road is on the right 100yds before the village.

The allotment car park is at the end of the blaze road (200 yds)

Admission: £3.50

SUNDAY 20 JUNE 10:00am - 4:00pm
SUNDAY 18 JULY 10:00am - 4:00pm
SUNDAY 15 AUGUST 10:00am - 4:00pm

Web Site: www.scotlandwellallotments.co.uk

Email Address: sgs@scotlandwellallotments.co.uk

Rachel House (CHAS) receives 40%, the net remaining to SGS Beneficiaries.

❀ ♿ 🐕 Carriage Driving, Ladies & Gents Toilets on Site ☕

17. ST. ANDREWS BOTANIC GARDEN Canongate, St Andrews KY16 8RT NEW

St. Andrews Botanic Garden

Guided tour of the Botanic Garden's rhododendron collection with Hon. Curator Bob Mitchell and Ian Douglas, Past President of the Scottish Rhododendron Society.

Tickets must be purchased in advance from the Secretary, Friends of the Botanic Garden, Canongate, St Andrews, KY16 8RT. Cheques payable to Friends of the Botanic Garden.

Route: On the Canongate, off A915

Admission: £15.00 per Head to Include Wine and Canape Reception and Garden Tour. Pre-booking Required.

FRIDAY 07 MAY 6:30pm - 8:30pm

FIFE

Web Site: www.st-andrews-botanic.org
Telephone: 01334 476452
Email Address: botanic@standbg.plus.com
Friends of St. Andrews Botanic Garden receives 40%, the net remaining to SGS Beneficiaries.

✿ ♿ ☕ Wine

18. ST. MONANS VILLAGE GARDENS KY10 2BX

The Gardeners of St. Monans

Seven or more gardens will be opening in this seaside village, a number of them for the first time. Cottage gardens, vegetable gardens, a collection of giant cacti and several hidden gardens in spectacular places. The medieval church will be open and welcomes visitors.

Route: Enter village, drive to harbour, turn right and follow the road to the top of the hill where tickets and plants can be bought from Mr and Mrs Gardner. Large church car park is just beyond.

Admission: £4.00

SUNDAY 30 MAY 2:00pm - 5:00pm

Telephone: 01333 730792

Auld Kirk, St. Monans receives 40%, the net remaining to SGS Beneficiaries.

✿ Medieval Church Open   ☕ Homemade by the Ladies of the Guild in the Church Hall

19. STRATHAIRLY HOUSE Upper Largo, Leven KY8 6ED

Mr and Mrs Andrew Macgill

A recently restored walled garden. Herbaceous and mixed planting schemes. Parkland and woodlands with views over Largo Bay.

Route: Located outside the village of Upper Largo on the A917 Leven to Elie coast road. Turning marked with SGS signs.

Admission: £5.00 per Person Including Tea and Biscuits. Children Under the Age of 16 Free when Accompanied by an Adult.

SUNDAY 23 MAY 2:00pm - 5:00pm

Email Address: strathairly@btconnect.com

SSAFA receives 40%, the net remaining to SGS Beneficiaries.

✿ ♿ Partial   🐕 ☕ Light Refreshments

20. TAYFIELD (IN CONJUNCTION WITH WILLOWHILL) Forgan, Newport-on Tay DD6 8HA

William and Elizabeth Berry

A wide variety of trees and shrubs established over the past 200 years in the grounds of Tayfield House.

Route: 1½ miles south of Tay Road Bridge. Take the B995 to Newport off the Forgan roundabout.

<u>Admission:</u> £4.00 (for admission to both gardens)

SUNDAY 16 MAY 2:00pm - 5:00pm

SUNDAY 12 SEPTEMBER 2:00pm - 5:00pm

Forgan Arts Centre receives 40% 16 May Opening, RIO Community Centre receives 40% 12 September Opening, the net remaining to SGS Beneficiaries.

❀ Forgan Arts Centre Craft Stall on 16 May   ☕ Homemade

21. TEASSES GARDENS Nr. Ceres KY8 5PG

Sir Fraser and Lady Morrison

Teasses Gardens have been developed by the present owners for 12 years and now extend to approximately 60 acres. In addition to the traditional oval walled garden with fruit, vegetables, cut flowers and large greenhouse, there are formal and informal areas of garden linked by numerous woodland walks with many woodland gardens. There are extensive areas of spring bulbs. Please allow at least two hours for a tour with a member of the gardening staff to enjoy these large and peaceful gardens.

<u>Route:</u> Between Ceres and Largo. Enter by farm entrance two miles west of New Gilston village. Follow tarmac road to Estate Office.

<u>Admission:</u> £5.00 includes tour

BY ARRANGEMENT ALL YEAR: INDIVIDUALS OR GROUPS

Telephone: 01334 828048

Email Address: joanie@teasses.com

All proceeds to SGS Beneficiaries

♿

22. WESTFIELD ROAD GARDENS Cupar KY15 5DS NEW

The Gardeners of Westfield Road

Cupar were 2009 winners of a special "Homecoming Award" and in the "Beautiful Scotland" Awards, the coveted Silver Gilt Trophy for best medium town. This has elevated the town to a higher level and is this year competing in the prestigious "Britain in Bloom" competition. The eight gardens open are all in Westfield Road, in easy walking distance from the car park and offer a selection from the very old large walled gardens to very modern on a new development, less than two years old.

<u>Route:</u> On the A91 between Auchtermuchty and St Andrews

<u>Admission:</u> £4.50 Children Free (Tickets and Maps Available at the Bonnygate Car Park and at Certain Gardens)

SUNDAY 06 JUNE 12:00pm - 5:00pm

Rotary Club of Cupar receives 40%, the net remaining to SGS Beneficiaries.

☕ Homemade in a Marquee at Belmore Lodge

23. WILLOWHILL (IN CONJUNCTION WITH TAYFIELD) Forgan, Newport-on-Tay DD6 8RA

Eric Wright & Sally Lorimore

An evolving 3 acre garden started in 2000. The house is surrounded by mixed borders of bulbs, shrubs, alpines and herbaceous perennials plus a vegetable plot. To the rear of the garden is a grassland area with wildlife pond and trees.

Route: 1½ miles south of Tay Road Bridge. Take the B995 to Newport off the Forgan roundabout. Willowhill is the first house on the left hand side next to the Forgan Arts Centre

Admission: £4.00 Willowhill and Tayfield (16 May and 12 September)

£3.00 Willowhill only (16-20 August)

SUNDAY 16 MAY 2:00pm - 5:00pm

SUNDAY 12 SEPTEMBER 2:00pm - 5:00pm

MONDAY 16 AUGUST – FRIDAY 20 AUGUST 2:00pm - 5:00pm (WILLOWHILL ONLY)

Forgan Arts Centre receives 40% 16 May Opening, RIO Community Centre receives 40% 12 September Opening, the net remaining to SGS Beneficiaries.

✿ Forgan Arts Centre Craft Stall on 16 May Opening ☕ Homemade Teas on 16 May and 12 September Only

23. WORMISTOUNE HOUSE Crail KY10 3XH

Baron and Lady Wormiston

17th century formal walled garden restored over the last 10 years including orchard, scent garden, parterre and potager. Woodland walk around natural lochan. Mosaic celtic cross in new pleasance garden. Splendid herbaceous border and largest listed Grisselinia in Scotland.

Route: On A917 Crail - St Andrews.

Admission: £4.00 Children Free

SUNDAY 11 JULY 12:00pm - 5:00pm

Email Address: gemmawormiston@aol.com

Crail Development Trust receives 40%, the net remaining to SGS Beneficiaries.

✿ 🐕 Except in walled garden ☕ Cream

PLANT SALES

11. HILL OF TARVIT ANNUAL SGS PLANT SALE AND FAIR Cupar KY15 5PB

The National Trust for Scotland

Interesting and wide selection of locally grown plants and clumps of herbaceous plants at bargain prices. See Fife entry No. 11 for details of the garden.

Route: 2 miles south of Cupar off A916

Admission: Adults £1.00 Children free

SUNDAY 03 OCTOBER 10:30am - 4:00pm

Seasons of Ceres receives 40%, the net remaining to SGS Beneficiaries.

Glasgow & District

'Gardens of Scotland' 2010 is sponsored by **Rensburg Sheppards Investment Management**

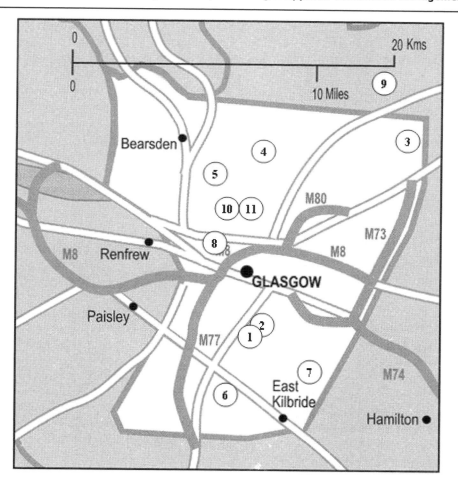

District Organiser: **Mrs A Barlow** 5 Auchencruive, Milngavie, Glasgow G62 6EE

Area Organisers: **Mrs S Elliott** 46 Corrour Road, Newlands G43 2DX

                                 Mrs P Macnair 36 Gartconnell Road, Bearsden G61 3BZ

                                 Mrs Jan Millar 3 Cochrane Court, Milngavie, Glasgow G62

                                 Mrs A Murray 44 Gordon Road, Netherlee G44 3TW

                                 Mr A Simpson 48 Thomson Drive, Bearsden G61 3NZ

Treasurer: **Mr J Murray** 44 Gordon Road, Netherlee G44 3TW

GLASGOW & DISTRICT

Gardens Open On a Specific Date

44 Gordon Road, Netherlee	Sunday 16 May	2:00pm - 5:00pm
Kirklee Circus Pleasure Garden and Beyond, Kirklee Circus	Saturday 22 May	2:30pm - 5:00pm
Kilsyth Gardens, Kilsyth	Sunday 23 May	2:00pm - 5:00pm
Kew Terrace Secret Gardens	Saturday 05 June	2:00pm - 5:00pm
46 Corrour Road, Newlands	Sunday 06 June	2:00pm - 5:00pm
Greenbank Garden, Clarkston	Tuesday 29 June	6:30pm - 9:30pm
Beanscroft, Ballmore	Sunday 11 July	1:00pm - 5:00pm
Garscube Allotments	Saturday 31 July	2:00pm - 5:00pm
Ingadi Enhle, Stewartfield	Sunday 08 August	2:00pm - 5:00pm
Greenbank Garden, Clarkston	Sunday 22 August	11:00am - 5:00pm

Gardens Open By Arrangement
When organising a visit to a garden open by arrangement, please enquire if there are facilities and catering available

5 Broomknowe, Balloch	On request	Tel: 01236 722 645

Plant Sales

Glasgow Botanic Gardens, Great Western Road, Glasgow	Saturday 12 June	11:00am - 4:00pm

1. 44 GORDON ROAD Netherlee G44 3TW
Anne and Jim Murray

Mature town garden of approximately one acre containing large trees, rhododendrons and herbaceous borders with many unusual plants. A Japanese garden and water feature are now established. Dovecot and new garden scultures. Garden as seen in "Beechgrove Garden".

Route: B767 Clarkston Road past Linn Park gates, turn at Williamwood Drive then second turning on the left.

Admission: £4.00 Children Free

SUNDAY 16 MAY 2:00pm - 5:00pm

Erskine Hospital receives 40%, the net remaining to SGS Beneficiaries.

✿ ♿ Partly ☕ Homemade

2. 46 CORROUR ROAD Newlands G42 2DX
Robert and Shona Elliot

A mature, fully stocked, walled town garden developed to provide all year interest with low maintenance. The emphasis is on shrubs and perennials with varied leaf shape and colour. Small pond with fish and frogs.

Route: From Glasgow take the A77 Kilmarnock Road. Turn left onto Newlands Road, then first left along St. Brides Road to Corrour Road.

Admission: £5.00 Including Teas

SUNDAY 06 JUNE 2:00pm - 5:00pm

Muscular Dystrophy Society receives 40%, the net remaining to SGS Beneficiaries.

❀ ♿ Partly 🐕 ☕ Homemade

3. 5 BROOMKNOWE Balloch, Cumbernauld G68 9AQ

Mrs Maureen Bingham

The garden has been developed over 20 years. It is completely organic with plants, shrubs and trees grown mostly from cuttings or seeds. There are raised vegetable beds, a new pond and a sheltered 'mirrored room' for soft fruit and tender vegetables.

Route: Take the A80 from Glasgow to Cumbernauld. Exit onto the A8011 signed Dullater. Follow Eastfield Road to Craigmarloch roundabout. Take first exit onto Balloch Loop Road. Broomknowe is 2nd on left.

Admission: By Donation

BY ARRANGEMENT ON REQUEST

Telephone: 01236 722 645

Macular Disease Society receives 40%, the net remaining to SGS Beneficiaries.

🐕

4. BEANSCROFT Fluchter Road, Ballmore, Torrance G64 4AS

Mr Robin Burnet

A pretty 200 year old cottage garden recreated and developed by the present owner to enhance its many features: herbaceous beds, lawns, paths to orchards and vegetable garden. There is an old bridge over a burn to a wildlife pond made by the owner, surrounded by an area stocked with rhododendrons, azaleas, trees, shrubs and grasses.

Route: From either the Allander Toll roundabout or from Torrance, take the A807 Balmore Road to the small village of Bardowie. In Bardowie, turn north down the narrow Craigmaddie Road signposted to Strathblane (A81) and with an additional sign for Baldernock Primary School. After ½ mile, in Barnellen, take the right turn and continue for about ½ mile towards the school. Beanscroft and a car park are behind the school.

Admission: £5.00

SUNDAY 11 JULY 1:00pm - 5:00pm

Playback Recording Service for the Blind receives 40%, the net remaining to SGS Beneficiaries.

❀ ♿ Partly 🐕 ☕ Homemade

5. GARSCUBE ALLOTMENTS Maryhill Road G20

University of Glasgow

The four acre site is owned by the University of Glasgow. It runs alongside the grounds of Acre House and has wonderful views northwestwards to the Kilpatrick Hills. The numerous plots show variety, character, imagination and individuality. A wide range of flowers, fruit and vegetables are grown.

Route: From Glasgow city centre take the A81 Garscube Road, which becomes Maryhill Road. Continue on Maryhill Road to the stretch of dual carriageway and then on as far as the roundabout at the entrance to the Science Park. Do a complete turn on the roundabout so as to head back towards Glasgow. The entrance to the allotments is almost immediately on the left just beyond a bus stop.

Admission: £5.00 - Includes admission to entire allotment area and teas.

SATURDAY 31 JULY 2:00pm - 5:00pm

Garscube Allotments Society receives 40%, the net remaining to SGS Beneficiaries.

 Produce Stall with Fruit & Vegetables Grown on Site

6. GREENBANK GARDEN Flenders Road, Clarkston G76 8RB

The National Trust for Scotland

A unique walled garden with plants and designs of particular interest to suburban gardeners. Fountains, woodland walk and special area for disabled visitors. Shop, plant sales, and gardening demonstrations throughout the year.

Walks at 11:30am, 1:30pm and 3:15pm

Tuesday 29 June: Join the Head Gardener for an interpretive walk through the garden followed by supper of soup and sandwich with tea and coffee. During supper there will be time for an informal gardeners question time then stay and have a visit to Greenbank House and learn the history of this fascinating property. Please book in advance.

Route: OS Ref: NS561566

Road: Flenders Road, off Mearns Road, Clarkston. Off M77 and A727, follow signs for East Kilbride to Clarkston Toll. 6m S of Glasgow city centre

Cycle: 4m from NCN 7, 75

Bus: No44a, Glasgow to Newton Mearns

Rail: Clarkston station, 1¼m

Admission: **Tuesday 29th June:** £35.00 (Booking Essential)

Sunday 22 August: £5.50 Concessions £4.50

TUESDAY 29 JUNE 6:30pm - 9:30pm

SUNDAY 22 AUGUST 11:00am - 5:00pm

Web Site: www.nts.org.uk

Telephone: 0844 493 2201 Email Address: dferguson@nts.org.uk

Donation to SGS Beneficiaries

Throughout Garden In Woodland Walk Only NCCPG Bergenia Species and Cultivars NTS Shop on Site

7. INGADI ENHLE 9 Brooklime Drive, Stewartfield, East Kilbride G74 4UD

Jim and Deidre Ozmond

Colourful town garden with mixed borders of interesting shrubs, perennials and a diverse range of annuals. Attractive hard landscaping adds interest to the whole scheme of the garden. Well stocked vegetable beds and greenhouse.

Route: Travel Stewartfield Way between the A726 at Centre 1 and Kingsgate, Junction off A749 and A725. At Heritage Park roundabout turn into Stewartfield Crescent, then take 1st right into Stewartfield Way. Brooklime Drive is to the end and right of the cul-de-sac/mini roundabout

<u>Admission:</u> £5.00 Including Teas

SUNDAY 08 AUGUST 2:00pm - 5:00pm

Guide Dogs receives 40%, the net remaining to SGS Beneficiaries.

❀ ♿ Partly 🐕 ☕ Homemade

8. KEW TERRACE SECRET GARDENS 19 Kew Terrace, Glasgow G12

Mr George Browning

Kew Terrace is one of the grand terraces that line Great Western Road and when built in 1845 to 1852 only one of the houses had a mews, the others had back gardens. Over the years the temptation to use them as car storage spaces has been resisted and now there is a series of 'Secret Gardens' all different in their handling, but all enhancing green living in a town environment. Access is from tree-lined, cobbled Kew Terrace Lane.

<u>Route:</u> From M8 take junction 17 (A82) and turn right onto Great Western Road. Continue for nearly one mile to cross over the Great Western Road/Byres Road junction. Kew Terrace is on the left and access is 250 yards beyond traffic lights.

<u>Admission:</u> £5.00 Includes admission to several gardens and teas.

SATURDAY 05 JUNE 2:00pm - 5:00pm

Kew Terrace Garden Owners Society receives 40%, the net remaining to SGS Beneficiaries.

❀ 🐕 ☕ Homemade

9. KILSYTH GARDENS Allanfauld Road, Kilsyth, G65 9DE

Mr and Mrs Geaorge Murdoch and Mr and Mrs Alan Patrick

Aeolia (Mr and Mrs G Murdoch) Has a garden of a third of an acre developed since 1960 by the present owners and contains many mature specimen trees and shrubs, a large variety of rhododendrons, primulas, hardy geraniums and herbaceous plants.

Blackmill (Mr and Mrs Alan Patrick) Blackmill is across the road from Aeolia and is an acre of mature and recent planting of specimen trees and shrubs developed on the site of an old mill. There are surprises at every turn and also an ornamental plant and rockpool. A further acre of natural woodland glen, paths alongside the Garrel Burn with views to the cascading waterfalls. WC available but not suitable for disabled.

<u>Route:</u> From Kirkintilloch take the A803 to Kilsyth. Continue on the A803 through the main roundabout in Kilsyth (Police Station on right). Just after the pedestrian crossing turn left into Parkburn Road. Follow the road up the hill until meeting Kingsway at the crossroads. The gardens are a short walk up Allanfauld Road, which is a continuation of Parkburn, but it is narrow and unsuitable for parking

<u>Admission:</u> £5.00 This includes admission to both gardens and homemade teas.

SUNDAY 23 MAY 2:00pm - 5:00pm

Telephone: 01236 821667

Strathcarron Hospice receives 40%, the net remaining to SGS Beneficiaries.

❀ ♿ Wheelchair Access to Some Parts of Blackmill 🐕 ☕ Homemade

10. KIRKLEE CIRCUS PLEASURE GARDEN AND BEYOND Kirklee Circus, Glasgow. G12 OTW

Lisella Hutton (Kirklee Circus Gardens Convenor)

Kirklee Circus Garden is a delightful oasis of calm enclosed by a discrete enclave of Victorian houses west of the Botanic Gardens. Over the years a dense circle of 32 lime trees has been reduced to five and replaced in stages with a large variety of interesting plants, many defying the shady location. This process will be continued into the future which will encourage a return visit. To the rear of the villas and terraced houses are the residents walled gardens, many of which will be on show. These display an amazing variety reflecting the aspirations and character of generations of owners as well as present residents.

Route: Enter from Kirklee Road, second on the right from the Great Western Road/ Kirklee Road junction and traffic lights. Parking on Kirklee Road. There are frequent bus services along Great Western Road. Nearest subway station is Hillhead Station on Byres Road. Kirklee Circus is a 10 minute walk from the station, either along Great Western Road or through the Botanic Gardens to the Kirklee Gate.

Admission: £5.00 - Includes the Circus Garden, a number of Residents Gardens and Teas with Homebaking.

SATURDAY 22 MAY 2:30pm - 5:00pm

Beatson Pebble Fund receives 20%, Save the Children Fund receives 20%, the net remaining to SGS Beneficiaries.

✿ ♿ To the Circus Garden ➴ ☕ Homemade

PLANT SALES

11. GLASGOW BOTANIC GARDENS Great Western Road, Glasgow G12 OUE

Glasgow City Council

Glasgow District's Annual Plant Sale will again be held in the spring. A large selection of indoor and outdoor plants and shrubs will be for sale. There will also be an opportunity to view the National Collection of Begonias and the extensive propogation areas. Scotland's largest collection of filmy ferns set in a fairy like grotto will also be open to view and this is particularly appealing to children.

ANY DONATION OF PLANTS BEFOREHAND WOULD BE WELCOME: PLEASE CONTACT 014 956 3109

Route: Leave M8 at Junction 17, follow signs for Dumbarton. The Botanic Garden is at the junction of Great Western Road A82 and Queen Margaret Drive.

Admission: Free - Donations Welcome

SATURDAY 12 JUNE 11:00am - 4:00pm

Friends of Botanic Gardens receives 40%, the net remaining to SGS Beneficiaries.

✿ ♿ ➴ ☕ Light Refreshments

'Gardens of Scotland' 2010 is sponsored by **Rensburg Sheppards Investment Management**

Isle of Arran

District Organiser: Mrs S C Gibbs Dougarie, Isle of Arran KA27 8EB
Treasurer: **Mrs E Adam** Bayview, Pirnmill, Isle of Arran KA217 8HP

Gardens Open On a Specific Date

Brodick Castle & Country Park, Brodick	Sunday 09 May	10:00am - 5:00pm
Strabane, Brodick	Sunday 23 May	11:00am - 5:00pm
Strabane, Brodick	Sunday 30 May	11:00am - 5:00pm
Dougarie	Sunday 27 June	2:00pm - 5:00pm
Brodick Castle & Country Park, Brodick	Sunday 11 July	10:00am - 5:00pm

1. BRODICK CASTLE & COUNTRY PARK Brodick KA27 8HY

The National Trust for Scotland

Exotic plants and shrubs. Walled garden. Woodland garden. Large collection of rhododendrons.

Route: Brodick 2 miles. Service buses from Brodick Pier to Castle. Regular sailings from Ardrossan and from Claonaig (Argyll). Information from Caledonian MacBrayne, Gourock. (Telephone 01475 650100)

Admission: £5.50, Concessions £4.50, Family £15.00, Single Parent Family £11.00

SUNDAY 09 MAY 10:00am - 5:00pm
SUNDAY 11 JULY 10:00am - 5:00pm

Web Site: www.nts.org.uk

Telephone: 0844 493 2152 Email Address: brodickcastle@nts.org.uk

Donation to SGS Beneficiaries

♿ Partial Shop ☕ Homemade Wine Light Refreshments in Tearoom

2. DOUGARIE KA27 8EB

Mr and Mrs S C Gibbs

Terraced garden in castellated folly. Tender shrubs, herbaceous border, traditional kitchen garden.

Route: Blackwaterfoot 5 miles. Regular ferry sailing from Ardrossan and Claonaig (Argyll). Information from Caledonian MacBrayne, Gourock. (Telephone 01475 650100)

Admission: £3.00 Children Free

SUNDAY 27 JUNE 2:00pm - 5:00pm

Pirnmill Village Association receives 40%, the net remaining to SGS Beneficiaries.
☕ Homemade in the Boathouse

ISLE OF ARRAN

3. STRABANE Brodick KA27 8DP
Lady Jean Fforde
Woodland Garden with fine rhododendrons and azaleas. Walled garden with good herbaceous borders.

<u>Route:</u> On east side of Brodick - Corrie road 100 yards before Duchess's Shopping Centre. Parking in front of house.

<u>Admission:</u> £4.00 Children Free

SUNDAY 23 MAY 11:00am - 5:00pm

SUNDAY 30 MAY 11:00am - 5:00pm

The Church of Scotland, Brodick receives 40%, the net remaining to SGS Beneficiaries.

☕

Visit Our Website at <u>www.gardensofscotland.org</u>

Master Class on Garden Management

With key members of the NTS Gardens Team

Thursday 11 March

at The National Trust for Scotland,

28 Charlotte Square, Edinburgh

£45.00 to include lunch

Tickets available from Mrs Barrrington: tel. 0131 243 9440

or email: <u>vbarrington@nts.or.uk</u>

'Gardens of Scotland' 2010 is sponsored by **Rensburg Sheppards Investment Management**

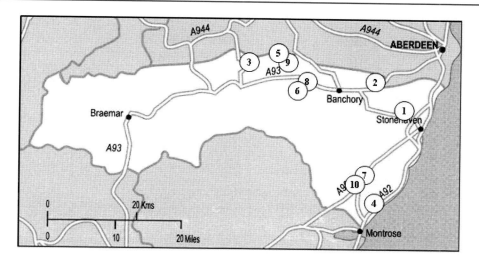

Kincardine & Deeside

District Organisers:	**Tina Hammond** Bardfield, Inchmarlo, Banchory AB31 4AT
	Julie Nicol Bogiesheil, Ballogie, Aboyne AB34 5DU
Area Organiser:	**Mrs Andrea Bond** Rosebank, Crathes, Banchory AB31 5JE
	Mrs Helen Jackson
	Ms. Frieda Morrison
Treasurer:	**Mr J Ludlow** Strutt & Parker LLP, St. Nicholas House, Banchory AB31 5YT

Gardens Open On a Specific Date

Ecclesgreig Castle, St Cyrus	Sunday 28 February	1:00pm - 4:00pm
Inchmarlo House Garden, Inchmarlo	Sunday 23 May	1:30pm - 4:30pm
The Burn House & The Burn, Glenesk	Sunday 30 May	2:00pm - 5:00pm
Kincardine, Kincardine O'Neil	Sunday 06 June	2:00pm - 5:00pm
Ecclesgreig Castle, St Cyrus	Sunday 20 June	1:00pm - 5:00pm
Crathes Castle, Banchory	Sunday 27 June	2:00pm - 5:30pm
Finzean House, Finzean	Sunday 27 June	2:00pm - 5:00pm
Findrack, Torphins	Sunday 04 July	2:00pm - 5:00pm
Douneside House, Tarland	Sunday 18 July	2:00pm - 5:00pm
Glenbervie House, Drumlithie	Sunday 01 August	2:00pm - 5:00pm
Inchmarlo House Garden, Inchmarlo	Sunday 24 October	1:30pm - 4:30pm

Gardens Open By Arrangement

When organising a visit to a garden open by arrangement, please enquire if there are facilities and catering available

4 Robert Street, Stonehaven	01 - 31 July	Tel: 01569 763877
Inchmarlo House Garden	For Charities & Groups	Tel: 01330 826242

1. 4 ROBERT STREET Stonehaven AB39 2DN

Sue and Michael Reid

Former walled orchard filled with a wide range of climbing plants, old-fashioned and species roses. Herbaceous borders, ferns and shrubs on several levels. Groups welcome.

Route: Off Evan Street from Stonehaven Market Square.

Admission: £3.50

BY ARRANGEMENT 01 - 31 JULY

Telephone: 01569 763877 Email Address: reid60@tiscali.co.uk

Scottish Meningitis Trust receives 40%, the net remaining to SGS Beneficiaries.

✿ ☕ Homemade

2. CRATHES CASTLE Banchory AB31 5QJ

The National Trust for Scotland

The walled garden is really eight gardens, ranging from the formal to the modern. The massive yew hedges were planted as early as 1702, while the Golden Garden was introduced by the Trust in 1973. Most famous of all are the June Borders, two lavish beds of herbaceous colour with the castle itself as a backdrop.

Guided walk at 3:00pm meet at garden entrance.

Route: OS Ref: NO735967 **Road:** On A93, 15m W of Aberdeen and 3m E of Banchory

Bus: Stagecoach Bluebird (No 201) from Aberdeen bus station stops at estate entrance

Rail: Aberdeen station 15m **Airport:** Aberdeen (Dyce) 12m

Admission: £8.50 Concessions £6.00

SUNDAY 27 JUNE 2:00pm - 5:30pm

Web Site: www.nts.org.uk

Telephone: 0844 493 2166 Email Address: crathes@nts.org.uk

Donation to SGS Beneficiaries

♿ NCCPG Pruning Workshop 10:00am - 12:00, Glasshouse Plant Workshop 1:00pm - 2:55pm, Garden Tour 3:00pm ☕ Light Refreshments

3. DOUNESIDE HOUSE Tarland AB34 4UD

The MacRobert Trust

The former home of Lady MacRobert who designed and developed the gardens from farmland in the early to mid 1900s. The house and gardens are now in Trust and from March to October are used exclusively by retired and serving Officers of The Armed Forces. Overlooking the Deeside Hills, ornamental terraced borders, woodland and water gardens surround a spectacular elevated lawn. The house is supplied with vegetables and cut flowers from the well-stocked walled garden, which also houses an ornamental greenhouse. There are fine walks along the beech belts with uninterrupted views over the Howe of Cromar.

Route: B9119 towards Aberdeen. Tarland 1½ miles.

Admission: £4.00 OAPs £2.00 Children Under 12 Free

SUNDAY 18 JULY 2:00pm - 5:00pm

Perennial receives 40%, the net remaining to SGS Beneficiaries.

❀ ♿   Local Pipe Band   ☕ Homemade

4. ECCLESGREIG CASTLE St Cyrus DD10 0DP

Mr Gavin Farquhar

Ecclesgreig Castle is Victorian Gothic on a 16th Century core. It is internationally famous and recognised as one of the inspirations for Bram Stoker's 'Dracula'.

The snowdrop walk starts at the castle, meanders around the estate, along woodland paths, around the pond, finishing at the garden. The woodlands contain some very interesting trees and shrubs.

The formal garden, which is in the Italian Renaissance style, sits below a terrace of decorative stone balustrades. It contains classical statues as well as round and sculptured topiary and offers spectacular views across St Cyrus to the sea.

The garden is in a constant course of development and has been undergoing renovation from a state of dereliction some ten years ago. The gardener and family will be happy to answer questions from visitors.

Route: Ecclesgreig will be signposted from the A92 Coast Road and from the A937 Montrose / Laurencekirk Road.

Admission: £3.00 Accompanied Children Free

SUNDAY 28 FEBRUARY FOR SNOWDROP FESTIVAL 1:00pm - 4:00pm

SUNDAY 20 JUNE 1:00pm - 5:00pm

Web Site: www.ecclesgreig.com   Email Address: enquiries@ecclesgreig.com

Scottish Civic Trust receives 20%, Christian Aid receives 20%, the net remaining to SGS Beneficiaries.

❀ 🐕 ⚘   Children's Colouring Competition, Archery, Bouncy Castle - Provisional on Weather and Availability   ☕ Homemade

5. FINDRACK Torphins AB31 4LB

Mr and Mrs Andrew Salvesen

The gardens of Findrack are set in beautiful wooded countryside and are a haven of interesting plants and unusual design features. There is a walled garden with circular lawns and deep herbaceous borders, stream garden leading to a wildlife pond, vegetable garden and woodland walk. Excellent selection of plants for sale all grown in the garden.

Route: Leave Torphins on A980 to Lumphanan after ½ mile turn off signposted Tornaveen. Stone gateway 1 mile up on left.

Admission: £4.00 Children under 12 £1.00

SUNDAY 04 JULY 2:00pm - 5:00pm

The Breadmaker receives 40%, the net remaining to SGS Beneficiaries.

❀ ♿ In Parts   ☕ Homemade

6. FINZEAN HOUSE Finzean, Banchory AB31 6NZ

Mr and Mrs Donald Farquharson

An evolving country house garden with beautiful views in a walled setting. Finzean House was the family home of Joseph Farquharson, the Victorian landscape painter, and the garden was the backdrop for several of his paintings. There are newly planted herbaceous borders and a recently laid out cutting garden alongside shrubs, trees and the historic holly hedge to the front.

Route: On B976, South Deeside Road, between Banchory and Aboyne

Admission: £4.00 OAPs £3.00 Children Free

SUNDAY 27 JUNE 2:00pm - 5:00pm

Forget Me Not Club receives 40%, the net remaining to SGS Beneficiaries.

✿ ♿ 🐕 ☕ Homemade

7. GLENBERVIE HOUSE Drumlithie, Stonehaven AB39 3YB

Mr and Mrs A Macphie

Nucleus of present day house dates from 15th century with additions in 18th and 19th centuries. A traditional Scottish walled garden on a slope with roses, herbaceous and annual borders along with fruit and vegetables. One wall is taken up with a fine Victorian style conservatory with many varieties of pot plants and climbers giving a dazzling display. There is also a woodland garden by a burn with primulas and ferns. Please note paths are quite steep in parts of the garden.

Route: Drumlithie 1 mile. Garden 1½ miles off A90

Admission: £4.00 Children £1.00

SUNDAY 01 AUGUST 2:00pm - 5:00pm

West Mearns Parish Church of Scotland receives 40%, the net remaining to SGS Beneficiaries.

✿ The Macallan Fine Oak Highland Single Malt Whisky Promotion   Baking Stall ☕

8. INCHMARLO HOUSE GARDEN Inchmarlo, Banchory AB31 4AL

Skene Enterprises (Aberdeen) Ltd

An ever-changing 5 acre Woodland Garden lies within the Inchmarlo Continuing Care Retirement Community. It was originally planted in the early Victorian era, featuring ancient Scots Pines, Douglas Firs and Silver Firs, one of which is over 42 metres tall, beeches and a wide variety of rare and unusual trees, including Pindrow Firs, Père David's Maple, Erman's Birch and a mountain snowdrop tree. They form a dramatic background to an early summer riot of mature azaleas and rhododendrons, producing a splendour of colour and scents. In autumn the colours of the trees and shrubs are breathtaking.

The Oriental Garden features a Kare Sansui, a dry slate stream designed by Peter Roger, a RHS Chelsea gold medal winner.

The new "Rainbow" Garden, within the keyhole-shaped purple Prunus Cerasifera hedge, has been designed by Billy Carruthers, an eight times gold medal winner at the RHS Scottish Garden Show. Over 1000 plants have been selected to reflect the colours of the rainbow throughout the four seasons of the year.

This garden will be open to the public in October for the first time.

Route: From Aberdeen via North Deeside Road on A93, one mile west of Banchory turn right at the main gate to Inchmarlo House.

Admission: £4.00, Concessions £3.00, Children under 14 Free

SUNDAY 23 MAY 1:30pm - 4:30pm

SUNDAY 24 OCTOBER 1:30pm - 4:30pm

ALSO BY ARRANGEMENT FOR CHARITIES AND GROUPS

Web Site: www.inchmarlo-retirement.co.uk

Telephone: 01330 826242 Email Address: info@inchmarlo-retirement.co.uk

Alzheimer Scotland Action on Dementia receives 40% May Opening, Royal Deeside Forget-me-Not Dementia Support receives 40% October Opening, the net remaining to SGS Beneficiaries.

✿ May only ♿ Limited Access ☕ Homemade and Homebakes £3.00

9. KINCARDINE Kincardine O'Neil AB34 5AE

Mr and Mrs Andrew Bradford

A woodland or wilderness garden in development with some mature rhododendrons and azaleas and new planting amongst mature trees. A walled garden with a mixture of herbaceous and shrub borders, a sensational laburnum walk, vegetables and fruit trees. Extensive lawns and wild - flower meadows and a thought-provoking Planetary Garden. All with a background of stunning views across Royal Deeside.

Route: Kincardine O'Neil on A93. Gates and lodge are opposite village school

Admission: £5.00 Children £2.00

SUNDAY 06 JUNE 2:00pm - 5:00pm

Children's 1st receives 20%, The Miss Edith Middleton Coutts' Trust (A Kincardine O'Neil Charity) receives 20%, the net remaining to SGS Beneficiaries.

✿ ♿ With Assistance ☕ Homemade

10. THE BURN HOUSE & THE BURN GARDEN HOUSE Glenesk DD9 7YP

David Wood, Bursar

Beautiful 18th century mansion house with magnificent walled garden nearby. Stunning 190 acre estate set in area of outstanding beauty including dramatic walk along the famous gorge in the North Esk river.

Route: 1 mile north of Edzell Village. 3 miles from the A90. Front entrance situated on North side of River North Esk Bridge on B966 between Edzell and Fettercairn.

Admission: £4.00

SUNDAY 30 MAY 2:00pm - 5:00pm

Telephone: 01356 648281 Email Address: burn@goodenough.ac.uk

McMillan Cancer Support receives 40%, the net remaining to SGS Beneficiaries.

♿ Partly Raffle, Tombola, Food Stalls ☕ Homemade Light Refreshments

BBQ - Not Included with Entrance Price

Kirkcudbrightshire

'Gardens of Scotland' 2010 is sponsored by **Rensburg Sheppards Investment Management**

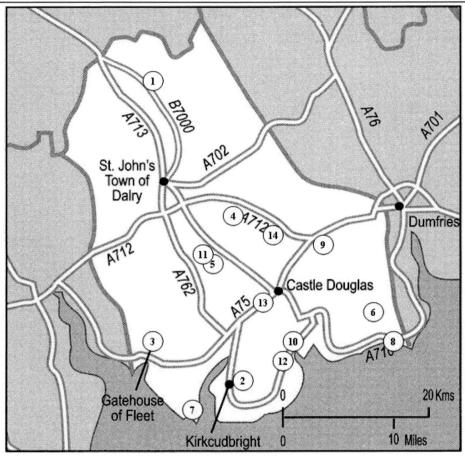

District Organiser: **Mrs C Cathcart** Culraven, Borgue, Kirkcudbright DG6 4SG

Area Organisers: **Mrs P Addison** Killeron Farm, Gatehouse of Fleet, Castle Douglas DG7 2BS

Mrs Val Bradbury Glenisle, Jubilee Path, Kippford DG5 4LW

Mrs W N Dickson Chipperkyle, Kirkpatrick, Durham DG7 3EY

Mrs R Elliot 18 Hanover Court, Castle Douglas DG7 1BU

Mrs B Marshall Cairnview, Carsphairn DG7 3TQ

Mrs M McIlvenna Braeneuk, Balmaclellan, Castle Douglas DG7 3QS

Mrs K Ross Slate Row, Auchencairn, Castle Douglas DG7 1QL

Mrs C V Scott 14 Castle Street, Kirkcudbright DG6 4JA

Treasurer: **Mr P Phillips** The Old Manse, Crossmichael DG7 3AT

Gardens Open On a Specific Date

Danevale Park, Crossmichael	Date to be Advised	1:00pm - 5:00pm
Walton Park, Castle Douglas	Sunday 25 April	2:00pm - 5:00pm
Threave Garden, Castle Douglas	Sunday 16 May	9:30am - 5:30pm
Spottes, Haugh of Urr	Sunday 23 May	2:00pm - 5:00pm
Corsock House, Corsock	Sunday 30 May	2:00pm - 5:00pm
Arndarroch, St John's Town of Dalry	Sunday 13 June	2:00pm - 5:00pm
Cally Gardens, Gatehouse of Fleet	Sunday 20 June	10:00am - 5:30pm
The Waterhouse Gardens at Stockarton	Sunday 27 June	1:00pm - 5:00pm
The Old Manse, Crossmichael	Sunday 04 July	2:00pm - 5:00pm
Southwick House, Southwick	Sunday 11 July	9:00am - 5:00pm
Southwick House, Southwick	Monday 12 July	9:00am - 5:00pm
Southwick House, Southwick	Tuesday 13 July	9:00am - 5:00pm
Southwick House, Southwick	Wednesday 14 July	9:00am - 5:00pm
Southwick House, Southwick	Thursday 15 July	9:00am - 5:00pm
Southwick House, Southwick	Friday 16 July	9:00am - 5:00pm
Glensone Walled Garden, Southwick	Sunday 18 July	2:00pm - 5:00pm
Threave Garden, Castle Douglas	Sunday 08 August	9:30am - 5:30pm
Broughton House, Kirkcudbright	Sunday 22 August	12:00pm - 5:00pm
Cally Gardens, Gatehouse of Fleet	Sunday 29 August	10:00am - 5:30pm
Arndarroch, St John's Town of Dalry	Sunday 05 September	2:00pm - 5:00pm

Gardens Open By Arrangement
When organising a visit to a garden open by arrangement, please enquire if there are facilities and catering available

Arndarroch, St John's Town of Dalry	July - September	Tel: 01644 460640
Corsock House, Castle Douglas	April - June & Autumn	Tel: 01644 440250
Danevale Park, Crossmichael	Until 1 June	Tel: 01556 670223
Manor Cottage, Ross, Borgue	June & July	Tel: 01557 870 381
Stockarton, Kirkcudbright	May, June and July	Tel: 01557 330 430

Gardens Open Regularly

Broughton House Garden	Summer Openings	Times Vary
Cally Gardens, Gatehouse of Fleet	03 Apr - 26 Sept.	
	Tues – Fridays	2:00pm - 5:30pm
	and Sats & Suns	10:00am – 5:30pm
Threave Garden, Castle Douglas	2 April - 31 October	9:30am - 5:30pm

KIRKCUDBRIGHTSHIRE

1. ARNDARROCH St John's Town of Dalry DG7 3UD
Annikki and Matt Lindsay

A 2¼ acre garden created since 1991 on a windswept hillside overlooking Kendoon Loch. A great variety of trees, some species roses and shrubs have been underplanted with herbaceous plants. Small kitchen garden. Collections of oriental and medicinal plants. Also a collection of over 20 different bamboos. A small woodland was planted in 2000. The aim has been to create a semi-natural, wildlife friendly environment.

Route: About 5 miles from St John's Town of Dalry or Carsphairn on the B7000. Follow signs to the Youth Hostel.

Admission: £3.00 Children Free

SUNDAY 13 JUNE 2:00pm - 5:00pm
SUNDAY 05 SEPTEMBER 2:00pm - 5:00pm
ALSO BY ARRANGEMENT JULY - SEPTEMBER

Telephone: 01644 460640

D&G Canine Rescue Centre receives 40%, the net remaining to SGS Beneficiaries.

✿ 🐕 Wildlife Display Indoors ☕ Homemade - June Opening Only

2. BROUGHTON HOUSE GARDEN 12 High Street, Kirkcudbright DG6 4JX
The National Trust for Scotland

Fascinating town house garden that belonged to E A Hornel - artist, collector and one of the 'Glasgow boys'. Full of colour, mostly herbaceous, old apple trees, greenhouse with old pelargonium varieties, fruit and vegetable garden. Open for the Snowdrop Festival on 7 and 8 February. The garden will be open in summer, times vary, please phone for details of garden walk.

Route: In Kirkcudbright High Street

Admission: £4.00 Children Free

SUNDAY 22 AUGUST 12:00pm - 5:00pm
SUMMER OPENINGS (TIMES VARY)

Web Site: www.nts.org.uk
Telephone: 01557 330 437 Email Address: broughtonhouse@nts.org.uk

Donation to SGS Beneficiaries

✿ ☕ Homemade

3. CALLY GARDENS Gatehouse of Fleet DG7 2DJ
Mr Michael Wickenden

A specialist nursery in a fine 2.7 acre 18th century walled garden with old vinery and bothy, all surrounded by the Cally Oak woods. Our collection of 3,500 varieties of plants can be seen and a selection will be available pot-grown. Excellent range of rare herbaceous perennials. Forestry nature trails nearby.

Route: From Dumfries take the Gatehouse turning off A75 and turn left through the Cally Palace Hotel gateway from where the gardens are well signposted.

Admission: £2.50

SUNDAY 20 JUNE 10:00am - 5:30pm

SUNDAY 29 AUGUST 10:00am - 5:30pm

03 APRIL - 26 SEPTEMBER, TUESDAYS - FRIDAYS 2:00pm - 5:30pm

03 APRIL - 26 SEPTEMBER, SATURDAYS & SUNDAYS 10:00am - 5:30pm

Web Site: www.callygardens.co.uk

Telephone: 01557 814703 Email Address: info@callygardens.co.uk

ROKPA Tibetan charity receives 40%, the net remaining to SGS Beneficiaries.

4. CORSOCK HOUSE Corsock, Castle Douglas DG7 3DJ

Mrs M L Ingall

Rhododendrons, woodland walks with temples, water gardens and loch. One acre formal walled garden being re-made. David Bryce turretted "Scottish Baronial" house in background.

Route: Off A75 Dumfries 14 miles, Castle Douglas 10 miles, Corsock village ½ mile on A712.

Admission: £4.00 Concessions £3.00 Children Free

SUNDAY 30 MAY 2:00pm - 5:00pm

ALSO BY ARRANGEMENT APRIL - JUNE & AUTUMN

Telephone: 01644 440250

Corsock & Kirkpatrick Durham Kirk receives 40%, the net remaining to SGS Beneficiaries.

 & Partial   Homemade

5. DANEVALE PARK Crossmichael DG7 2LP

Mrs M R C Gillespie

Open for snowdrops. Mature policies with woodland walks alongside the River Dee. Walled garden.

Route: A713. Crossmichael 1 mile, Castle Douglas 2 miles.

Admission: £2.50

DATE TO BE ADVISED 1:00pm - 5:00pm

ALSO BY ARRANGEMENT UNTIL 1 JUNE

Telephone: 01556 670223 Email Address: danevale@tiscali.co.uk

Poppyscotland receives 40%, the net remaining to SGS Beneficiaries.

 & Partly   Homemade In the House

6. GLENSONE WALLED GARDEN Southwick, Dumfries DG2 8AW NEW

William & Josephine Millar

A recently restored walled garden complete with central water feature. Borders of perennials & shrubs with beds interspersed through the lawn. A large kitchen garden with a variety of vegetables & fruit occupies a section of the garden. Bee Bowls, a very unique feature, are positioned in two opposite corners of the wall. Set in an idyllic valley with views of the Solway Firth and the Cumbrian hills.

Route: Off the A710 Dumfries to Dalbeattie coast road at Caulkerbush. Take the B793 to Dalbeattie for two miles then turn right & follow the arrows

Admission: £3.50 Children Free

SUNDAY 18 JULY 2:00pm - 5:00pm

Telephone: 01387 780215 Email Address: josephine.millar@btconnect.com

Combat Stress receives 40%, the net remaining to SGS Beneficiaries.

♿ 🐕 ☕ Homemade

7. MANOR COTTAGE, ROSS Borgue DG6 4TR NEW

Mrs Susan Finlay

Situated within a working stock farm on the shore of a windswept coastal bay off the Solway River Dee the garden is a haven for wildlife. Developed since 1993 it comprises lawns, a sunken garden created from scratch, shrubs and a wonderfield view

Route: Off the B727 Kirkcudbright to Gatehouse of Fleet road, 4 miles from Kirkcudbright follow the signs to Ross Bay. Go through Ross Farm and follow track to the end of the bay

Admission: By Donation

BY ARRANGEMENT JUNE & JULY

Web Site: www.baycottage.net

Telephone: 01557 870 381 Email Address: finlay.baycottage@btinternet.com

Marie Curie receives 40%, the net remaining to SGS Beneficiaries.

✿ ♿ Partial 🐕 ☕

8. SOUTHWICK HOUSE Southwick DG2 8AH

Mr and Mrs R H L Thomas

Traditional formal walled garden with lily ponds, herbaceous borders, shrubs, vegetables, fruit and greenhouses. Fine trees and lawns through which flows the Southwick burn. New developments in water garden.

Route: On A710 near Caulkerbush. Dalbeattie 7 miles, Dumfries 17 miles.

Admission: £4.00 Children Free

SUNDAY 11 JULY – FRIDAY 16 JULY 9:00am - 5:00pm

Loch Arthur receives 20%, Perennial (GRBS) receives 20%, the net remaining to SGS Beneficiaries.

✿ 🐕 ☕ Homemade

9. SPOTTES Haugh of Urr DG7 3JX NEW

Mr & Mrs Herries

Walled garden, lake, beech walk and policies originally laid out to complement 18th century house in the same family since construction. Extensive restoration and additions ongoing since 1995 include Far Eastern additions, Japanese tea house etc.

Towering yew hedges and mature trees are enhanced with new plantings of bulbs, rhododendrons, herbaceous and bog beds. Sensible footwear advised.

Route: Off A75 three miles East of Castle Douglas take B794 to Haugh of Urr & Dalbeattie. Entrance nearly 1 mile by stone bridge, gateposts & white fence - follow parking directions

Admission: £4.00

SUNDAY 23 MAY 2:00pm - 5:00pm

Telephone: 01556 660202 Email Address: amanda.herries@spottes.co.uk

Loch Arthur Community receives 40%, the net remaining to SGS Beneficiaries.

❀ ♿ Partial 🐕 ☕ Homemade

10. STOCKARTON Kirkcudbright DG6 4XS

Lt. Col. and Mrs Richard Cliff

A garden begun in 1994. Our aim has been to create informal and small gardens around a Galloway farmhouse, leading down to a loch.

Route: On B727 Kirkcudbright to Gelston Road. Kirkcudbright 3 miles, Castle Douglas 7 miles.

Admission: By Donation

BY ARRANGEMENT MAY, JUNE AND JULY

Telephone: 01557 330 430

Friends of Loch Arthur Community receives 40%, the net remaining to SGS Beneficiaries.

❀ ♿ 🐕

11. THE OLD MANSE Crossmichael DG7 3AT

Mr and Mrs Peter Phillips

Roses, shrubs, azaleas, herbaceous, rock garden in a constantly developing working garden created over the past dozen years. Splendid views to River Dee.

Route: On A713 Castle Douglas/Ayr on edge of Crossmichael Village.

Admission: £3.00 Children Free

SUNDAY 04 JULY 2:00pm - 5:00pm

Abbeyfield Stewartry Society receives 40%, the net remaining to SGS Beneficiaries.

❀ ♿ 🐕 ☕ Homemade In Village Hall

12. THE WATERHOUSE GARDENS AT STOCKARTON Kirkcudbright DG6 4XS

Martin Gould & Sharon O'Rourke

One acre of densely planted terraced cottage style gardens attached to a Galloway cottage. Three ponds surround the oak framed eco-polehouse 'The Waterhouse' available to rent 52 weeks a year. Climbing roses, clematis and honeysuckles are a big feature as well as pond-side walk. Over 50 photos on website. Featured on BBC Scotland's 'Beechgrove Garden' 2007

Route: On B727 Kirkcudbright to Gelston & Dalbeattie road. Kirkcudbright 3 miles,

KIRKCUDBRIGHTSHIRE

Castle Douglas 7 miles
Admission: £3.00
SUNDAY 27 JUNE 1:00pm - 5:00pm
Web Site: www.waterhousekbt.co.uk
Telephone: 01557 331266 Email Address: waterhousekbt@aol.com
Loch Arthur Community receives 40%, the net remaining to SGS Beneficiaries.
❁ 🐕 Paintings by Martin Gould for Sale ☕ Homemade Light Refreshments
Served in 'The Waterhouse', Open for Viewing. Toilet in The Waterhouse

13. THREAVE GARDEN Castle Douglas DG7 1RX

The National Trust for Scotland
Home of the Trust's School of Practical Gardening. Spectacular daffodils in spring,
Colourful herbaceous borders in summer, striking autumn trees and heather garden.
Route: Off A75, one mile west of Castle Douglas.
Admission: £6.00 Concessions £5.00
SUNDAY 16 MAY 9:30am - 5:30pm
SUNDAY 08 AUGUST 9:30am - 5:30pm
2 APRIL - 31 OCTOBER DAILY 9:30am - 5:30pm
Web Site: www.nts.org.uk
Telephone: 01556 502 575 Email Address: threave@nts.org.uk
Donation to SGS Beneficiaries
❁ ♿ ☕ Homemade Wine Light Refreshments

14. WALTON PARK Castle Douglas DG7 3DD

Mr Jeremy Brown
Walled garden, gentian border. Flowering shrubs, rhododendrons and azaleas.
Route: B794 to Corsock, 3½ miles from A75
Admission: £3.00 Children Free
SUNDAY 25 APRIL 2:00pm - 5:00pm
Corsock & Kirkpatrick Durham Church receives 40%, the net remaining to SGS Beneficiaries.
❁ ♿ Partly 🐕 ☕ Homemade

A good way to get rid of green fly and black fly on plants is to use some left over soap as an insecticide, pop it into a spray bottle with some hot water and a little vinegar, leave to cool and mist spray the entire plant.

Lanarkshire

'Gardens of Scotland' 2010 is sponsored by **Rensburg Sheppards Investment Management**

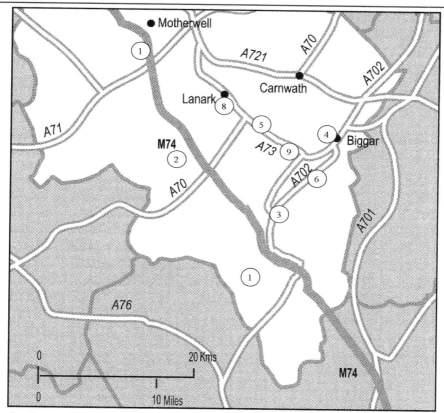

District Organiser: Mrs M Maxwell Stuart Baitlaws, Lamington ML12 6HR
Press Officer: **Mr G Crouch** 2 Castlehill Court, Symington, Biggar ML12 6JR
Treasurer: **Mrs E Munro** High Meadows, Nemphlar, Lanark ML11 9JF

Gardens Open On a Specific Date

The Scots Mining Company House	Sunday 02 May	2:00pm - 6:00pm
20 Smithycroft, Hamilton	Sunday 09 May	1:00pm - 5:00pm
Dippoolbank Cottage, Carnwath	Sunday 20 June	2:00pm - 6:00pm
New Lanark Roof Garden, Lanark	Sunday 20 June	5:00pm - 8:00pm
Symington House, By Biggar	Sunday 27 June	2:00pm - 5:00pm
Auchlochan House, Lesmahagow	Sunday 04 July	1:00pm - 5:00pm
Baitlaws, Lamington	Sunday 18 July	2:00pm - 5:00pm
Dippoolbank Cottage, Carnwath	Sunday 25 July	2:00pm - 6:00pm
Culter Allers, Coulter	Sunday 08 August	2:00pm - 5:00pm

LANARKSHIRE

Gardens Open By Arrangement
When organising a visit to a garden open by arrangement, please enquire if there are facilities and catering available

Baitlaws, Lamington, Biggar	June - August	Tel: 01899 850240
Biggar Park, Biggar	May - July - Groups	Tel: 01899 220185
Carmichael Mill, Hyndford Bridge	On request	Tel: 01555 665880
The Scots Mining Company House	On request	Tel: 01659 74235

Gardens Open Regularly

New Lanark Roof Garden, Lanark	All Year (Ex. 25 Dec & 1 Jan) Groups Welcome 11:00am - 5:00pm

1. 20 SMITHYCROFT Hamilton ML3 7UL
Mr and Mrs R I Fionda

A plantswoman's garden which has developed into a mature oasis. Eucalyptus, phormiums and clematis abound and there is a large range of unusual plants which only flourish in sheltered parts of Scotland. The garden won a number of awards in South Lanarkshire Council's 2009 Annual Garden Competition - Overall Winner for "Best Floral and Ornamental Garden" in Hamilton South Area, First for "Best Newcomer", First for "Vegetable Garden" and First for "Floral and Ornamental Garden".

Route: Off M74 at Junction 6. 1 mile on A72 – well signed.
Admission: £3.50
SUNDAY 09 MAY 1:00pm - 5:00pm
St Mary's Church, Hamilton for Mary's Meals receives 40%, the net remaining to SGS Beneficiaries.
✿ ♿ 🐕 Painting Exhibition, Jewellry, Book and Home-made Card Stalls
☕ Homemade

2. AUCHLOCHAN HOUSE New Trows Road, Lesmahagow ML11 0GJ
MHA Auchlochan

A beautiful and well stocked walled garden that was completely restored in 1994 and now forms the centre point of this unique 85 acre retirement village.

Attractive woodland and lakeside walks, stunning herbaceous borders, terrace gardens, rhododendron and heather gardens.

Featured in "Scotland for Gardeners".

Route: From M74 North take junction 9. From M74 South take junction 10. Follow B7078, take Lesmahagow sign. From village follow New Trows Road for 1½ miles
Admission: £4.00
SUNDAY 04 JULY 1:00pm - 5:00pm
All entrance takings to SGS Beneficiaries. Plant Stall 20% to Auchlochan Residents AC and 20% to SGS Beneficiaries.
✿ Extensive ♿ 🐕 ☕ In Courtyard Coffee Shop

3. BAITLAWS Lamington, Biggar ML12 6HR

Mr and Mrs M Maxwell Stuart

The garden is set at over 900 ft. above sea level and has been developed over the past 25 years with a particular emphasis on colour combinations of shrubs and herbaceous perennials which flourish at that height. A small pond is a recent addition. The surrounding hills make an imposing backdrop. Featured in "Good Gardens Guide".

Route: Off A702 above Lamington Village. Biggar 5 miles, Abington 5 miles, Lanark 10 miles.

Admission: £4.00

SUNDAY 18 JULY 2:00pm - 5:00pm
ALSO BY ARRANGEMENT JUNE - AUGUST

Telephone: 01899 850240

Biggar Museum Trust, Lamington Chapel Restoration Fund receives 40%, the net remaining to SGS Beneficiaries.

✿ Large 🐕 ☕ Homemade

4. BIGGAR PARK Biggar ML12 6JS

Mr and Mrs David Barnes

Ten acre garden starred in "Good Gardens Guide", featured on "The Beechgrove Garden" and in "Country Life" "Scottish Field" and many others. Incorporating traditional walled garden with long stretches of herbaceous borders, shrubberies, fruit, vegetables and a potager. Lawns, walks, pools, small Japanese garden and other interesting features. Glades of rhododendrons, azaleas and blue poppies in May and June. Good collection of old fashioned roses in June and July; interesting young trees.

Route: on A702, quarter mile south of Biggar.

Admission: £4.50

BY ARRANGEMENT MAY - JULY - GROUPS WELCOME

Telephone: 01899 220185

Email Address: sue@smbarnes.com

Donation to SGS Beneficiaries

♿ In Parts

5. CARMICHAEL MILL Hyndford Bridge, Lanark ML11 8SJ

Chris, Ken & Gemma Fawell

Riverside gardens which surround the only remaining workable water powered grain mill in the whole of Clydesdale. Admission charge includes entry to the mill which will be turning, river levels permitting. Diverse plant habitats from saturated to bone dry allow a vast range of trees and shrubs, both ornamental and fruit, with a vegetable garden. Herbaceous perennials, annuals and biennials with ornamental/wildlife pond complementing the landscape. Also to be seen are the archaeological remains of medieval grain mills from C.1200 and foundry, lint mill and threshing mill activity within the curtilage of the Category B Listed Building.

Route: Just off A73 Lanark to Biggar Road ½ mile east of the Hyndford Bridge.

Admission: £4.00 Children Over 12 £2.00
BY ARRANGEMENT ON REQUEST
Telephone: 01555 665880
Email Address: ken.fawell@btinternet.com
Donation to SGS Beneficiaries
♿ Partial ☕ Light Refreshments by Prior Booking

6. CULTER ALLERS Coulter, Biggar ML12 6PZ

The McCosh Family
Culter Allers, a late-Victorian baronial house, has maintained its traditional one-acre
walled kitchen garden, half with fruit and vegetables, the other half with mainly cut
flowers and herbaceous. The policies of the house are open and include woodland
walks and an avenue of 125 year old lime trees leading to the Village Church.
Route: In the village of Coulter, 3 miles south of Biggar on A702
Admission: £4.00 Children Free
SUNDAY 08 AUGUST 2:00pm - 5:00pm
Coulter Library Trust receives 40%, the net remaining to SGS Beneficiaries.
❀ ♿ Partial ☕ Homemade

7. DIPPOOLBANK COTTAGE Carnwath ML11 8LP

Mr Allan Brash
Artist's intriguing cottage garden. Vegetables grown in small beds. Herbs, fruit,
flowers, pond in woodland area with tree house and summer house. Fernery completed
in 2007. This is an organic garden mainly constructed with recycled materials.
Route: Off B7016 between Forth and Carnwath near the village of Braehead on the
Auchengray road. Approx 8 miles from Lanark. Well signed.
Admission: £3.00
SUNDAY 20 JUNE 2:00pm - 6:00pm
SUNDAY 25 JULY 2:00pm - 6:00pm
The Little Haven receives 40%, the net remaining to SGS Beneficiaries.
❀ ☕ Homemade

8. NEW LANARK ROOF GARDEN New Lanark Mills, Lanark ML11 9DB

New Lanark Visitor Centre
This amazing 9,000 square feet Roof Garden has been created on the roof of the
historic A Listed Mill No. 2, in the heart of the New Lanark World Heritage Site.
Designed by Douglas Coltart of Viridarium to meet these challenging conditions, the
garden and viewing platform offer splendid and seasonally changing views. The Roof
Garden is part of the New Lanark Visitor Centre, and is accessed by lift or stairs from
the Textile Machinery Exhibition Area in the adjacent Mill No. 3.
Sunday 20 June - Special Midsummer Roof Garden Evening Event - Admission
will include access to the stunning Roof Garden, a glass of wine/soft drink and live
musical entertainment. The textile machinery exhibition area will be open as will New
Lanark Gift Shop and the Edinburgh Woollen Mill store. Plus you'll be able to purchase

refreshments and light snacks from the Mill Pantry Coffee shop. Come and join us on Scotland's largest Rooftop Garden.

Route: New Lanark is 1 mile south of Lanark and around an hour from Glasgow (M74/A72) and Edinburgh (A70). From the south, the village is 30 mins from M74 Junction 13/Abington - main trunk road to Edinburgh.

Admission: **Midsummer Event:** £5.00

Normal: £6.95, Concessions £5.95, Families (2+2) £21.95, (2+4) £27.95 - includes entrance to exhibitions

SUNDAY 20 JUNE 5:00pm - 8:00pm

ALL YEAR (EXC. 25 DEC & 1 JAN) GROUPS WELCOME 11:00am - 5:00pm

Web Site: www.newlanark.org

Telephone: 01555 661345   Email Address: trust@newlanark.org

Donation to SGS Beneficiaries

♿ [B&B] New Lanark Mill Hotel   Waterhouses - Self Catering ☕ Cream Wine Light Refreshments   Lunches at Mill Pantry Coffee Shop or New Lanark Mill Hotel

9. SYMINGTON HOUSE By Biggar ML12 6LW

Mr and Mrs James Dawnay

Restored walled garden and greenhouses. Close to River Clyde

Route: Entrance East of Symington Village on A72 between Biggar and Symington.

Admission: £4.00

SUNDAY 27 JUNE 2:00pm - 5:00pm

Elizabeth Finn Care receives 40%, the net remaining to SGS Beneficiaries.

❀ ♿ Partial 🐕 ☕

10. THE SCOTS MINING COMPANY HOUSE Leadhills, Biggar ML12 6XP [NEW]

Charlie & Greta Clark

The site is c.400m (1280 - 1300 ft) above sea level, which is high for a cultivated garden. The surrounding landscape is open moorland with sheep grazing. The garden is largely enclosed by dense planting, but the various walks, assisted by the elevated position of the house, allow views through the trees into the surrounding countryside. Historic Scotland in their register of "Gardens and Designed Landscapes" describe the garden as "An outstanding example of a virtually unaltered, small, 18th-century garden layout connected with James Stirling, the developer of the profitable Leadhills mining enterprise, and possibly William Adam."

Say goodbye to spring walking among what must be the last daffodils of the year.

Route: On Main Street, Leadhills (B797) 6 miles from M74 junction 13 (Abington).

Admission: £3.50 Children Under 12 Free

SUNDAY 02 MAY 2:00pm - 6:00pm

BY ARRANGEMENT ON REQUEST

Telephone: 01659 74235

Scots Mining Company House Trust receives 40%, the net remaining to SGS Beneficiaries.

❀ Limited ♿ Partial 🐕 ☕

Lochaber & Badenoch

'Gardens of Scotland' 2010 is sponsored by **Rensburg Sheppards Investment Management**

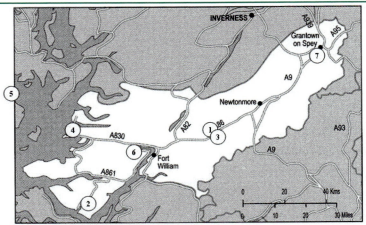

District Organiser: Mr and Mrs Norrie Maclaren Ard-Daraich, Ardgour,
Nr. Fort William PH33 7AB

Area Organisers: **Mrs Sally MacDonald** Keppoch House, Roy Bridge PH31 4AE
Mrs Philip MacKenzie Glenkyllachy, Tomatin IV13 7YA

Treasurer: **Mr Norrie Maclaren** Ard-Daraich, Ardgour,
Nr. Fort William PH33 7AB

Gardens Open On a Specific Date

Camusdarach, Arisaig	Sunday 23 May	2:00pm - 6:00pm
Aberarder, Kinlochlaggan	Sunday 06 June	2:00pm - 5:30pm
Ardverikie, Kinlochlaggan	Sunday 06 June	2:00pm - 5:30pm
Conaglen, Ardgour	Sunday 13 June	2:00pm - 5:00pm
Mockbeggar, Grantown-on-Spey	Sunday 20 June	2:00pm - 6:00pm

Gardens Open Regularly

Ardtornish, By Lochaline, Morvern	All Year	10:00am - 6:00pm
Canna House Walled Garden,	Last Wed Apr-Aug incl. &	
Isle of Canna	First Sat May–Aug incl.	10:30am - 4:00pm

1. ABERARDER (JOINT OPENING WITH ARDVERIKIE) Kinlochlaggan PH20 1BX

The Feilden Family
The garden has been laid out over the last twenty years to create a mixture of spring and autumn plants and trees, including rhododendrons, azaleas and acers. The elevated view down Loch Laggan from the garden is exceptional.
<u>Route:</u> On A86 between Newtonmore and Spean Bridge at east end of Loch Laggan.

Admission: £4.50 (entrance to both properties)
SUNDAY 06 JUNE 2:00pm - 5:30pm
Marie Curie receives 20%, Kinlochlaggan Village Hall receives 20%, the net remaining to SGS Beneficiaries.
✿ ♿ ☕ Homemade

2. ARDTORNISH By Lochaline, Morvern PA34 5UZ
Mrs John Raven
Wonderful gardens of interesting mature conifers, rhododendrons, deciduous trees, shrubs and herbaceous set amidst magnificent scenery.
Route: A884 Lochaline 3 miles
Admission: £3.50
ALL YEAR 10:00am - 6:00pm
Donation to SGS Beneficiaries

3. ARDVERIKIE (JOINT OPENING WITH ABERARDER) Kinlochlaggan PH20 1BX
Mrs P Laing and Mrs E T Smyth-Osbourne
Lovely setting on Loch Laggan with magnificent trees. Walled garden with large collection of acers, shrubs and herbaceous. Architecturally interesting house (not open). Site of the filming of the TV series "Monarch of the Glen".
Route: On A86 between Newtonmore and Spean Bridge. Entrance at east end of Loch Laggan by gate lodge over bridge.
Admission: £4.50 (entrance to both properties)
SUNDAY 06 JUNE 2:00pm - 5:30pm
Marie Curie receives 20%, Kinlochlaggan Village Hall receives 20%, the net remaining to SGS Beneficiaries.
✿ ♿ ☕ Homemade at Aberarder Only

4. CAMUSDARACH Arisaig, Inverness-shire PH39 4NT
A Simpson
Seaside garden of approximately 2 acres still in development. Several different parts around the house. Shrubs, trees, wild flower area full of orchids. Large vegetable, fruit and picking flower area. Outside the garden are bluebell woods, beaches and a farm walk with many wild flowers
Route: From Fort William take A830 towards Mallaig. 4 miles past Arisaig turn left signed to Camusdarach. After 1½ miles turn right at Camusdarach sign and proceed down drive.
Admission: £4.00
SUNDAY 23 MAY 2:00pm - 6:00pm
Help for Heroes receives 40%, the net remaining to SGS Beneficiaries.
✿ ♿ 🐕 ☕ Cream Light Refreshments

LOCHABER & BADENOCH

5. CANNA HOUSE WALLED GARDEN Isle of Canna PH44 4RS NEW
National Trust for Scotland

Formerly derelict 2 acre walled garden 2 years into a 5 year restoration. Soft fruit, top fruit, vegetables, ornamental lawns and flower beds. 80ft Escallonia arch. Woodland walks outside walls. Spectacular views of neighbouring islands.

Route: Access Isle of Canna via Calmac ferry from Mallaig pier. Head gardener will meet boat at Canna pier for tour of garden.

Admission: £3.00

LAST WEDNESDAY OF EVERY MONTH APRIL - AUG INCLUSIVE 10:30am - 4:00pm
FIRST SATURDAY MAY - AUG INCLUSIVE 10:30am - 4:00pm

Telephone: 01687 462998 Email Address: nbaker@nts.org.uk

Donation to SGS Beneficiaries

☕ Light Refreshments Available at Adjacent Island Tearoom

6. CONAGLEN Ardgour, By Fort William PH33 7AH
Mr & Mrs J Guthrie

A fabulous west coast garden. Rhododendrons, azaleas, herbaceous borders, herb and cut flower gardens, shrubs and mature conifers.

Route: From Fort William or Glencon cross Corran Ferry. Turn right and proceed for 4½ miles. From Glenfinnan turn right along west side of Loch Eil then alongside Loch Linnhe for 6 miles

Admission: £4.00

SUNDAY 13 JUNE 2:00pm - 5:00pm

Telephone: 01855 841234

Abernethy Trust receives 40%, the net remaining to SGS Beneficiaries.

✿ ♿ 🐕 Baking Stall & Other Activities ☕ Homemade

7. MOCKBEGGAR Woodside Avenue, Grantown-on-Spey PH26 3JR NEW
Mr and Mrs J S C Hamlett

An interesting garden created in last five years from a derelict site with a wide selection of perennials, shrubs, annuals and herbs. Greenhouse featuring propagation with a collection of fuchsias. Vegetables in four raised beds, fruit cage, polytunnel. Water feature.

Route: From the south: Enter Grantown, turn right at the lights then first right into Woodside Avenue. Continue along until you see a sign parallel to the road saying 1-11 Woodpark. Exactly opposite is our lane marked by sign 8mph. Mockbeggar is a grey house on the right, half way down the lane.

Admission: £3.50

SUNDAY 20 JUNE 2:00pm - 6:00pm

Email Address: hammies@tiscali.co.uk

Highland Hospice receives 40%, the net remaining to SGS Beneficiaries.

✿ ☕ Cream

Midlothian

'Gardens of Scotland' 2010 is sponsored by **Rensburg Sheppards Investment Management**

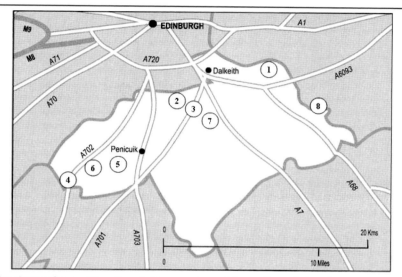

District Organiser: **Mrs Sarah Barron** Laureldene, Kevock Road, Lasswade EH18 1HT

Area Organisers: **Mrs K Drummond** Pomathorn House, Penicuik EH26 8PJ

Mrs A M Gundlach Fermain, 4 Upper Broomieknowe, Lasswade EH18 1LP

Mrs R Hill Law House, 27 Biggar Road, Silverburn EH26 9LJ

Mrs E Watson Newlandburn House, Newlandrig, Gorebridge EH23 4NS

Treasurer: **Mr A M Gundlach** Fermain, 4 Upper Broomieknowe, Lasswade EH18 1LP

Gardens Open On a Specific Date

Kevock Garden, Lasswade	Sunday 28 February	12:00pm - 3:00pm
Kevock Garden, Lasswade	Saturday 17 April	2:00pm - 5:00pm
Kevock Garden, Lasswade	Sunday 18 April	2:00pm - 5:00pm
Mount Ceres, Broomieknowe	Saturday 01 May	2:00pm - 6:00pm
Mount Ceres, Broomieknowe	Tuesday 01 June	2:00pm - 6:00pm
Penicuik House, Penicuik	Sunday 06 June	2:00pm - 5:00pm
Cousland Smiddy and Village Gardeners	Saturday 12 June	12:00pm - 5:00pm
The Old Sun Inn, Newbattle	Sunday 27 June	2:00pm - 5:00pm
Mount Ceres, Lasswade,	Thursday 01 July	2:00pm - 6:00pm
Newhall, Carlops	Sunday 18 July	2:00pm - 6:00pm
Mount Ceres, Lasswade,	Sunday 01 August	2:00pm - 6:00pm
Silverburn Village	Sunday 01 August	12:30pm - 5:00pm

MIDLOTHIAN

Gardens Open By Arrangement
When organising a visit to a garden open by arrangement, please enquire if there are facilities and catering available

Mount Ceres, Lasswade	Private Viewing for large groups	Tel: 0131 663 8700
Newhall, Carlops	June, July and August	Tel: 01968 660206

Plant Sales

SGS Plant Sale, Oxenfoord Mains	Saturday 9 October	9:30am - 1:30pm

1. COUSLAND SMIDDY AND VILLAGE GARDENERS Cousland EH22 NEW

Cousland Smiddy Trust & The Gardeners of Cousland

Cousland Village near Dalkeith is home to the oldest working smiddy in Scotland which has been in continuous use since 1703. The Cousland Smiddy Trust, established in 1989, now runs the Smiddy preserving it for future generations. There are 13 Organic allotments in the garden grounds behind the Smiddy, which are let to local villagers, some of whom will be on hand to answer questions. Some of the village gardens will be open along with the Smiddy and Smith's Cottage Museum. Demonstrations will be given by the Blacksmith.

Route: Route: 1.5 miles east of Dalkeith on A68 then A6124 or 1.5 miles south of Whitecraig on A6124. Local bus service available.

Admission: £4.00 Children Under 16 Free

SATURDAY 12 JUNE 12:00pm - 5:00pm

Cousland Smiddy Trust and Cousland Village Hall Association receive 40%, the net remaining to SGS Beneficiaries.

 Homemade in Village Hall

2. KEVOCK GARDEN 16 Kevock Road, Lasswade EH18 1HT

David and Stella Rankin

A wonderful hillside garden overlooking the North Esk Valley and Mavisbank Estate. There are several mature trees, rhododendrons, azaleas and unusual shrubs all underplanted with a wide range of woodland plants. On the higher section of the south facing slope there are terraces with rockeries and troughs, below this there is a pond with primula, iris, and other damp loving plants. The garden has featured in several television programmes and magazine articles.

Kevock Garden is open in February for the snowdrops and wide range of other early spring flowering bulbs and primulas as well as in the summer for interesting perennials and shrubs.

Route: Kevock Road lies to the south of A678 Loanhead/Lasswade Road.

Admission: £3.00 Children Free

SUNDAY 28 FEBRUARY (FOR SNOWDROP FESTIVAL) 12:00pm - 3:00pm

SATURDAY 17 APRIL 2:00pm - 5:00pm
SUNDAY 18 APRIL 2:00pm - 5:00pm
Web Site: www.kevockgarden.co.uk
Telephone: 0131 454 0660 Email Address: info@kevockgarden.co.uk
St. Paul's and St.George's Project 21 receives 40%, the net remaining to SGS
Beneficiaries.
✿ Interesting plant stall with rare and unusual plants ⚘ ☕ Soup in Winter Teas in spring

3. MOUNT CERES 3 Lower Broomieknowe, Lasswade, EH18 1LW `NEW`
Mrs. Ruth Mehlsen
Tucked away in Lower Broomieknowe, this charming garden is a plant person's paradise. A romantic semi-formal garden of over an acre, there is something here for everyone. The garden, which surrounds a large Victorian house, is designed as a series of garden rooms like a patchwork – some bright and beautiful, others ideal for quiet contemplation. There is a white garden, alpine scree garden, boxed hedge garden, sunken garden, fern garden, several small ponds, water features and a waterfall. Many interesting trees and shrubs, with a variety of unusual herbaceous plants reflecting colour, foliage and form. Lots of ideas for keen gardeners in this continuously developing garden.
The opening times reflect the garden at its peak. In the words of the owner "Welcome to Paradise"
Route: Off B704 (Broomieknowe) Between Lasswade and Bonnyrigg. Lothian Region Transport Bus No. 31 to Cockpen (get off at Nazareth House Nursing home, before Bonnyrigg Town).
No parking in Lower Broomieknowe but please park at the top of the road.
Admission: £2.00 Children Under 5 Free
SATURDAY 01 MAY 2:00pm - 6:00pm
TUESDAY 01 JUNE 2:00pm - 6:00pm
THURSDAY 01 JULY 2:00pm - 6:00pm
SUNDAY 01 AUGUST 2:00pm - 6:00pm
ALSO BY ARRANGEMENT PRIVATE VIEWING FOR LARGE GROUPS
Telephone: 0131 663 8700 Email Address: ruthmehlsen@googlemail.com
Orbis (Flying Eye Hospital) receives 40%, the net remaining to SGS Beneficiaries.
✿ Large Selection of Plants Propagated Wholly From the Garden and Packets of Seeds ♿ Most Parts of Garden ☕ And Biscuits (Cost £1.00) in the Conservatory or Seats Available in the Garden

MIDLOTHIAN

4. NEWHALL Carlops EH26 9LY

John and Tricia Kennedy

Traditional 18th century walled garden with huge herbaceous border, shrubberies, fruit and vegetables. Many unusual plants for sale. Stunning glen running along River North Esk in process of restoration (stout shoes recommended). Large pond with planting evolving. Young arboretum and collection of Rosa pimpinellifolia. As in Good Gardens Guide 2010, Scottish Field, Gardens Monthly, Scotland on Sunday

Route: On A702 Edinburgh/Biggar, a quarter of a mile after Ninemileburn and a mile before Carlops. Follow signs.

Admission: £4.00

SUNDAY 18 JULY 2:00pm - 6:00pm

ALSO BY ARRANGEMENT JUNE, JULY AND AUGUST

Telephone: 01968 660206 Email Address: tricia.kennedy@newhalls.co.uk

William Steel Trust receives 40%, the net remaining to SGS Beneficiaries.

✿ ♿ Partial 🐕 Treasure Hunt Teddy Bear Hunt ☕ Homemade

Light Lunches are Available on Request on By Arrangement Visits

5. PENICUIK HOUSE Penicuik EH26 9LA

Sir Robert and Lady Clerk

Outstanding designed landscape with ornamental lakes, rhododendrons, azaleas and wonderful walks.

Route: On A766 road to Carlops, Penicuik 1 mile.

Admission: £5.00

SUNDAY 06 JUNE 2:00pm - 5:00pm

The Church of St. James the Less, Penicuik receives 20%, The Penicuik House Preservation Trust receives 20%, the net remaining to SGS Beneficiaries.

✿ ♿ 🐕 ☕ Homemade in the House

6. SILVERBURN VILLAGE Silverburn Village EH26 9LJ

The Gardeners of Silverburn

Nestling in the foothills of the Pentlands, Silverburn has a selection of village gardens of varying size and planting style growing at 800ft. Wonderful views and many ideas for growing plants in exposed locations. Come and have tea in the new Silverburn Village Hall and enjoy the Beechgrove 2008 Community Garden.

Route: A702, Edinburgh/Biggar Road, 13 miles south of Edinburgh and 1 mile before Ninemileburn

Admission: £3.50 Children Free

SUNDAY 01 AUGUST 12:30pm - 5:00pm

Silverburn Community Ltd receives 40%, the net remaining to SGS Beneficiaries.

✿ ♿ In Most Gardens 🐕 ☕ Homemade Light Refreshments Soup and Rolls

7. THE OLD SUN INN Newbattle, Dalkeith EH22 3LH

Mr and Mrs James Lochhead

Small half acre garden of island and raised beds containing a collection of species lilies, rock plants and some unusual bulbs - there are also two small interconnecting ponds and a conservatory.

Route: From Eskbank take B703 (Newtongrange). The garden is immediately opposite entrance to Newbattle Abbey College.

Admission: £3.00 Children Free

SUNDAY 27 JUNE 2:00pm - 5:00pm

Telephone: 0131 663 2648 Email Address: randjlochhead@uwclub.net

All proceeds to SGS Beneficiaries

✿ ♿ ☕ Homemade

PLANT SALES

8. SGS PLANT SALE Oxenfoord Mains, Near Pathhead EH22 2PF

Held under cover

Excellent selection of garden and house plants donated from private gardens.

Contact telephone number: Mrs Parker 01620 824788 or Hon Michael Dalrymple 01875 320844 (office hours)

Route: On A6093 signed off A68 4 miles south of Dalkeith.

Admission: Free

Donations to Scotland's Garden Scheme welcome

SATURDAY 9 OCTOBER 9:30am - 1:30pm

Cancer Research receives 40%, the net remaining to SGS Beneficiaries.

♿ 🐕 Compost Making, Vegetables and Homemade Jams ☕ Light Refreshments Soup and Rolls, Homebaking

---

Master Class on Garden Management

With key members of the NTS Gardens Team

Thursday 11 March

at The National Trust for Scotland,

28 Charlotte Square, Edinburgh

£45.00 to include lunch

Tickets available from Mrs Barrrington: tel. 0131 243 9440 or email: vbarrington@nts.or.uk

Moray & Nairn

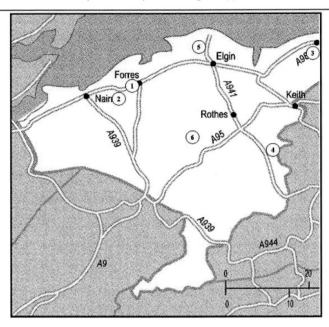

District Organiser: **Mr David Carter** The Old Granary, Letterfourie, Buckie AB56 5JP

Area Organiser: **Mrs Lorraine Dingwall** Bents Green, 10 Pilmuir Road West, Forres IV36 2HL

Treasurer: **Mr Michael Barnett** Drumdelnies, Nairn, IV12 5NT

Gardens Open On a Specific Date

Bents Green, Forres	Sunday 16 May	10:00am - 7:00pm
Carestown Steading, Deskford	Sunday 13 June	2:00pm - 5:00pm
Castleview, Auchindoun	Sunday 13 June	2:00pm - 5:00pm
Knocknagore, Knockando	Sunday 20 June	2:00pm - 5:00pm
Applegrove Primary School, Forres	Sunday 27 June	2:00pm - 4:30pm
Bents Green, Forres	Sunday 25 July	9:00am - 7:00pm
Castleview, Auchindoun	Sunday 01 August	2:00pm - 5:00pm
Gordonstoun, Duffus	Sunday 29 August	2.00pm - 4.30pm

Gardens Open By Arrangement

When organising a visit to a garden open by arrangement, please enquire if there are facilities and catering available

Bents Green, Forres   15 Feb - 14 March
                               and 02 May – 19 Sept   Tel: 01309 674634

1. APPLEGROVE PRIMARY SCHOOL Orchard Road, Forres IV36 1PJ

Applegrove Primary School

Vegetable/fruit garden, bottle greenhouse, shrub beds, sunshine bed, flower arrangers garden. Several beds including annuals, dried, pressed, foliage, fragrant tubs and window boxes. RHS "Britain in Bloom" Young Persons Award 2008

Route: School on Orchard Road. Turn left at sunken garden when approaching from East and follow road to roundabout, straight across, school on left.

Admission: £4.00 (includes tea)

SUNDAY 27 JUNE 2:00pm - 4:30pm

Telephone: 01309 672367

Macmillan Cancer Support receives 40%, the net remaining to SGS Beneficiaries.

2. BENTS GREEN 10 Pilmuir Road West, Forres IV36 2HL

Mrs Lorraine Dingwall

Plantsman's small town garden with circa hundred varieties of Snowdrops in April, over three hundred cultivars of Hostas, an extensive collection of hardy Geraniums together with many other unusual plants. Managed entirely without the use of artificial fertilizers or chemicals, the owner encourages hedgehogs, toads and wild birds to control slugs.

Route: From Tesco roundabout at Forres continue along Nairn Road. Take first left onto Ramflat Road then right at the bottom, then first left onto Pilmuir Road West.

Admission: £3.00

SUNDAY 16 MAY 10:00am - 7:00pm

SUNDAY 25 JULY 9:00am - 7:00pm

BY ARRANGEMENT 15 FEBRUARY - 14 MARCH 10:00am - 4:00pm FOR THE SNOWDROP FESTIVAL

AND BY ARRANGEMENT 02 MAY - 19 SEPTEMBER

Web Site: www.simplesite.com/hosta

Telephone: 01309 674634 Email Address: fixanddig@aol.com

Macmillan Nurses receives 40%, the net remaining to SGS Beneficiaries.

3. CARESTOWN STEADING Deskford, Buckie AB56 5TR

Rora Paglieri

The best compliment to Carestown garden was paid by "The Garden History Society in Scotland" when it described it as "Garden history in the making". The garden was started in 1990 and has received accolades ever since from the press, TV and web. Every year a new addition is made, the latest being the epitome of the modern vegetable plot which is proving to be a great success: four year rotation, raised beds, seeping irrigation. Meanwhile trees and shrubs are maturing, the maze is growing, the ducks are reproducing in the three ponds and the atmosphere is as happy as ever. Not to be forgotten is the "pearl" of the garden, the courtyard with knot beds and topiary now fully mature.

Route: East of B9018 Cullen/Keith (Cullen 3 miles, Keith 9½ miles). Follow SGS signs towards Milton and Carestown.

Admission: £4.00

SUNDAY 13 JUNE 2:00pm - 5:00pm

Web Site: www.CarestownSteading.com

Email Address: rora403@btinternet.com

All proceeds to SGS Beneficiaries

☕

4. CASTLEVIEW Auchindoun, Dufftown AB55 4DY

Mr and Mrs Ian Sharp

A small secluded riverside garden, created on three levels from scrub land by two enthusiastic beginners in 2005. The garden consists of two interconnected ponds, one formal, one natural and an abundance of herbacious plants and shrubs. The garden features many sitting areas where you can admire the garden from many view points.

Route: From Dufftown on the A920, travel approx. three miles towards Huntly. Drive until a small cluster of houses is reached, garden on the left approx. 20 yards off the main road.

Admission: £3.00

SUNDAY 13 JUNE 2:00pm - 5:00pm
SUNDAY 01 AUGUST 2:00pm - 5:00pm

Telephone: 01340 820 941 Email Address: ian@castleviewdufftown.co.uk

Cat Protection League receives 40%, the net remaining to SGS Beneficiaries.

Cat Protection League Charity Stall ☕ Light Refreshments

5. GORDONSTOUN Duffus, near Elgin IV30 5RF

The Headmaster, Gordonstoun School

Gardens: Good formal herbaceous borders around lawns, terrace, orchard

School grounds: Gordonstoun House (Georgian House of 1775/6 incorporating earlier 17th century house built for 1st Marquis of Huntly) and school chapel - both open.

Unique circle of former farm buildings known as the Round Square. Scenic lake.

Route: Entrance off B9012, 4 miles from Elgin at Duffus Village

Admission: £3.50 Children £1.50

SUNDAY 29 AUGUST 2.00pm - 4.30pm

Web Site: www.gordonstoun.org.uk

Telephone: 01343 837837 Email Address: lambies@gordonstoun.org.uk

All proceeds to SGS Beneficiaries

✿ ♿ 🐕 ☕ Homemade

6. KNOCKNAGORE Knockando AB38 7SG

Dr and Mrs Eckersall

A series of gardens created from rough pasture and moorland since 1995 comprising trees, herbaceous beds, rockery, courtyard garden and "Sittie Ooterie". Vegetable plot and two ponds, all surrounded by stunning views.

Route: Entrance from "Cottage Road" which connects the B9102 Archiestown to Knockando Road with the Knockando to Dallas Road.

Admission: £3.00

SUNDAY 20 JUNE 2:00pm - 5:00pm

Telephone: Fax: 01340 810554

Dialysis Unit Doctor Gray's Hospital, Elgin receives 40%, the net remaining to SGS Beneficiaries.

✿ 🐕 ☕ Cream

Peeblesshire

'Gardens of Scotland' 2010 is sponsored by **Rensburg Sheppards Investment Management**

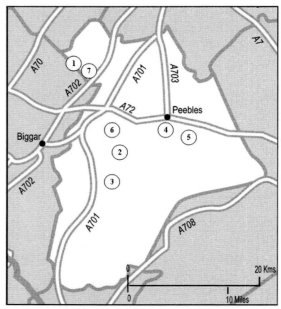

District Organiser: Mrs Mary Carrel 14 Leeburn View, Cardrona, Peebles EH45 9LS

Area Organisers: Mrs D Balfour-Scott Dreva Craig, Broughton, Biggar ML12 6HH

Mr Graham Buchanan-Dunlop The Potting Shed, Broughton Place, Broughton ML12 6HJ

Mrs H B Marshall Garden Cottage, Baddinsgill, West Linton EH46 7HL

Mr K St C Cunningham Hallmanor, Peebles, Tweeddale EH45 9JN

Treasurer: Mr J Birchall The Old Manse, Drumelzier, Biggar ML12 6JD

Gardens Open On a Specific Date

Drumelzier Place, Broughton	Sunday 21 February	1:00pm - 4:00pm
Kailzie Gardens, Peebles	Sunday 28 February	10:00am - 4:00pm
Baddinsgill, West Linton	Sunday 30 May	12:30pm - 5:00pm
Haystoun, Peebles	Sunday 30 May	1:30pm - 5:00pm
West Linton Village Gardens	Sunday 13 June	2:00pm - 5:00pm
Dawyck Botanic Garden, Stobo	Sunday 03 October	10:00am - 5:00pm
Stobo Japanese Water Garden	Sunday 17 October	12:30pm - 4:00pm

Gardens Open Regularly

Kailzie Gardens, Peebles
Wild Garden   All Year   11:00pm – 5:00pm
Kailzie Gardens, Peebles
Walled Garden   Mid March - 31 October 11:00pm - 5:00pm

1. BADDINSGILL West Linton EH46 7HL

Gavin and Elaine Marshall

Beautiful woodland garden 1,000 feet up in the Pentland Hills above West Linton - a stunning situation. Woodland and riverside walks, several reclaimed recently. Bluebells, azaleas and rhododendrons. Water garden. Sculpture Exhibition in conjunction with Edinburgh Sculpture Workshop.

Route: A702 to West Linton. Uphill past golf course for 2½ miles.

Admission: £3.50 Children Free

SUNDAY 30 MAY 12:30pm - 5:00pm

Telephone: 01968 660698

Oxfam (The Mongu Water Project) receives 40%, the net remaining to SGS Beneficiaries.

♿ Limited 🐕 Sculpture Exhibition ☗ Homemade   Light Lunches

2. DAWYCK BOTANIC GARDEN Stobo EH45 9JU

Royal Botanic Gardens Edinburgh

Stunning collection of rare trees and shrubs. With over 300 years of tree planting Dawyck is a world famous arboretum with mature specimens of Chinese conifers, Japanese maples, Brewer's spruce, the unique Dawyck beech and Sequoiadendrons from North America which are over 45 metres tall. Bold herbaceous plantings run along the burn. Range of trails and walks. Fabulous autumn colours

Autumn Magic Guided Walks at 11.30am and 2pm - £2.00 (Please book with Dawyck Botanics).

Route: 8 miles south west of Peebles on B712

Admission: £4.00 Concessions £3.50 Family £9.00

Guided Walks £2.00

SUNDAY 03 OCTOBER 10:00am - 5:00pm

Telephone: 01721 760 254

Donation to SGS Beneficiaries

☘ NCCPG Shop ☗ Light Refreshments   Restaurant

3. DRUMELZIER PLACE Broughton ML12 6JD NEW

Mr and Mrs Michael Lukas

Carpets of woodland snowdrops in a farmhouse garden on the banks of the River Tweed. Riverside walks.

Route: On B712, 3 miles east of Broughton overlooking River Tweed. Follow signs.

Admission: £3.00

PEEBLESSHIRE

SUNDAY 21 FEBRUARY FOR THE SNOWDROP FESTIVAL 1:00pm - 4:00pm

The Rock Trust receives 40%, the net remaining to SGS Beneficiaries.

♿ Very Limited, Gravel Path ☘ ☕

4. HAYSTOUN Peebles EH45 9JG

Mr and Mrs David Coltman

A 16th century house (not open) has a charming walled garden with an ancient yew tree, herbaceous beds and vegetable garden. There is a wonderful burnside walk, created since 1980, with azaleas, rhododendrons and primulas leading to a small ornamental loch (cleared in 1990), with stunning views up Glensax valley.

Route: Cross River Tweed in Peebles to south bank and follow garden open sign for approx 1 mile.

Admission: £4.00

SUNDAY 30 MAY 1:30pm - 5:00pm

St. Columba's Hospice receives 40%, the net remaining to SGS Beneficiaries.

❀ ♿ Partial - Walled Garden Only 🐕 ☕ Homemade

5. KAILZIE GARDENS Peebles EH45 9HT

Lady Buchan-Hepburn

Semi -formal walled garden with shrub and herbaceous borders. Rose garden. Well stocked greenhouse. Woodland and burnside walks amongst massed spring bulbs, rhododendrons and azaleas. The garden is set among fine old trees including an old larch planted in 1724.

Route: On B7062 2.5 miles east of Peebles

Admission: **1 Jan-14 Mar & 1 Nov-31 Dec** £2.50, Children (5-12) £1.00

15 Mar-31 May £3.50, Conc. £3.00, Children (5-12) £1.00

1 Jun-31 Oct £4.00, Conc. £3.50 (Children (5-12) £1.00

Children under 5 Free

Group Rates (Over 15)

15 Mar-31 May £2.80

1 Jun-31 Oct £3.20

SUNDAY 28 FEBRUARY 10:00am - 4:00pm

1 - 27 FEB & 1 - 14 MARCH FOR THE SNOWDROP FESTIVAL 11:00am - 5:00pm

WOODLAND & WILD GARDEN: ALL YEAR 11:00pm - 5:00pm

WALLED GARDEN: MID MARCH - 31 OCTOBER 11:00am - 5:00pm

Web Site: www.infokailziegardens.com

Telephone: 01721 720007 Email Address: angela.buchanhepburn@btinternet.com

Erskine Hospital receives 40% on 28 February, the net remaining to SGS Beneficiaries.

Donation to SGS Beneficiaries on other dates

❀ ♿ 🐕 ☘ B&B Holiday Cottage Shop, Putting Green, Fishing Ponds ☕ Cream Wine Light Refreshments   Restaurant/Tea Room, Groups & Large Parties Welcome

6. STOBO JAPANESE WATER GARDEN Home Farm, Stobo EH45 8NX

Hugh & Charles Seymour

Garden was originally laid out 100 years ago and features magnificent trees and shrubs, Japanese artifacts, such as lanterns, a tea house and oriental style bridges. A spendid waterfall cascades from the lake at one end. The water divides between two burns which are crossed in several places by stepping stones as well as bridges. The Autumn colours of the maples, azaleas, cercidiphyllums (with their aroma of burnt sugar) reflect in the pools of water adding to the tranquility of this garden. **PLEASE WEAR SENSIBLE SHOES**.

Route: 7 miles west of Peebles on the B712. 1½ miles from Dawyck Botanical Garden.
Admission: £4.00 Children Free
SUNDAY 17 OCTOBER 12:30pm - 4:00pm
Telephone: 01721 760245
Email Address: hugh.seymour@btinternet.com
Combat Stress receives 40%, the net remaining to SGS Beneficiaries.
✿ ♿ Very Limited 🐕 B&B ☕ Homemade Light Refreshments

7. WEST LINTON VILLAGE GARDENS West Linton EH46 7EL

West Linton Village Gardeners

Seven gardens with a wide range of spring flowering plants and shrubs including a vegetable garden, rhododendrons, azaleas, meconopsis, alliums and other interesting plants.

Route: A701 or A702 and follow signs.
Admission: £5.00
SUNDAY 13 JUNE 2:00pm - 5:00pm
Ben Walton Trust receives 40%, the net remaining to SGS Beneficiaries.
✿ ♿ Partial 🐕 ☕ Homemade in Church Hall

To make cut flowers last longer don't use water straight from the tap, let the water lie for a while to get it to room temperature and then add an aspirin to the water.

Perth & Kinross

'Gardens of Scotland' 2010 is sponsored by **Rensburg Sheppards Investment Management**

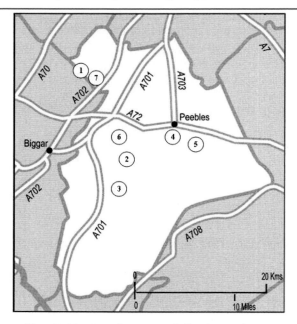

District Organisers: **Mrs D J W Anstice** Broomhill, Abernethy PH2 9LQ

The Hon Mrs Ranald Noel-Paton Pitcurran House, Abernethy PH2 9LH

Area Organisers: **Mrs C Arbuthnott** The Old Manse, Caputh, PH1 4JH

Mrs C Dunphie Wester Cloquhat, Bridge of Cally, Perthshire PH10 7JP

Miss Henrietta Harland Easter Carmichael Cottage, Forgandenny Road, Bridge of Earn PH2 9EZ

Mrs T Holcroft Glenbeich, Lochearnhead FK19 8PZ

Mrs M Innes Kilspindie Manse, Kilspindie PH2 7RX

Mrs J Landale Clatnic House, By Crieff PH7 4JY

Lady Livesay Bute Cottage, Academy Road, Crieff PH7 4AT

Mrs D Nichol Rossie House, Forgandenny PH2 9EH

Miss Judy Norwell 20 Pitcullen Terrace, Perth PH2 7EG

Miss Bumble Ogilvy Wedderburn Garden Cottage, Lude, Blair Atholl PH18 5TR

Treasurer: **Mr Cosmo Fairbairn** Alleybank, Bridge of Earn PH2 9EZ

Gardens Open On a Specific Date

Rossie House, Forgandenny	Thursday 18 February	2:00pm - 5:00pm
Rossie House, Forgandenny	Thursday 18 March	2:00pm - 5:00pm
Megginch Castle, Errol	Sunday 11 April	2:00pm - 5:00pm
Rossie House, Forgandenny	Thursday 15 April	2:00pm - 5:00pm
Glendoick, by Perth	Sunday 02 May	2:00pm - 5:00pm
Branklyn, Perth	Sunday 09 May	10:00am - 4:00pm
Rossie House, Forgandenny	Thursday 13 May	2:00pm - 5:00pm
Glendoick, by Perth	Sunday 16 May	2:00pm - 5:00pm
Pitcurran House, Abernethy	Sunday 16 May	2:00pm - 6:00pm
Dowhill, Kelty	Sunday 23 May	12:00am - 4:00pm
Achnacloich, by Aberfeldy	Sunday 30 May	1:00pm - 5:00pm
Cloan, by Auchterarder	Sunday 30 May	1:30pm - 5:30pm
Farleyer Field House, By Aberfeldy	Sunday 30 May	1:00pm - 5:00pm
Murthly Castle, Murthly	Saturday 05 June	2:00pm - 6:00pm
Bradystone House, Murthly	Sunday 13 June	11:00am - 4:00pm
Explorers Garden, Pitlochry	Sunday 13 June	10:00am - 5:00pm
Carig Dhubh, Bonskeid	Sunday 20 June	2:00pm - 5:30pm
Blair Castle Gardens, Blair Atholl	Saturday 26 June	9:30am - 5:30pm
Lands of Loyal Hotel, Alyth	Sunday 27 June	11:00am - 7:00pm
The Cottage, Longforgan	Sunday 27 June	2:00pm - 5:00pm
Glenlyon House, Fortingall	Sunday 04 July	2:00pm - 5:00pm
Wester Cloquhat , Bridge of Cally	Sunday 11 July	2:00pm - 5:00pm
Auchleeks House, Calvine	Sunday 18 July	2:00pm - 5:30pm
Boreland, Killin	Sunday 25 July	2:00pm - 5:30pm
Mount Tabor House, Perth	Sunday 01 August	10:00am - 5:00pm
Scone Palace, Perth	Saturday 07 August	9:30am - 5:00pm
Drummond Castle Gardens, Crieff	Sunday 08 August	1:00pm - 5:00pm
Scone Palace, Perth	Sunday 08 August	9:30am - 5:00pm

Gardens Open By Arrangement
When organising a visit to a garden open by arrangement, please enquire if there are facilities and catering available

Auchleeks House, Calvine	01 June - 30 Sep.	Tel: 01796 483263
Carig Dhubh, Bonskeid	01 May - 31 August	Tel: 01796 473469
Easter Meikle Fardle, Meikleour	Large Groups Welcomed	Tel: 01738 710330
Glendoick, by Perth	For dates not listed in main entry	Tel: 01738 860 205
Glenlyon House, Fortingall	01 June - 30 Sept.	Tel: 01887 830233
Parkhead House, Perth	03 May - 30 Sept.	Tel: 01738 625983

PERTH & KINROSS

Gardens Open Regularly

Ardvorlich, Lochearnhead	01 May - 31 May	9:00am – Dusk
Blair Castle Gardens, Blair Atholl	05 Jan - 23 March	
	Tuesdays & Saturdays	
	and Sun 14 March	9:30am - 2:30pm
	Also 28 Mar. - 29 Oct.	9:30am - 5:30pm
Bolfracks, Aberfeldy	01 April - 31 Oct.	10:00am - 6:00pm
Braco Castle, Braco	01 Feb. – 31 Oct.	10:00am - 5:00pm
Cluny House, Aberfeldy	20 Feb. - 14 March	10:00am - 4:00pm
	and 15 Mar. - 31 Oct.	10:00am - 6:00pm
Drummond Castle Gardens, Crieff	01 May - 31 October	1:00pm - 6:00pm
Easter Meikle Fardle, Meikleour	05 April - 31 July	
	Mondays and Fridays	10:00am - 6:30pm
Explorers Garden, Pitlochry	01 April - 31 Oct.	10:00am - 5:00pm
Glendoick, by Perth	15 – 19 February	10:00am - 4:00pm
	22 - 26 February	10:00am - 4:00pm
	05 April - 11 June	10:00am - 4:00pm
Glendoick Garden Centre, by Perth	All Year	10:00am - 4:00pm
Lands of Loyal Hotel, Alyth	All Year Plant Sales	
Scone Palace, Perth	20, 21, 26, 27 &	
	28 February	11:00am - 5:00pm
	01 April - 31 Oct.	9:30am - 5:00pm
	Nov. - March (Grounds	
	only open every Friday)	10:00am - 4:00pm

1. ACHNACLOICH (JOINT OPENING WITH FARLEYER FIELD HOUSE) Balhomais, by Aberfeldy PH15 2JE NEW

Mr and Mrs D Lee

Set in a scenic part of Perthshire. Achnacloich is a glorious young garden of 1½ acres, consisting of an interesting mix of trees, shrubs and perennials.

Route: From Weem, 1½ miles west.

Admission: £4.00 to include Farleyer Field House

SUNDAY 30 MAY 1:00pm - 5:00pm

Guide Dogs for the Blind receives 40%, the net remaining to SGS Beneficiaries.

✿ 🐕 Plant Quiz ☕ Homemade

2. ARDVORLICH Lochearnhead FK19 8QE

Mr and Mrs Sandy Stewart

Beautiful glen with rhododendrons (species and many hybrids) grown in wild conditions amid oaks and birches. Quite steep in places. Gumboots advisable when wet.

Route: On South Loch Earn Road 3 miles from Lochearnhead, 5 miles from St Fillans.

Admission: £3.00

01 MAY - 31 MAY 9:00AM - DUSK
The Gurkha Welfare Trust receives 40%, the net remaining to SGS Beneficiaries.

3. AUCHLEEKS HOUSE Calvine PH18 5UF
Mr and Mrs Angus MacDonald
Auchleeks is a classical Georgian house with a large herbaceous walled garden in a beautiful glen setting surrounded by hills and mature trees.
<u>Route:</u> North of Blair Atholl turn off A9 at Calvine. B847 towards Kinloch Rannoch, 5 miles on right.
<u>Admission:</u> £4.00 Children Free
SUNDAY 18 JULY 2:00pm - 5:30pm
ALSO BY ARRANGEMENT 01 JUNE - 30 SEPTEMBER
Telephone: 01796 483263
Sandpiper Trust receives 40%, the net remaining to SGS Beneficiaries.
 Homemade

4. BLAIR CASTLE GARDENS Blair Atholl PH18 5TL
Blair Charitable Trust
Blair Castle stands as the focal point in a designed landscape of some 2,500 acres within a large and traditional estate. Hercules Garden is a walled enclosure of about 9 acres recently restored to its original 18th Century form with landscaped ponds, plantings, fruit trees, vegetables, herbaceous gardens and landscape features. Diana's Grove is a magnificent stand of tall trees including grand fir, Douglas fir, larch and wellingtonia in just two acres. The Grove is home to the UK's second tallest tree, a grand fir measuring 62.70 metres.
In February, enjoy the seasonal delight of snowdrops in bloom on a walk around the castle grounds. A gentle meandering route passes through the Hercules Garden and weaves along to St Brides Kirk. The walk also includes access to two new paths (only open to the public at snowdrop time). Then step inside and enjoy the indoor flowers. The castle's entrance hall, Banvie Hall and restaurant will be filled with bowls of scented daffodils, hyacinths and tulips.
<u>Route:</u> Off A9, follow signs to Blair Castle, Blair Atholl.
<u>Admission:</u> £4.75 Children £2.25 Families £11.00 Special rates for groups of 12 or more. Free entry from November to end of March.
SATURDAY 26 JUNE 9:30am - 5:30pm
05 JANUARY - 23 MARCH (TUES & SATS) & SUN 14 MARCH 9:30am - 2:30pm
28 MARCH - 29 OCTOBER 9:30am - 5:30pm
Web Site: www.blair-castle.co.uk
Telephone: 01796 481207 Email Address: office@blair-castle.co.uk
Donation to SGS Beneficiaries
Cream Wine Light Refreshments Free access to the Castle's Tullibardine Restaurant. Please come in when you visit

5. BOLFRACKS Aberfeldy PH15 2EX

The Douglas Hutchison Trust

Very special 3 acre north facing garden with wonderful views overlooking the Tay valley. Burn garden with rhododendrons, azaleas, primulas, meconopsis, etc. in woodland setting. Walled garden with shrubs, herbaceous borders, old fashioned roses and clematis. Great selection of bulbs in the spring and good autumn colour with sorbus, gentians and cyclamen. Slippery paths and bridges in wet weather.

<u>Route:</u> 2 miles west of Aberfeldy on A827. White gates and Lodge on left. Brown tourist signs.

<u>Admission:</u> £4.00 Children under 16 Free

01 APRIL - 31 OCTOBER 10:00am - 6:00pm

Web Site: www.bolfracks.com

Telephone: 01887 820344 Email Address: athel@bolfracks.com

Donation to SGS Beneficiaries

 Refreshments for groups by arrangement

6. BORELAND Killin FK21 8TT

Mrs Angus Stroyan

A varied garden with borders as the main feature. Very pretty walk along river leading to arboretum.

<u>Route:</u> Off A827 through Killin, first turning left at Bridge of Lochay Hotel. House approx. 2 miles on left.

<u>Admission:</u> £3.00 Children over 12 £1.00

SUNDAY 25 JULY 2:00pm - 5:30pm

Cancer Research U.K. (Killin Branch) receives 40%, the net remaining to SGS Beneficiaries.

 ♿ 🐩 Cream

7. BRACO CASTLE Braco FK15 9LA

Mr & Mrs M van Ballegooijen

A 19th Century landscaped garden comprising woodland and meadow walks with a fine show of spring flowering bulbs, many mature specimen trees and shrubs, with considerable new planting. The partly walled garden is approached on a rhododendron and tree-lined path and features an ornamental pond, extensive hedging and lawns with shrub and herbaceous borders. The planting is enhanced by spectacular views over the castle park to the Ochils. Good autumn colour.

<u>Route:</u> 1 to 1½ mile drive from gates at north end of Braco Village, just west of bridge on A822

<u>Admission:</u> £3.00 Children Free

1 FEBRUARY - 31 OCTOBER 10:00am - 5:00pm

Telephone: 01786 880437

The Woodland Trust receives 40%, the net remaining to SGS Beneficiaries.

♿ Partly   No Catering Facilities

8. BRADYSTONE HOUSE Murthly PH1 4EW

Mr and Mrs James Lumsden

True cottage courtyard garden converted 14 years ago from derelict farm steadings. Ponds, free roaming ducks and hens and many interesting shrubs and ornamental trees.

Route: From south/north follow A9 to Bankfoot, then sign to Murthly. At crossroads in Murthly take private road to Bradystone.

Admission: £3.50 Children Free

SUNDAY 13 JUNE 11:00am - 4:00pm

Help for Heroes receives 40%, the net remaining to SGS Beneficiaries.

❀ ♿ Stalls ☕ Soup, Filled Rolls and Teas

9. BRANKLYN 116 Dundee Road, Perth PH2 7BB

The National Trust for Scotland

This attractive garden in Perth was once described as "the finest two acres of private garden in the country". It contains an outstanding collection of plants particularly rhododendrons, alpine, herbaceous and peat-loving plants, which attract gardeners and botanists from all over the world.

Route: On A85 Perth/Dundee road

Admission: £5.00, Concessions £4.00, Family Ticket £14.00

SUNDAY 09 MAY 10:00am - 4:00pm

Web Site: www.nts.org.uk

Telephone: 0844 493 2193 Email Address: smcnamara@nts.org.uk

Donation to SGS Beneficiaries

❀ ♿ Partial

10. CARIG DHUBH Bonskeid PH16 5NP

Mr and Mrs Niall Graham-Campbell

The garden is comprised of mixed shrubs and herbaceous plants with meconopsis and primulas. It extends to about one acre on the side of a hill with some steep paths and uneven ground. The soil is sand overlying rock - some of which projects through the surface. Beautiful surrounding country and hill views.

Route: Take old A9 between Pitlochry and Killiecrankie, midway turn west on the Tummel Bridge Road B8019, 3/4 mile on north side of the road.

Admission: £3.50 Children under 16 Free

SUNDAY 20 JUNE 2:00pm - 5:30pm
ALSO BY ARRANGEMENT 01 MAY - 31 AUGUST

Telephone: 01796 473469 Email Address: niallgc@btinternet.com

Tenandry Kirk receives 40%, the net remaining to SGS Beneficiaries.

❀ 🐕 ☕ Homemade

11. CLOAN by Auchterarder PH3 1PP

Mr and Mrs Richard Haldane

Gardens and policies extending to roughly 7 acres, originally laid out in the 1850s.

PERTH & KINROSS

Mature trees, rhododendrons and azaleas. Walled, water and wild gardens and delightful woodland walks.

Route: South out of Auchterarder (Abbey Road) then follow yellow signs.
Admission: £4.00 OAPs £3.00 Children Under 16 £0.50
SUNDAY 30 MAY 1:30pm - 5:30pm
Telephone: 01764 662299
Friends of St. Margaret's Hospital, Auchterarder receives 40%, the net remaining to SGS Beneficiaries.
♿ Minimal 🐕 ☕ Homemade

12. CLUNY HOUSE Aberfeldy PH15 2JT

Mr J and Mrs W Mattingley
A wonderful, wild woodland garden overlooking the scenic Strathtay valley. Experience the grandeur of one of Britain's widest trees, the complex leaf variation of the Japanese maple, the beauty of the American trillium or the diversity of Asiatic primulas. A good display of snowdrops. Cluny's red squirrels are usually very easily seen. A treasure not to be missed.

Route: 3½ miles from Aberfeldy on Weem to Strathtay Road
Admission: £4.00 Children Under 16 Free
20 FEBRUARY - 14 MARCH FOR THE SNOWDROP FESTIVAL 10:00am - 4:00pm
15 MARCH - 31 OCTOBER 10:00am - 6:00pm
Web Site: www.clunyhousegardens.com
Telephone: 01887 820795 Email Address: wmattingley@btinternet.com
Donation to SGS Beneficiaries
✿ Seed Sold ♿ Limited 🐕 Not Suitable for Excercising Dogs

13. DOWHILL Kelty KY4 0HZ

Mr and Mrs Colin Maitland Dougall
The garden has grown so well over the last 20 years that the owners are now fighting their way out! Ponds and primulas enhanced by a background of wonderful old trees. Woodland walks to the ruins of Dowhill Castle. A demonstration with trained gun dogs (not the owners') will be held during the afternoon.

Route: 3/4 mile off M90, exit 5, towards Crook of Devon
Admission: £4.00 Children Under 16 Free
SUNDAY 23 MAY 12:00pm - 4:00pm
Gun Dog Rescue receives 40%, the net remaining to SGS Beneficiaries.
✿ 🐕 Soup and Rolls

14. DRUMMOND CASTLE GARDENS Crieff PH7 4HZ

Grimsthorpe & Drummond Castle Trust Ltd
The Gardens of Drummond Castle were originally laid out in 1630 by John Drummond, 2nd Earl of Perth. In 1830 the Parterre was changed to an Italian style. One of the most interesting features is the multi-faceted sundial designed by John Mylne, Master Mason

to Charles I. The formal garden is said to be one of the finest in Europe and is the largest of its type in Scotland.

Route: Entrance 2 miles south of Crieff on Muthill road (A822).

Admission: £4.00 OAPs £3.00 Children £2.00

SUNDAY 08 AUGUST 1:00pm - 5:00pm

01 MAY - 31 OCTOBER 1:00pm - 6:00pm

Web Site: www.drummondcastlegardens.co.uk

British Limbless Ex-Servicemen's Association receives 40%, the net remaining to SGS Beneficiaries.

✿ ♿ Restricted 🐕 Raffle, Stalls, Entertainments, Pipe Band ☕

15. EASTER MEIKLE FARDLE Meikleour PH2 6EF

Rear Admiral and Mrs John Mackenzie

A delightful old fashioned 2 acre garden. Herbaceous borders backed by soft sandstone walls or beech hedges. Small enclosed garden with raised beds and recently formed water and bog garden. Walks through maturing woodland.

Route: Take A984 Dunkeld to Coupar Angus 1½ miles, from Spittalfield towards Meikleour, third house on left after turning to Lethendy.

Admission: £4.00 Children Free

05 APRIL - 31 JULY - MONDAYS AND FRIDAYS 10:00am - 6:30pm

ALSO BY ARRANGEMENT - LARGE GROUPS WELCOMED

Telephone: 01738 710330

Seafarers UK receives 40%, the net remaining to SGS Beneficiaries.

♿ Partial ☕ Homemade Light Refreshments Available on Request

16. EXPLORERS GARDEN Pitlochry PH16 5DR

Pitlochry Festival Theatre

This six acre woodland garden, now seven years old, is maturing nicely. More and more visitors are coming to see the wonders this four star VisitScotland attraction reveals - art and architecture, wildlife and birds, exotic plants, peat and rock gardens, extraordinary landscaping and magnificent views. Try the guided tours that reveal the stories of the Scottish Plant Hunters who risked their lives travelling the globe in search of new plants and trees. In this garden, which is divided into different parts of the world, you will see the plants they collected for cultivation, commerce and conservation.

Route: A9 to Pitlochry town, follow signs to Pitlochry Festival Theatre.

Admission: £3.00 Children £1.00 Guided Tour £4.00

SUNDAY 13 JUNE 10:00am - 5:00pm

01 APRIL - 31 OCTOBER 10:00am - 5:00pm (last entry 4:30pm)

Web Site: www.explorersgarden.com

Acting for Others receives 40%, the net remaining to SGS Beneficiaries.

✿ ♿ 🐕 ☕ At Theatre

17. FARLEYER FIELD HOUSE (JOINT OPENING WITH ACHNACLOICH) By Aberfeldy PH15 2JE [NEW]

Mr and Mrs D Stewart

Set in a scenic part of Perthshire the garden is 3½ acres and still evolving after 10 years. There are herbaceous borders, ponds, woodland paths and plenty of shrubs and roses.

Route: From Weem, 1½ miles west.

Admission: £4.00 to include Achnacloich

SUNDAY 30 MAY 1:00pm - 5:00pm

Guide Dogs for the Blind receives 40%, the net remaining to SGS Beneficiaries.

✿ 🐕 Plant Quiz 🍰 Homemade

18. GLENDOICK by Perth PH2 7NS

Peter, Patricia, Kenneth and Jane Cox

Glendoick was recently included in the "Independent on Sunday" exclusive survey of Europe's top 50 gardens and boasts a unique collection of plants collected by 3 generations of the Cox family from their plant-hunting expeditions to China and the Himalayas. Fine collection of rhododendrons, magnolia, meconopsis, kalmia, hydrangea and sorbus in the enchanting burnside woodland garden. Extensive peat garden, nursery and hybrid trial garden.

On Sunday open days only, 2 and 16 May, as well as the gardens, visitors can walk round the nursery production areas and members of the Cox family will be available to answer questions.

Route: Follow brown signs to Glendoick Garden Centre off A90 Perth - Dundee road. Gardens are ½ mile behind Garden Centre. Please drive up and park at gardens (free parking)

Admission: £4.00 (£5.00 Including Guide Book) School Children Free. Tickets from Garden Centre except on Sundays 2 and 16 May when tickets will be at the garden entrance.

SUNDAY 02 MAY 2:00pm - 5:00pm

SUNDAY 16 MAY 2:00pm - 5:00pm

15 FEBRUARY - 19 FEBRUARY FOR SNOWDROP FESTIVAL 10:00am - 4:00pm

22 FEBRUARY - 26 FEBRUARY FOR SNOWDROP FESTIVAL 10:00am - 4:00pm

05 APRIL - 11 JUNE 10:00am - 4:00pm

DAILY FOR GARDEN CENTRE 10:00am - 4:00pm

ALSO BY ARRANGEMENT FOR DATES NOT LISTED

Web Site: www.glendoick.com

Telephone: 01738 860 205 Email Address: orders@glendoick.com

Donation to SGS Beneficiaries

♿ Only by the House ✿ [NCCPG] Rhododendron x 4 🍰 Light Refreshments at Garden Centre Cafe

19. GLENLYON HOUSE Fortingall PH15 2LN

Mr and Mrs Iain Wotherspoon

Interesting garden framed by hedges, with colourful herbaceous borders and fruit trees underplanted with perennials and annuals. Kitchen and cutting garden. Wild life pond.
Route: Take A827 Aberfeldy, B846 Coshieville then turn off for Fortingall and Glen Lyon.
Admission: £4.00
SUNDAY 04 JULY 2:00pm - 5:00pm
ALSO BY ARRANGEMENT 01 JUNE - 30 SEPTEMBER
Telephone: 01887 830233
Fortingall Church receives 40%, the net remaining to SGS Beneficiaries.
✿ ♿ Partial 🐕 ☕ Homemade

20. LANDS OF LOYAL HOTEL Loyal Road, Alyth, Blairgowrie PH11 8JQ NEW

David & Verity Webster

The main garden faces south overlooking the Vale of Strathmore and the town of Alyth. Two terraces with wide herbaceous borders provide lots of colour and interest all year round. In summer the walls are draped with spectacular roses. Plants for sale all year round, although occasionally a large event at the hotel may prevent garden viewing.
Route: From Alyth Market Square, cross the burn following B952/Commerce St. Continue up steep hill/Toutie St. right on to Hill St. Slight left on to Loyal Rd; Hotel 200 years on right.
Admission: £3.50 Children Free
SUNDAY 27 JUNE 11:00am - 7:00pm
ALL YEAR PLANT SALES
Web Site: www.landsofloyal.com
Telephone: 01828 633151 Email Address: info@landsofloyal.com
Help for Heroes receives 40%, the net remaining to SGS Beneficiaries. Also 20% of annual plant sales to SGS Beneficiaries.
✿ All Year Round ♿ Partial 🐕 B&B Full Hotel Facilities, Local Stalls, BBQ (something delicious in a bun) ☕ Cream Wine Light Refreshments Fully Licensed Bar & Restaurant. Food Served All Day. Non Residents Welcome

21. MEGGINCH CASTLE Errol PH2 7SW

Mr Giles Herdman & The Hon. Mrs Drummond-Herdman of Megginch

15th century turreted castle (not open) with Gothic stable yard and pagoda dovecote. 19th century formal front garden, topiary and ancient yews. Splendid array of daffodils and rhododendrons. Double Walled kitchen garden and orchard.
Route: Approach from Dundee only, directly off A90, on south side of carriageway ½ mile on left after Errol flyover, between lodge gatehouses. 7 miles from Perth, 8 from Dundee.
Admission: £4.00 Children Free
SUNDAY 11 APRIL 2:00pm - 5:00pm
All Saints Church, Glencarse receives 40%, the net remaining to SGS Beneficiaries.
♿ 🐕 ☕ Light Refreshments

PERTH & KINROSS

22. MOUNT TABOR HOUSE Mount Tabor Road, Perth PH2 7DE

Mr and Mrs John McEwan

Mature terraced town garden originally laid out in the late 19th Century surrounded by trees and herbaceous borders. Water feature

Route: From Dundee Road in Perth at Isle of Skye Hotel, turn right into Manse Road, over mini-roundabout and into Mount Tabor Road.

Admission: £3.50

SUNDAY 01 AUGUST 10:00am - 5:00pm

The Katie McKerracher Trust receives 40%, the net remaining to SGS Beneficiaries.

❀ ♿ Mostly 🐕 Craft Stall ☕ Homemade Soup and Rolls from 12 - 2pm Teas from 2 - 5pm

23. MURTHLY CASTLE Murthly PH1 4HP

Mr & Mrs T. Steuart Fothringham

The walled garden at Murthly Castle was first laid out in the 17th Century and retains the original fountain, yew trees and summer house. The extensive landscaped policies include many avenues of mature conifers, including the Douglas firs planted in the 1840s and the ancient 'Dead Walk' leading to the private chapel.

Route: Access via Murthly or Caputh. (Please note NO access from A9)

Admission: £4.00 Children under 12 Free

SATURDAY 05 JUNE 2:00pm - 6:00pm

Help for Heroes receives 40%, the net remaining to SGS Beneficiaries.

❀ ♿ No Toilet Access No Dogs Please Castle Bric-a-Brac Stall ☕ Homemade

24. PARKHEAD HOUSE Parkhead Gardens, Burghmuir Road, Perth PH1 1JF

Mr & Mrs M.S. Tinson

The garden surrounds a 300 year old house with mature trees, one of which is an outstanding Spanish Chestnut. Meandering paths lead to secluded corners through beds of interesting and unusual plants and shrubs - a real plant lovers' haven. A small vegetable plot includes container grown vegetables and a greenhouse. This is a hidden gem of a garden with always something in flower.

Route: Parkhead Gardens is a small lane off the west end of Burghmuir Road in Perth. More detailed directions on request.

Admission: £3.50

BY ARRANGEMENT 03 MAY - 30 SEPTEMBER

Telephone: 01738 625983   Email Address: maddy.tinson@gmail.com

All proceeds to SGS Beneficiaries

❀ When Plants are Available ♿ Limited Guide Dogs Only ☕ Homemade by Prior Arrangement

25. PITCURRAN HOUSE Abernethy PH2 9LH NEW

The Hon Ranald & Mrs Noel-Paton

New garden (created 2005) with many interesting and unusual plants. Behind the house semi-hardy euphorbia mellifera, melianthus major and sophora davidii grow happily amongst cistus and hebes. The garden also includes many ericaceous shrubs, meconopsis, paeonies, primulas and smilacina racemosa. A rose pergola is covered with Blush Noisette, Felicite Perpetue and Paul's Himalayan Musk, and a large west facing hydrangea border brightens up the late summer.

Route: SE of Perth. From M90 (exit 9) take A912 towards Glenfarg, left at roundabout onto A913 to Abernethy. Pitcurran House is at far eastern end of village.

Admission: £4.00 Children Free

SUNDAY 16 MAY 2:00pm - 6:00pm

St. John's Episcopal Church, Perth receives 40%, the net remaining to SGS Beneficiaries.
Good ♿ Partial 🐕 The Macallan Fine Oak Highland Single Malt Whisky Promotion 🍵 Homemade

26. ROSSIE HOUSE Forgandenny PH2 9EH

Mr & Mrs David B. Nichol

Rossie dates from 1657. Many of the trees in the garden and surrounding park date back to this time. The undulating terrain is full of magnificent trees, shrubs and many beautiful rhododendrons which are all set off by a carpet of bluebells, trillium and other woodland plants. Paths take you down by the stream, over bridges and eventually into the walled garden. Sculptures by Nigel Ross and David Annand grace the garden whilst Castlemilk sheep graze the paddocks.

Carpets of snowdrops in glorious surroundings.

Route: Forgandenny is on the B935 between Bridge of Earn and Dunning

Admission: £4.00 Children Free

THURSDAY 18 FEBRUARY (SNOWDROP FESTIVAL) 2:00pm - 5:00pm
THURSDAY 18 MARCH (HELLEBORES AND SCILLAS) 2:00pm - 5:00pm
THURSDAY 15 APRIL (EARLY RHODODENDRONS) 2:00pm - 5:00pm
THURSDAY 13 MAY (RHODODENDRONS AND BLUEBELLS) 2:00pm - 5:00pm

Web Site: www.aboutscotland.com   Email Address: judynichol@rossiehouse.co.uk

Camphill Village Trust receives 40%, the net remaining to SGS Beneficiaries.
Small ♿ Limited 🐕 👶 [B&B] 🍵 Groups Please Pre-warn. Tel: 01738 812265

27. SCONE PALACE Perth PH2 6BD

The Earl & Countess of Mansfield

Extensive and well laid out grounds and a magnificent pinetum dating from 1848; there is a Douglas fir raised from the original seed sent from America in 1824. There is also a Plant Hunters' pavilion dedicated to Douglas and other Scottish Plant Hunters. The woodland garden has attractive walks amongst the rhododendrons and azaleas and leads into the Monks' Playgreen and Friar's Den of the former Abbey of Scone. Good snowdrops.

Route: A93. Perth 2 miles. Perth/Braemar Road

Admission: Prices correct at time of going to press

Grounds Only: £5.10, Concessions £4.50, Children £3.50

PERTH & KINROSS

Palace and Grounds: £9.00, Concessions £7.90, Children £6.00
SATURDAY 07 AUGUST FOR ORCHID FESTIVAL 9:30am - 5:00pm
SUNDAY 08 AUGUST FOR ORCHID FESTIVAL 9:30am - 5:00pm
20, 21, 26, 27 & 28 FEBRUARY FOR SNOWDROP FESTIVAL 11:00am - 5:00pm
01 APRIL - 31 OCTOBER 9:30am - 5:00pm
NOVEMBER - MARCH (FRIDAYS - GROUNDS ONLY) 10:00am - 4:00pm
Web Site: www.scone-palace.co.uk
Telephone: 01738 552300 Email Address: visits@scone-palace.co.uk
Donation to SGS Beneficiaries
♿ Limited 🐕 🌸 Children's Adventure Playground, Pinetum, Murray Star Maze
☕ Cream Wine Light Refreshments Only Available Within Opening Hours 1 April -
31 October

28. THE COTTAGE 36 Main Street, Longforgan DD2 5ET

Dr and Mrs Andrew Reid
This two acre garden faces south and has views of the Tay and Fife Hills. It is designed
for year round interest with rhododendron and azalea beds, herbaceous borders and
roses. There are water features and many interesting trees.
Route: Turn off A90 at Longforgan sign between Perth (15 miles) and Dundee (5 miles).
Situated in the middle of Longforgan Main Street. Street Parking.
Admission: £3.00 Children 50p
SUNDAY 27 JUNE 2:00pm - 5:00pm
Barnardo's receives 40%, the net remaining to SGS Beneficiaries.
🌸 ♿ No Dogs Raffle ☕ Homemade Light Refreshments Cake & Candy

29. WESTER CLOQUHAT Bridge of Cally PH10 7JP

Brigadier and Mrs Christopher Dunphie
Terraced garden enlarged in 2001 to include a water garden. Lawns, mixed borders
with a wide range of shrubs, roses and herbaceous plants. Splendid situation with fine
view down to the River Ericht.
Route: Turn off A93 just north of Bridge of Cally and follow signs for ½ mile
Admission: £4.00 Children Under 16 Free
SUNDAY 11 JULY 2:00pm - 5:00pm
Royal Scottish National Orchestra receives 40%, the net remaining to SGS Beneficiaries.
🌸 ☕ Homemade

Renfrewshire

'Gardens of Scotland' 2010 is sponsored by **Rensburg Sheppards Investment Management**

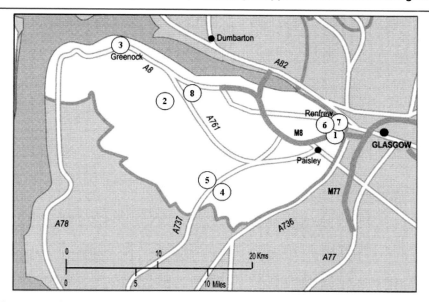

District Organisers: **Mrs Rosemary Leslie** High Mathernock Farm, Auchentiber Road, Kilmacolm PA13 4SP. Tel: 01505 874032

Mrs Alexandra MacMillan Langside Farm, Kilmacolm PA13 4SA. Tel: 01475 540423

Area Organisers: **Mrs B McLean** 49 Middlepenny Road, Langbank PA14 6XE

Mr J A Wardrop DL St Kevins, Victoria Road, Paisley PA2 9PT

Treasurer: **Mrs Jean Gillan** Bogriggs Cottage, Carlung, West Kilbride KA23 9PS

Gardens Open On a Specific Date

Lochside, Lochwinnoch	Sunday 21 February	2:00pm - 5:00pm
Duchal, Kilmacolm	Sunday 23 May	2:00pm - 5:00pm
Greenock Gardens, Greenock	Sunday 20 June	2:00pm - 5:00pm
Lochwinnoch Gardens	Sunday 04 July	2:00pm - 5:00pm
Sma' Shot Cottages Heritage Centre, Paisley	Sunday 11 July	12:00pm - 4:00pm
Paisley Gardens, Paisley	Sunday 25 July	2:00pm - 5:00pm
Barshaw Park Walled Garden, Paisley	Sunday 22 August	2:00pm - 5:00pm

RENREWSHIRE

Plant Sales

St Fillan's Episcopal Church Kilmacolm   Saturday 18 September 10:00am - 1:00pm

1. BARSHAW PARK WALLED GARDEN Paisley PA1 1UG

Environmental Services Department, Renfrewshire Council

Walled garden displaying a varied selection of plants, some of which are suitable for the blind to smell and feel. These include a colourful layout of summer bedding plants, herbaceous borders, mixed shrub borders and rose beds.

Route: From Paisley town centre along the Glasgow road (A737) pass Barshaw Park and take first left into Oldhall Road and then first left again into walled garden car park. Pedestrian visitors can also approach from Barshaw Park by mid gate in Glasgow Road.

Admission: By donation

SUNDAY 22 AUGUST 2:00pm - 5:00pm

Erskine Hospital receives 40%, the net remaining to SGS Beneficiaries.

  Homemade

2. DUCHAL Kilmacolm PA13 4RA

Lord Maclay

18th Century garden with walls particularly well planted and maintained, entered by footbridge over the Greenwater. Specie trees, hollies, old fashioned roses, shrubs and herbaceous borders with fruit orchards and vegetable garden. Lily pond.

Route: On B788 1 mile from Kilmacolm (this road links B786 Lochwinnoch Rd and A761 Bridge of Weir road) Greenock/Glasgow bus via Bridge of Weir. Knapps Loch stop is quarter mile from garden.

Admission: £4.00 Children Under 16 Free

SUNDAY 23 MAY 2:00pm - 5:00pm

Ardgowan Hospice receives 20%, Strathcarron Hospice, Denny receives 20%, the net remaining to SGS Beneficiaries.

 Partial Homemade

3. GREENOCK GARDENS Greenock PA16 NEW

Mr & Mrs Arhimandritis and Mr & Mrs Wood

66 Union Street - Newly landscaped by owners over past 3 years. Divided into three sections with different theme and colours in each. A large selection of perennials and a mediterranean flavour.

27 Denholm Terrace - a small traditional 1930s lay-out garden. In the process of being reclaimed and adapted with a wide variety of features including herbaceous borders, water feature and small vegetable plot.

Route: **Union Steet**: take signs for Greenock Golf Course from main A770 (Brougham St), turn right into Union St, No 66 is between Margaret & Fox Streets

Denholm Terrace: take signs for Greenock Golf course from main A770 (Brougham St), to top of Forsyth St. Denholm Tce on left opp. clubhouse. Parking on Forsyth St.

Admission: £4.00 Children Under 16 Free

SUNDAY 20 JUNE 2:00pm - 5:00pm
Ardgowan Hospice receives 40%, the net remaining to SGS Beneficiaries.
✿ �") 🍵Homemade Wine Light Refreshments   Teas at Union Street and Wine/Refreshments at Denholm Terrace

4. LOCHSIDE Lochwinnoch PA12 4JH

Keith and Kate Lough
Mature woodland gardens carpeted with snowdrops (Waterproof footwear advised)
<u>Route:</u> From A737 200 yards east of Lochwinnoch/Largs roundabout. White railings on north side of road. Also direct pedestrian access via RSPB Lochwinnoch Reserve.
<u>Admission:</u> £3.00 Children Free
SUNDAY 21 FEBRUARY 2:00pm - 5:00pm
Alzheimers Scotland receives 40%, the net remaining to SGS Beneficiaries.
✿ Snowdrops 🐾 🍵 Homemade

5. LOCHWINNOCH GARDENS Lochwinnoch PA12

The Gardeners of Lochwinnoch
35a Calder Street (Mr and Mrs Hunt) Colourful garden, sympathetic to wildlife with relaxing atmosphere!
41 Church Street (Mr and Mrs J Watson) Long, interesting garden containing a variety of plants. Pond with bridge.
Hillfoot Cottage, 95 High Street (Mr and Mrs Cole) Village garden. Perennial and herbaceous. A true cottage garden.
36 Calder Street (Mr and Mrs Gordon Nicholl) Walled garden stretching back from old cottage (1838) containing an astonishing selection of plants.
Novar, Harvey Square (Mr and Mrs Drummond) L-shaped walled garden of ¼ acre. Fruit trees, soft fruit, greenhouse, lawns and shrubs.
RSPB Wildlife Garden Small garden with variety of plants suitable for wildlife.
Community Garden (c/o Gordon Nicholl) **Church Street**
<u>Route:</u> On A760 Johnstone to Largs Road. Watch for yellow signs in village. Maps at every garden.
<u>Admission:</u> £4.00 includes entry to all gardens. Children under 16 free.
SUNDAY 04 JULY 2:00pm - 5:00pm
St Vincent's Hospice receives 20%, Teenage Cancer Trust receives 20%, the net remaining to SGS Beneficiaries.
✿ In Community Garden, Church Street 🐾 🍵 Homemade at Our Lady of Fatima Church Hall, High Street

6. PAISLEY GARDENS Paisley PA2

Gardeners of Paisley
38 Calside (Dr Ahmed) - Walled garden with many attractive shrubs and decorative trees. Variety of plants and fruit trees around house. Croquet lawn.
18 Calside Avenue (Mr and Mrs Hamilton) - Bedding and alpines in rockery. Filled baskets

and pots. Lots of interest.

8A Calside Avenue (Mr and Mrs Rowand) - Family garden with mature flower beds & display of annuals, fish pond and greenhouse collection of citrus plants and begonias.

6 Calside Avenue (Mr and Mrs Paul) - Large beautiful garden, full of colour and interest.

Route: Proceed south by Causeyside St from ring road at Canal Street. Calside is main road to Glennifer Braes. Calside Av is off main road.

Admission: £3.00 Children Under 10 Free

SUNDAY 25 JULY 2:00pm - 5:00pm

St Vincent's Hospice receives 20%, Accord Hospice receives 20%, the net remaining to SGS Beneficiaries.

✿ At 4 Calside Avenue (Mrs Francesca Stewart) ♿ Partial 🐕 ☕ Homemade at 4 Calside Avenue (Mrs Francesca Stewart)

7. SMA' SHOT COTTAGES HERITAGE CENTRE 11/17 George Place, Paisley PA1 2HZ

Old Paisley Society

Small enclosed courtyard garden. Enjoy the 19th century weaver's garden designed to celebrate the 21st anniversary of Sma' Shot Cottages. All plants are true to the period. Assistance in the creation of the garden was provided by the "Beechgrove Garden". Visitors may also see the rare "Paisley Gem" (Dianthus) and the new "Viola Sma' Shot Cottages" bred by local gardener, Hugh Boyd.

Route: Off New Street in Paisley Town Centre.

Admission: £2.00

SUNDAY 11 JULY 12:00pm - 4:00pm

Web Site: www.smashot.co.uk

Old Paisley Society receives 40%, the net remaining to SGS Beneficiaries.

♿ Gift Shop, Heritage Centre Tours (Free) ☕ Homemade Light Refreshments

PLANT SALES

8. ST FILLAN'S EPISCOPAL CHURCH Moss Road, Kilmacolm PA13

St Fillan's Episcopal Church

Plant sale with a wide variety of locally grown plants and shrubs.

Route: Moss Road, Kilmacolm, PA13 - turn off A761 Port Glasgow-Bridge of Weir Rd in centre of Kilmacolm into Moss Road.

Admission: Free

SATURDAY 18 SEPTEMBER 10:00am - 1:00pm

St Fillan's Episcopal Church receives 40%, the net remaining to SGS Beneficiaries.

✿ ☕ Homemade

Ross, Cromarty, Skye & Inverness

'Gardens of Scotland' 2010 is sponsored by **Rensburg Sheppards Investment Management**

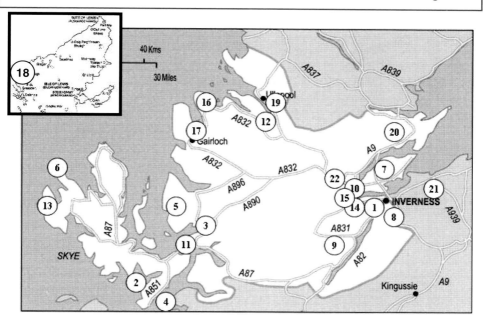

District Organiser: **Lady Lister-Kaye** House of Aigas, Beauly, IV4 7AD
Treasurer: **Mrs Sheila Kerr** Lilac Cottage, Struy, By Beauly, IV4 7JU

Gardens Open On a Specific Date

Dundonnell House, Dundonnell	Thursday 15 April	2:00pm - 5:00pm
Attadale, Strathcarron	Saturday 22 May	2:00am - 5:00pm
Inverewe, Poolewe	Tuesday 25 May	10:00am - 5:00pm
House of Gruinard, Laide	Wednesday 26 May	2:00pm - 5:00pm
Croc na Boull, Muir of Ord	Sunday 30 May	2:00pm - 5:00pm
Inverewe, Poolewe	Tuesday 1 June	10:00am - 5:00pm
Dundonnell House, Dundonnell	Thursday 03 June	2:00pm - 5:00pm
Field House, Belladrum	Sunday 06 June	2:00pm - 5:00pm
Applecross Walled Garden, Strathcarron	Saturday 12 June	2:00pm - 5:00pm
Novar, Evanton	Sunday 13 June	2:30pm - 5:00pm
Cardon, Balnafoich	Saturday 19 June	1:00pm - 5:00pm
Brackla Wood, Culbokie	Friday 25 June	2:00pm - 5:30pm
House of Aigas and Field Centre, by Beauly	Sunday 27 June	2:00pm - 5:00pm
Dundonnell House, Dundonnell	Thursday 01 July	2:00pm - 5:00pm
Applecross Walled Garden, Strathcarron	Saturday 10 July	2:00pm - 5:00pm

ROSS, CROMARTY, SKYE & INVERNESS

House of Aigas and Field Centre, by Beauly	Sunday 25 July	2:00pm - 5:00pm
House of Gruinard, Laide	Wednesday 28 July	2:00pm - 5:00pm
Applecross Walled Garden, Strathcarron	Saturday 07 August	2:00pm - 5:00pm
Dundonnell House, Dundonnell	Thursday 12 August	2:00pm - 5:00pm
Woodview, Highfield	Sunday 29 August	2:00pm - 5:00pm

Gardens Open By Arrangement
When organising a visit to a garden open by arrangement, please enquire if there are facilities and catering available

Brackla Wood, Culbokie	03 - 31 July (other dates possible)	Tel: 01349 877765
Dundonnell House, Dundonnell	On request	Tel: 07789 390028
Dunvegan Castle and Gardens	16 Oct. - 31 Dec, Weekdays (ex. Christmas & New Year)	Tel: 01470 521206
House of Aigas and Field Centre, by Beauly	For Groups of a Minimum of 8 People	Tel: 01463 782443
Leathad Ard, Upper Carloway	Please Phone Mon - Sat	Tel: 01851 643204
Novar, Evanton	For Groups of a Minimum of 8 People	Tel: 01349 831062
West Lodge, Kilravock, Croy	20 May - 20 August	Tel: 01667 493736

Gardens Open Regularly

Abriachan Garden Nursery, Loch Ness Side	01 Feb - 30 Nov	9:00am - 7:00pm
An Acarsaid, Ord, Sleat	01 April - 31 Oct	10:00am - 5:30pm
Applecross Walled Garden, Strathcarron	01 March - 31 Oct.	2:00pm - 5:00pm
Armadale Castle Gardens	Jan – Mar & Nov - Dec	Dawn – Dusk
	April - October	9:30am - 5:30pm
Attadale, Strathcarron	01 April - 31 October (except Sundays)	10:00am - 5:30am
Balmeanach House, Struan	02 May - 31 October Weds & Sats	11:00am - 4:30pm
Coiltie Garden, Divach	18 June - 18 July	12:00pm - 6:00pm
Duirinish Lodge & Gardens, Kyle of Lochalsh	31 May - 05 June	2:00pm - 6:00pm
Dunvegan Castle and Gardens, Isle of Skye	01 April - 15 October	10:00am - 5:30pm
Leathad Ard, Upper Carloway	05 June - 28 August, Tues, Thurs & Sats	1:45pm - 6:00pm
Leckmelm Shrubbery & Arboretum, By Ullapool	01 April - 31 October	10:00am - 6:00pm

1. ABRIACHAN GARDEN NURSERY Loch Ness Side IV3 6LA

Mr and Mrs Davidson

An outstanding garden. Over 4 acres of exciting plantings, with winding paths through native woodlands. Seasonal highlights - snowdrops, hellebores, primulas, meconopsis, hardy geraniums and colour-themed summer beds. Views over Loch Ness. New path to pond through the Bluebell Wood. The garden will close at 5pm during the winter months.

Route: On A82 Inverness/Drumnadrochit road, approximately 8 miles south of Inverness.

Admission: £2.00

01 FEBRUARY - 30 NOVEMBER 9:00am - 7:00pm

Web Site: www.lochnessgarden.com

Telephone: 01463 861232

Highland Hospice receives 40%, the net remaining to SGS Beneficiaries.

Working Retail Nursery Tea/Coffee Machine

2. AN ACARSAID Ord, Sleat, Isle of Skye IV44 8RN

Mrs Eileen MacInnes (Garden Manager: Mr Tim Godfrey)

A two acre garden perched on low cliffs above the shore of Loch Eishort with stunning views to the Cuillins. Informal mixed plantings, started in the 1960s, with shrubbery and viewpoint, lawns, borders and scree bed and many cobbled paths.

Route: Take A851 from Broadford or Armadale. Ord is signposted 5 miles from Armadale.

Admission: By Donation Box

01 APRIL - 31 OCTOBER 10:00am - 5:30pm

Email Address: t.godfrey@virgin.net

Crossroads Care, Skye receives 40%, the net remaining to SGS Beneficiaries.

3. APPLECROSS WALLED GARDEN Strathcarron IV54 8ND **NEW**

Applecross Organics

Walled garden of 1.25 acres in spectacular surroundings. Derelict for 50 years but lovingly restored since 2001. Lots of herbaceous borders, fruit trees and raised vegetable beds. We try to have an interesting plant table in this wonderful peaceful setting

Route: Take the spectacular Bealach na Ba hill road after Kishorn. At the T junction in Applecross, turn right for half a mile. Entrance to Applecross House is immediately in front of you.

Admission: £3.00

SATURDAY 12 JUNE 2:00pm - 5:00pm
SATURDAY 10 JULY 2:00pm - 5:00pm
SATURDAY 07 AUGUST 2:00pm - 5:00pm
01 MARCH - 31 OCTOBER. 2:00pm - 5:00pm

ROSS, CROMARTY, SKYE & INVERNESS

Telephone: 01520 744440

Lymphodema Society receives 40%, the net remaining to SGS Beneficiaries.

✿ ♿ 🐴 ☕ Cream Wine Light Refreshments Award Winning Cafe/Restaurant in Garden: Open 11.00 - 20.30 daily 1 March - 31 October

4. ARMADALE CASTLE GARDENS Armadale, Isle of Skye IV45 8RS NEW

Clan Donald Lands Trust

The 40 acres of exotic trees, shrubs and flowers are remarkable for their beauty and for their very existence. The warm, generally frost-free, climate of the west coast of Scotland - a result of the Gulf Stream - and the work of our professional staff allow the sheltered gardens to flourish. Although there have been gardens at Armadale since the 17th century, it was just over 200 years ago that the planting began which was to create the gardens you see today. There was further development in Victorian times with expanses of lawn intermittently planted with trees and shrubbery. When the Clan Donald Lands Trust took over, the gardens were overgrown and neglected. Several years of hard pruning, rebuilding and planting around the centrepiece of Armadale Castle has resulted in 40 acres of fascinating woodland gardens and lawns that provide a tranquil place to sit or walk. Underneath the now majestic trees thrives a carpet of bluebells, orchids and wild meadow flowers, in spring and summer, forming a gentle backdrop to the formally planted areas such as the sunny terraced walk and herbaceous borders. Water plants flourish in and around the ponds and shrubs from around the world thrive throughout. The gardens and the area are also home to birds and wildlife not generally found on the Isle of Skye. Leading off from the formal gardens, visitors can enjoy woodland walks and nature trails, from short walks to much longer walks with beautiful views of the Sound of Sleat.

Route: From the Skye Bridge, (A87) head north, turning left just before Broadford onto A851. Armadale is signposted and can be found 15 miles down this road before you reach the ferry terminal.

From Armadale Pier, drive ¼ mile north on A851 to Gardens entrance and car park.

Admission: £6.95 Concessions £4.95 Children £4.95 Under 5 Free Family £20.00 Free admission Jan-March & Nov-December

JAN - MARCH AND NOV – DEC DAWN - DUSK

APRIL - OCTOBER 9:30am - 5:30pm

Web Site: www.clandonald.com

Telephone: 01471 844305 Email Address: office@clandonald.com

Donation to SGS Beneficiaries

✿ ♿ 🐴 Three Retail Outlets - One Specifically Garden ☕ Homemade Wine Light Refreshments Catering Facilities at Stables Restaurant - Lunches, Teas, Alcoholic Beverages

5. ATTADALE Strathcarron IV54 8YX

Mr and Mrs Ewen Macpherson

The Gulf Stream and surrounding hills and rocky cliffs create a microclimate for 20 acres of outstanding water gardens, old rhododendrons, unusual trees and fern collection in a geodesic dome. Japanese garden and sculpture collection. Giant sundial.

Route: On A890 between Strathcarron and South Strome.

Admission: £4.50 Concessions £3.00 Children £1.00

SATURDAY 22 MAY 2:00am - 5:00pm

01 APRIL - 31 OCTOBER (EXCEPT SUNDAYS) 10:00am - 5:30pm

Web Site: www.attadalegardens.com

Telephone: 01520 722603 Email Address: geoffattgdns@yahoo.co.uk

Howard Doris Centre receives 40% (22 May Opening), the net remaining to SGS Beneficiaries.

❀ On Most Days ♿ Partial 🐕 Raffle ☕ Homemade on Open Day and D.I.Y. Tearoom with History of Garden April - October

6. BALMEANACH HOUSE Struan, Isle of Skye IV56 8FH

Mrs Arlene Macphie

A garden with herbaceous border, bedding and a small azalea/rhododendron walk. To make this garden, one third of an acre of croft land was fenced in during the late 1980s and there is now a woodland dell with fairies, three ponds and a small shrubbery.

Route: A87 to Sligachan, turn left, Balmeanach is 5 miles north of Struan and 5 miles south of Dunvegan

Admission: £3.00

02 MAY - 31 OCTOBER WEDNESDAYS & SATURDAYS 11:00am - 4:30pm

Web Site: www.skye-holiday.com

Telephone: 01470 572320 Email Address: info@skye-holiday.com

S.S.P.C.A. receives 40%, the net remaining to SGS Beneficiaries.

❀ At Plants 'n Stuff, Atholl Service Station **B&B** Tourist Board 4 star ☕

7. BRACKLA WOOD Culbokie, Dingwall IV7 8GY

Susan and Ian Dudgeon

Mature 1 acre plot consisting of woodland, wildlife features, ponds, mixed borders, a kitchen garden, a rockery and a mini-orchard. Spring bulbs and hellebores, rhododendron, wisteria and roses followed by crocosmia, clematis and deciduous trees provide continuous colour and interest throughout the season. New pond for 2010.

Route: From the North: Take the A9 and turn off to Culbokie. At the far end of the village, turn right after the playing fields signposted "Munlochy". Two miles up the road, turn right into "No Through Road" signposted "Upper Braefindon" From the South: Take the A9 and turn off to Munlochy. At the far end of the village, turn right and then sharp left up road signposted "Culbokie" and "Killen". After about 4½ miles turn left onto road signposted "Upper Braefindon" Brackla Wood is first house on left.

Admission: £3.00

FRIDAY 25 JUNE 2:00pm - 5:30pm

BY ARRANGEMENT 03 - 31 JULY (OTHER DATES MAY BE POSSIBLE - PLEASE RING TO CHECK)

Telephone: 01349 877765 Email Address: smdbrackla@aol.com

Highland Heartbeat Support Association receives 40%, the net remaining to SGS Beneficiaries.

✿ ♿ Partial With Assistance ☕ Homemade

8. CARDON Balnafoich, Farr IV2 6XG

Caroline Smith

Set in approximately 5 acres of woodlands. Feature pond and lawn area. Rockeries, wild woodland areas, cottage style planting.

Route: From Inverness **either:** take A9 South. In approx. 7 miles turn right into Daviot. Proceed through Daviot to single track road heading for Balnafoich crossroads. Cardon is approx. 3½ miles on right. If you reach crossroads you have gone too far. **Or:** from Inverness Academy roundabout take B861 heading for Inverarnie. Approx 4½ miles from Academy take left at crossroads signed Daviot. Cardon is 400 yds. on left in dip on road.

Admission: £3.00 Children Free

SATURDAY 19 JUNE 1:00pm - 5:00pm

Telephone: 01808 521389 Email Address: csmith@kitchens01.fsnet.co.uk

Local Charities receive 40%, the net remaining to SGS Beneficiaries.

✿ ♿ 🐕 ☕ Homemade   Homemade Cakes, Scones, Home Baking, Jam, etc

9. COILTIE GARDEN Divach, Drumnadrochit IV63 6XW

Gillian and David Nelson

A garden made over the past 25 years from a long neglected Victorian garden, now being somewhat reorganised to suit ageing gardeners. Many trees, old and new, shrub and herbaceous borders, wall beds, roses, all set in beautiful hill scenery with a fine view of 100ft. Divach Falls.

Route: Take turning to Divach off A82 in Drumnadrochit village. Proceed two miles uphill, passing Falls. 150m beyond Divach Lodge.

Admission: £3.00 Children Free

18 JUNE - 18 JULY 12:00pm - 6:00pm

Amnesty International receives 40%, the net remaining to SGS Beneficiaries.

✿ ♿

10. CROC NA BOULL Muir of Ord IV6 7TW

Mr & Mrs Richard Constanduros

3 acre garden currently being established within an existing natural setting of mature trees. New features include azaleas, rhododendrons, hosta bed and orchard.

Route: Coming from Inverness, cross railway bridge in Muir of Ord, turn very sharp left (signposted Corry Road), entrance to the garden is at the fourth passing place.

Admission: £3.00 Children Free

SUNDAY 30 MAY 2:00pm - 5:00pm

Urray House receives 40%, the net remaining to SGS Beneficiaries.

 Limited ♞ ☕ Homemade

11. DUIRINISH LODGE & GARDENS Kyle of Lochalsh IV40 8BE

William Roe

A work-in-progress of the restoration and development of an 18 acre garden with interesting plants and wildlife and fabulous West Highland views.

<u>Route:</u> Off the minor road between Reraig/Balmacara and Plockton.

<u>Admission:</u> £5.00 Children and Disabled Free

31 MAY - 05 JUNE 2:00pm - 6:00pm

Email Address: william@duirinish.com

Local Charities receive 40%, the net remaining to SGS Beneficiaries.

♞ ☕ Homemade

12. DUNDONNELL HOUSE Dundonnell, Little Loch Broom, Wester Ross IV23 2QW

Dundonnell Estates

Camellias and magnolias and bulbs in spring, rhododendrons and laburnum walk in this ancient walled garden. Exciting planting in new borders gives all year colour centred around one of the oldest yew trees in Scotland. Midsummer roses, restored Edwardian glasshouse, riverside walk, arboretum - all in the valley below the peaks of An Teallach.

<u>Route:</u> Off A835 at Braemore on to A832. After 11 miles, take Badralloch turn for half a mile.

<u>Admission:</u> £3.50 Children Free

THURSDAY 15 APRIL 2:00pm - 5:00pm

THURSDAY 03 JUNE 2:00pm - 5:00pm

THURSDAY 01 JULY 2:00pm - 5:00pm

THURSDAY 12 AUGUST 2:00pm - 5:00pm

ALSO BY ARRANGEMENT ON REQUEST

Telephone: 07789 390028

Stroke Association receives 40% on two days, Fauna & Flora International receives 40% on two days, the net remaining to SGS Beneficiaries.

✿ 15 April and 3 June only ☕ Homemade   3 June at Dundonnell House. Other days at Maggie's Tearoom 4 miles towards Little Loch Broom

13. DUNVEGAN CASTLE AND GARDENS Isle of Skye IV55 8WF

Hugh Macleod of Macleod

Dunvegan Castle's five acres of formal gardens began life in the 18th century. In stark contrast to the barren moorland and mountains which dominate Skye's landscape, the gardens are a hidden oasis featuring an eclectic mix of plants as you make your way through woodland glades, past shimmering pools fed by waterfalls and streams flowing down to the sea. Having experienced the Water Garden with its ornate bridges and islands replete with a rich and colourful plant variety, you can take a stroll through the elegant surroundings of the formal Round Garden featuring a Box-wood Parterre as its centrepiece.

Route: Dunvegan Village 1 mile, 23 miles west of Portree.

Admission: **Gardens Only:** £6.00 Concessions £5.00 Children (5-15) £3.00

Castle & Gardens: £8.00 Concessions £6.50 Children £4.00

01 APRIL - 15 OCTOBER - DAILY (LAST ENTRY 5.00pm) 10:00am - 5:30pm

ALSO BY ARRANGEMENT 16 OCTOBER - 31 DECEMBER WEEK DAYS Ex. XMAS

Web Site: www.dunvegancastle.com

Telephone: 01470 521206 Email Address: info@dunvegancastle.com

Donation to SGS Beneficiaries

& 🐕 Craft, Woollen & Gift Shops, Clan Exhibition, Audio Visual Theatre, Boat Trips to Seal Colony 🍵 Light Refreshments Wine

14. FIELD HOUSE Belladrum, Beauly IV4 4BA NEW

Mr & Mrs D Paterson

Informal country garden in one acre site. Mixed borders with some unusual plants - a plantsman's garden

Route: 4 miles from Beauly on A833 Beauly to Drumnadrochit road, then follow signs to Belladrum.

Admission: £3.00

SUNDAY 06 JUNE 2:00pm - 5:00pm

Highland Hospice receives 20%, C.H.S. receives 20%, the net remaining to SGS Beneficiaries.

🌸 🍵 Light Refreshments

15. HOUSE OF AIGAS AND FIELD CENTRE by Beauly IV4 7AD

Sir John and Lady Lister-Kaye

Aigas has a woodland walk overlooking the Beauly River with a collection of named Victorian specimen trees now being restored and extended with a garden of rockeries, herbaceous borders and shrubberies. Guided walks on nature trails

Route: 4½ miles from Beauly on A831 Cannich/Glen Affric road.

Admission: £3.00 Children Free

SUNDAY 27 JUNE 2:00pm - 5:00pm

SUNDAY 25 JULY 2:00pm - 5:00pm

BY ARRANGEMENT FOR GROUPS OF A MINIMUM OF 8 PEOPLE (LUNCH/TEAS AVAILABLE ON REQUEST)

Telephone: 01463 782443

Email Address: sheila@aigas.co.uk

Highland Hospice (Aird branch) receives 40%, the net remaining to SGS Beneficiaries.

🌸 & Partial No Dogs 🍵 Homemade

16. HOUSE OF GRUINARD Laide IV22 2NQ

The Hon Mrs A G Maclay

Superb hidden and unexpected garden developed in sympathy with stunning west coast estuary location. Wide variety of interesting herbaceous and shrub borders with water garden and extended wild planting.

Route: On A832 12 miles north of Inverewe and 9 miles south of Dundonnell.

Admission: £3.50 Children Under 16 Free

WEDNESDAY 26 MAY 2:00pm - 5:00pm

WEDNESDAY 28 JULY 2:00pm - 5:00pm

Telephone: 01445 731235

MacMillan Nurses receives 40%, the net remaining to SGS Beneficiaries.

✿ ☕ Homemade   On 26th May Only

17. INVEREWE Poolewe IV22 2LG

The National Trust for Scotland

Magnificent 54 acre Highland garden, surrounded by mountains, moorland and sea-loch. Created by Osgood Mackenzie in the late 19th century, it now includes a wealth of exotic plants, from Australian tree ferns to Chinese rhododendrons to South African bulbs.

There will be a walk with the Head Gardener to focus on woodland gardening on Tuesday 25 May and a walk led by the First Gardener on Tuesday 1 June to view some of the National Collection plantings. Meet at the Visitor Centre at 1pm.

Route: Signposted on A832 by Poolewe, 6m NE of Gairloch.

Admission: £8.50 Concessions £5.50

TUESDAY 25 MAY 10:00am - 5:00pm

TUESDAY 1 JUNE 10:00am - 5:00pm

Web Site: www.nts.org.uk

Telephone: 0844 493 2225 Email Address: inverewe@nts.org.uk

Donation to SGS Beneficiaries

♿ NCCPG Visitor Centre, Normal Opening Hours ☕ Light Refreshments   Normal Restaurant Availability

18. LEATHAD ARD Upper Carloway, Isle of Lewis HS2 9AQ

Rowena and Stuart Oakley

A ¾ acre sloping garden with stunning views over East Loch Roag. The garden has evolved as shelter hedges have grown, dividing the garden into a number of separate areas. The growth of the shelter and the formation of raised beds has created a range of different conditions allowing a wide variety of plants to be grown. Beds include herbaceous borders; cutting borders; bog gardens; grass garden; exposed beds; patio and vegetable and fruit patches. It is hoped to extend the bog garden this year and build a pond. Some plants will be available for sale

Route: Take A858 from Shawbost to Carloway. First right after entering village

ROSS, CROMARTY, SKYE & INVERNESS

(opposite football pitch). First house on right. The Westside circular bus from Stornoway will drop you at the road end. (Ask for the Carloway football pitch).
Admission: Donations Welcome (Recommended Minimum £3.00)
05 JUNE - 28 AUGUST, TUES, THURS & SATS 1:45pm - 6:00pm
ALSO BY ARRANGEMENT CALL TO ARRANGE A SUITABLE TIME (NOT SUNDAYS)
Telephone: 01851 643204 Email Address: oakley1a@clara.co.uk
Red Cross (Scotland) receives 40%, the net remaining to SGS Beneficiaries.

19. LECKMELM SHRUBBERY & ARBORETUM By Ullapool IV23 2RH

Mr and Mrs Peter Troughton
The restored 12 acre arboretum, planted in the 1880s, is full of splendid and rare trees including 2 "Champions", specie rhododendrons, azaleas and shrubs. Warmed by the Gulf Stream, this tranquil woodland garden has alpines, meconopsis, palms, bamboos and winding paths which lead down to the sea.
Route: Situated by the shore of Loch Broom 3 miles south of Ullapool on the A835 Inverness/Ullapool road. Parking in walled garden.
Admission: Recommended donation £3.00 Children under 16 free
01 APRIL - 31 OCTOBER 10:00am - 6:00pm
Donation to SGS Beneficiaries and Local Charities

20. NOVAR Evanton IV16 9XL

Mr and Mrs Ronald Munro Ferguson
Water gardens with flowering shrubs, trees and plants, especially rhododendrons and azaleas. Large, five acre walled garden with formal 18th century oval pond (restored).
Route: Off B817 between Evanton and junction with A836: turn west up Novar Drive.
Admission: £5.00 Children Free
SUNDAY 13 JUNE 2:30pm - 5:00pm
ALSO BY ARRANGEMENT FOR GROUPS OF A MINIMUM OF 8 PEOPLE
Telephone: 01349 831062
Diabetes Charities receives 40%, the net remaining to SGS Beneficiaries.
❀ ♿ To Most Areas Raffle/Tombola ☕ Homemade

21. WEST LODGE Kilravock, Croy IV2 5PG

Mr and Mrs C Buss
Small, pretty, cottage style garden, packed with an interesting mixture of plants for long seasonal interest. Island and raised beds, small wildlife pond, vegetable/fruit area. Largest private collection in the area of over 250 Daylilies (at their best during July).
CHILDREN AND DOGS NOT ADMITTED
Route: From Inverness take B9006 towards Culloden/Cawdor. At Croy, turn left into village, second right up hill past shop, last cottage on right, opposite war

memorial/village hall. Parking available in driveway at front of cottage.

<u>Admission:</u> £3.00

BY ARRANGEMENT 20 MAY - 20 AUGUST

Telephone: 01667 493736 Email Address: buss.shelter@virgin.net

Cats Protection League receives 40%, the net remaining to SGS Beneficiaries.

✿ ☕Homemade

22. WOODVIEW Highfield, Muir of Ord IV6 7UL

Miss Lynda Macleod

Award winning well-stocked mature garden of approximately one third of an acre, containing many unusual trees. It comprises various "rooms" Italian inspired with sculptured trees. Pergola clad with golden hop, overlooking still water feature containing one white water lily. Chinese room very calm and relaxing with acers. Formal borders of twilight (white). Large exotic border. Abundance of colour from spring to autumn. Pond with waterside plants. Raised vegetable beds. Greenhouse. New borders and features ongoing every year.

<u>Route:</u> Follow signs to Ord Distillery on the A832 Muir of Ord to Marybank. House opposite Clashwood Forest Walk. Parking in Clashwood.

<u>Admission:</u> £3.00 Children Free

SUNDAY 29 AUGUST 2:00pm - 5:00pm

Telephone: 01463 871928

Email Address: lynwoodview@yahoo.co.uk

Highland Hospice receives 40%, the net remaining to SGS Beneficiaries.

✿ 🐴 ☕ Homemade Light Refreshments

Stirling Autumn Lecture

At the Albert Hall, Stirling

Tuesday 14 September 10:30am – 4:00pm

3 Keynote Speakers (To be Announced)

Morning Coffee, Sandwich Lunch, Wine and Stalls

Tickets £45.00

From Lady Edmonstone

Tel: 01360 770215 or Email: Juliet@edmonstone.com

Roxburghshire

'Gardens of Scotland' 2010 is sponsored by **Rensburg Sheppards Investment Management**

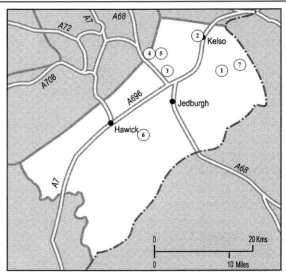

District Organiser: **Mrs Sally Yonge** Newtonlees, Kelso TD5 7SZ
Treasurer: **Mr Peter Jeary** Kalemouth House, Eckford, Kelso TD5 8LE

Gardens Open On a Specific Date

Stable House, Maxton	Sunday 06 June	2:00pm - 6:00pm
Corbet Tower, Morebattle	Saturday 03 July	2:00pm - 5:00pm
West Leas, Bonchester Bridge	Sunday 04 July	2:00pm - 5:30pm
St Boswells Village Gardens	Saturday 10 July	11:00am - 6:00pm
Yetholm Village Gardens	Sunday 18 July	2:00pm - 6:00pm

Gardens Open By Arrangement
When organising a visit to a garden open by arrangement, please enquire if there are facilities and catering available

Stable House, Maxton, St Boswells	For Groups	Tel: 01835 823024

Gardens Open Regularly

Floors Castle, Kelso	02 April - 05 April	
	& 01 May - 31 Oct.	11:00am - 5:00pm
Monteviot, Jedburgh	01 April - 31 Oct.	12:00pm - 5:00pm

1. CORBET TOWER Morebattle, Nr Kelso TD5 8AQ

Simon and Bridget Fraser

Scottish Victorian garden set in parklands in the foothills of the Cheviots. The garden includes formal box parterred rose garden with old fashioned roses, a well stocked traditional walled vegetable and cutting garden, lawns with medieval peel tower and an attractive woodland walk.

Route: From A68 north of Jedburgh take A698 for Kelso. At Kalemouth follow B6401 to Morebattle then road marked Hownam to Corbet Tower.

Admission: £4.00

SATURDAY 03 JULY 2:00pm - 5:00pm

The Childrens Society receives 40%, the net remaining to SGS Beneficiaries.

Limited but Disabled Parking Near House and Access to Teas Home-made Cakes and Preserves   Ann Fraser Cards Homemade

2. FLOORS CASTLE Kelso TD5 7SF

The Duke of Roxburghe

The largest inhabited house in Scotland enjoys glorious views across parkland, the River Tweed and the Cheviot Hills. Woodland garden, riverside and woodland walks, formal French style Millennium Parterre and the traditional walled garden. The walled garden contains colourful herbaceous borders, vinery and peach house, and in keeping with the tradition, the kitchen garden still supplies vegetable and soft fruit for the castle.

Route: Floors Castle can be reached by following: the A6089 from Edinburgh; the B6397 from Earlston or the A698 from Coldstream. Tourism signs direct you through the town to the Golden Gates and the Drive. Entrance to the Walled Gardens, Garden Centre and Terrace Café can be reached via a second entrance on the B6397

Admission: Grounds and Gardens Only: (individual rates) Adults £3.50 Senior Citizens/Students £3.00 Children 16 and under free

02 APRIL - 05 APRIL & 01 MAY - 31 OCTOBER 11:00am - 5:00pm (LAST ADMISSION 4.30pm)

Web Site: www.floorscastle.com

Telephone: 01573 223333

Donation to SGS Beneficiaries

Garden Centre situated next to Terrace Café Terrace Café specialising in Homemade Dishes prepared by the Duke's Chef.

3. MONTEVIOT Jedburgh TD8 6UQ

Marquis & Marchioness of Lothian

Series of differing Gardens including Herb Garden, Rose Garden, Water Garden linked by bridges, and River garden with herbaceous Shrub Borders. Dene Garden featuring ponds and bridges and planted with a variety of foliage plants.

Route: Turn off A68, 3 miles north of Jedburgh B6400.

Admission: £3.50. Children under 16 free

ROXBURGHSHIRE

01 APRIL - 31 OCTOBER (LAST ENTRY 4:00PM) 12:00pm - 5:00pm
Web Site: www.monteviot.com
Telephone: 01835 830380
Donation to SGS Beneficiaries
♿ Partial

4. ST BOSWELLS VILLAGE GARDENS St Boswells TD6 0ET

St Boswells Gardeners
St Boswells lies beside the River Tweed in the heart of the Scottish Borders. Much of the charm of the village in summer depends upon the variety, interest and contrast of its many gardens. Parking on the Village Green ONLY where tickets will be available.
Route: Off A68 into village on B6404.
Admission: £4.00
SATURDAY 10 JULY 11:00am - 6:00pm
St Boswells Parish Church (Scottish Charity No: SC010210) receives 40%, the net remaining to SGS Beneficiaries.
♿ 🐕

5. STABLE HOUSE Maxton, St Boswells TD6 0EA

Lt. Col and Mrs M D Blacklock
Half acre garden and courtyard planted around converted stables. Garden with interesting plant combinations, grouping shrubs, trees and perennials in sunny and cool shady beds. Decorative vegetable garden.
Route: Two minutes from A68 on A699 to Kelso
Admission: £3.00 Children Free
SUNDAY 06 JUNE 2:00pm - 6:00pm
ALSO BY ARRANGEMENT FOR GROUPS
Telephone: 01835 823024
Maxton & Mertoun Kirk receives 40%, the net remaining to SGS Beneficiaries.
✿ and Produce Stall ♿ Face Painting for Children ☕ Homemade

6. WEST LEAS Bonchester Bridge TD9 8TD

Mr and Mrs Robert Laidlaw
The visitor to West Leas can share in the exciting and dramatic project on a grand scale still in the making. At its core is a passion for plants allied to a love and understanding of the land in which they are set. Collections of perennials and shrubs, many in temporary holding quarters, lighten up the landscape to magical effect. New landscaped water features, bog garden and extensive new shrub and herbaceous planting. A recently planted orchard, with underplantings of spring bulbs demonstrates that the productive garden can be highly ornamental.
Route: Signed off the Jedburgh/Bonchester Bridge Road.
Admission: £4.00
SUNDAY 04 JULY 2:00pm - 5:30pm

Telephone: 01835 862524

Email Address: ann.laidlaw@btconnect.com

Macmillan Cancer Relief, Borders Appeal receives 40%, the net remaining to SGS Beneficiaries.

✿ & Very Limited 🐕 ☕ Wine

7. YETHOLM VILLAGE GARDENS Town Yetholm TD5 8RL

The Gardeners of Yetholm Village

A variety of gardens with their own unique features have joined the Yetholm Village Gardens Open Day this year. Village gardens open will include: **Copsewood, Almond Cottage, 5 Yew Tree Lane, Rosebank, The Old Manse, The Hall House, 2 Yew Tree Bank, Thirlestane, Crookedshaws, Hazeldean and Grafton House**. In addition **"The Allotments"** running along the High Street will again open this year in turn providing an ever popular feature. Other events will include "The Yetholm Wind Quintet", who will perform in one of the gardens during the afternoon. There will also be poetry readings at The Old Manse.

The Village of Town Yetholm is situated at the north end of the Pennine Way and lies close to the Bowmont Water in the dramatic setting of the foothills of the Cheviots. Yetholm Village Gardens Open Day offers visitors the chance to walk through several delightful gardens planted in a variety of styles and reflecting many distinctive horticultural interests. From newly established, developing and secret gardens to old and established gardens there is something here to interest everyone. The short walking distance between the majority of the gardens provides the added advantage of being able to enjoy the magnificence of the surrounding landscape to include "Staerough" and "The Curr" which straddle both the Bowmont and Halterburn Valleys where evidence of ancient settlements remain.

Tickets will be sold on the Village Green. Ample parking available on the High Street.

<u>Route:</u> South of Kelso take the B6352 to Yetholm Village.

<u>Admission:</u> £3.50 Includes All Gardens Children Under 10 Free

SUNDAY 18 JULY 2:00pm - 6:00pm

RDA - Riding for the Disabled Association Borders Group receives 40%, the net remaining to SGS Beneficiaries.

✿ Produce & Plant Stall Offering Plants, Vegetables and Home Baking & Limited Access 🐕 Bric-a-Brac and Book Stall ☕ Homemade   Served in the Village Hall During the Afternoon £2.00

To keep compost warm use some bubble wrap to line pots and containers

Stirlingshire

'Gardens of Scotland' 2010 is sponsored by **Rensburg Sheppards Investment Management**

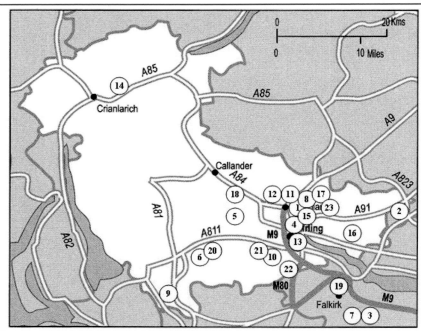

District Organisers: **Carola Campbell** Kilbryde Castle, Dunblane FK15 9NF
Lesley Stein Southwood, Southfield Crescent, Stirling FK8 2JQ

Area Organisers: **Rebecca East** Camallt, Fintry G63 0XH
Fleur McIntosh 8 Albert Place, Stirling FK8 2QL
Iain Morrison Clifford House, Balkerach Street, Doune FK16 6DE
Douglas Ramsay The Tors, 2 Slamannan Road, Falkirk FK1 5LG
Catherine Simpson 4 Randolph Road, Stirling FK8 2AJ
Carly Speirs 5 Randolph Road, Stirling FK8 2AJ
Sue Stirling-Aird Old Kippenross, Dunblane FK15 0LQ

Treasurer: **John McIntyre** 18 Scott Brae, Kippen FK8 3DL

Gardens Open On a Specific Date

West Plean House, By Stirling	Sunday 07 February	1:00pm - 4:00pm
West Plean House, By Stirling	Sunday 14 February	1:00pm - 4:00pm
West Plean House, By Stirling	Sunday 21 February	1:00pm - 4:00pm
Kilbryde Castle, Dunblane,	Sunday 28 February	1:00pm - 4:00pm
Milseybank, Bridge of Allan	Sunday 11 April	1:00pm - 5:00pm
Avonmuir House, Muiravonside	Sunday 18 April	2:00pm - 5:00pm
The Pass House, Kilmahog	Sunday 02 May	2:00pm - 5:00pm

Kilbryde Castle, Dunblane	Sunday 09 May	2:00pm - 5:00pm
Touch, Stirling	Sunday 16 May	2:00pm - 5:00pm
Yellowcraig Wood Bluebell Walk, Nr. Causewayhead	Sunday 16 May	1:00pm - 5:00pm
Glenorchard, Dunblane	Sunday 23 May	2:00pm - 5:00pm
Bridge of Allan Gardens	Sunday 06 June	1:00pm - 5:00pm
Kilbryde Castle, Dunblane,	Sunday 13 June	2:00pm - 5:00pm
King's Park Gardens, Stirling	Sunday 20 June	1:00pm - 5:00pm
Coldoch, Blairdrummond	Sunday 27 June	2:00pm - 5:00pm
32 Ledcameroch Gardens, Dunblane	Sunday 04 July	2:00pm - 5:00pm
Dunblane Gardens, Dunblane	Sunday 04 July	2:00pm - 5:00pm
Drumbroider Moss, Easter Greencraigs	Sunday 11 July	2:00pm - 5:00pm
The Tors and 33 High Station Rd. Falkirk	Sunday 25 July	2:00pm - 5:00pm
The Gean House, Alloa	Tuesday 27 July	2:00pm - 5:00pm
Thorntree, Arnprior	Sunday 08 August	2:00pm - 5:00pm
Avonmuir House, Muiravonside	Sunday 05 September	2:00pm - 5:00pm
Gargunnock House, Gargunnock	Sunday 26 September	2:00pm - 5:00pm

Gardens Open By Arrangement
When organising a visit to a garden open by arrangement, please enquire if there are facilities and catering available

Arndean, By Dollar	Mid May - Mid June	Tel: 01259 743525
Culbuie, Buchlyvie	May – Oct for Groups	Tel: 01360 850232
Duntreath Castle, Blanefield	On request	Tel: 01360 770215
Gargunnock House, Gargunnock	Guided Tour for Groups	Tel: 01786 860392
Kilbryde Castle, Dunblane,	On request	Tel: 01786 824897
Lochdochart, Crianlarich	01 May - 30 Sept.	Tel: 01838 300274
Milseybank, Bridge of Allan	On request	Tel: 01786 833866
The Linns, Sheriffmuir	01 Feb – 11 March & 19 May - 29 June	Tel: 01786 822295
Thorntree, Arnprior	On request	Tel: 01786 870710

Gardens Open Regularly

Gargunnock House, Gargunnock	01 Feb - 11 Mar Weds & Suns	11:00am - 4:00pm
	Mid April - Mid June & 01 Sept. - 31 Oct. Weds	2:00pm - 5:00pm
Lochdochart, Crianlarich	15 May - 13 June Sats & Suns	12:00pm - 4:00pm

Plant Sales

Gargunnock House, Gargunnock	Sunday 26 September	2:00pm - 5:00pm

STIRLINGSHIRE

1. 32 LEDCAMEROCH GARDENS Dunblane FK15 OGZ

Mark & Miranda Goodwin

This property is at one end of a delightfully secluded recent development. The gardens are on a small scale and occupy the kind of space that lots of people have and can give ideas to visitors. No 32 has a very pretty front garden and a small rear garden, which was once a grassy slope, and is now terraced with over 100 railway sleepers. Interesting plants and shrubs.

Route: Off Perth Road in Dunblane.

Admission: £3.00

SUNDAY 04 JULY 2:00pm - 5:00pm

All proceeds to SGS Beneficiaries

✿ ☕ Homemade

2. ARNDEAN By Dollar FK14 7NH

Johnny and Katie Stewart

Flowering shrubs, rhododendrons, azaleas, a mile woodland walk

Route: Off A977 and A91

Admission: £4.00

BY ARRANGEMENT MID MAY - MID JUNE

Telephone: 01259 743525 Email Address: johnny@arndean.co.uk

Scots Guards Colonel's Fund receives 40%, the net remaining to SGS Beneficiaries.

♿ 🐕

3. AVONMUIR HOUSE Muiravonside, by Linlithgow EH49 6LN NEW

Mark & Jan Strudwick

The house and gardens are the old Manse of Muiravonside built about 1795. There is a walled garden with fruiting trees and a north and a south facing border. The gardens then lead through shrubs and young trees towards an old ruin with a walk along the burnside back towards the house. Good daffodils in spring.

Route: Junction 4 M9. Follow A803 to Linlithgow for about half a mile and turn right signposted Whitecross. Follow road to Whitecross. In centre of Whitecross take first right, past a small football ground, round a sharp corner and just before the bridge over the Union Canal turn right, towards Muiravonside Kirk and Cemetery and immediately right again into a parking area in the field.

Admission: £4.00

SUNDAY 18 APRIL 2:00pm - 5:00pm

SUNDAY 05 SEPTEMBER 2:00pm - 5:00pm

Telephone: 07831 242992

Combat Stress receives 40%, the net remaining to SGS Beneficiaries.

✿ ♿ Produce Stall ☕ Homemade

4. BRIDGE OF ALLAN GARDENS Bridge of Allan FK9

The Bridge of Allan Gardeners

Plaka, Pendreich Road, FK9 4LY (Malcolm and Ann Shaw)

½ acre of semi-terraced gardens divided into outdoor rooms with wild spaces. In addition, there are rhododendrons, perennials and interesting stone and other features.

Garvia, 10 Fishers Green, FK9 4PU (Garth and Sylvia Broomfield)

½ acre specialist's garden with beach garden, oriental section, extensive rockeries with alpines and dwarf conifers, several water features with stream and ponds and a fruit and vegetable area. New feature - Gothic stone folly!

Kenilworth, 7 Kenilworth Road, FK9 4DU (Bill and Sheila Anderson)

This fine traditional garden has been kept true to its original layout dating back to the 1850s. Kenilworth is one of the three oldest houses in Kenilworth Road and was a lodging to young Robert Louis Stevenson and his family during May 1858. The garden boasts a number of specimen trees including a magnificent deodar cedar tree all of which make it delightfully secluded. There are also open spaces and many different areas of interest. Plants include rhododendrons, azaleas, herbaceous and several varieties of annuals. An elegant and sturdy fruit cage serves as adequate protection from the birds.

Kilmun Cottage, 1b Pendreich Rd, FK9 4PZ (Frances Fielding)

Designed and beautfiully landscaped by the owner within the last two years, this third of an acre garden on a slope has much variety. A terraced garden with an attractive rockery and pond, raised beds with herbaceous plants including a fine Fothergilla major, vegetable plot with 3 handsome espalier apple trees and a potential fruit garden with blueberry and other bushes leading to a wild area.

St Saviour's Rectory Garden & St Saviour's Church Garden, Keir Street FK9 (Dominic and Anna Ind)

The attractive Rectory garden was redesigned 3 years ago by the present Rector and his wife. The addition of a trellis, a raised bed and a sweeping herbaceous border filled with interesting plants gives the garden instant form and colour. It is sheltered on one side by the Church and another by the Rectory. The Church garden has a well laid out semi-walled garden with interesting plants and an attractive beech hedge. The Church, over 150 years old, will be open to all visitors.

Maps & tickets available at all gardens

<u>Route:</u> Signposted from village.

<u>Admission:</u> £5.00 Children Free

SUNDAY 06 JUNE 1:00pm - 5:00pm

Email Address: annshaw@mac.com

St Saviour's Church receives 30%, Strathcarron Hospice receives 10%, the net remaining to SGS Beneficiaries.

 🐕 ☕ Cream at St Saviours Church Hall

5. COLDOCH Blairdrummond, Stirling FK9 4XD [NEW]

Mr and Mrs David Stewart

The garden at Coldoch is sheltered by belts of mature woodland on three sides and looks South over the Carse of Stirling. There is a new parterre courtyard garden and border replacing old farm buildings and garaging that then leads directly onto a new parterre kitchen garden created using three old walls of an earlier rose garden. Otherwise the various parts of the policies which include a stream, a pond, a bog, paddocks and woodland are delineated by hedges of beech, hornbeam, privet, cotoneaster and laurel. The roads are lined with very old oaks and sycamores mixed with new trees from Eastern Europe, Central Asia and mature Cherry trees.

Route: From the A84 Stirling to Doune road turn west on to the A873 towards Aberfoyle. Stay on this road for just under 1 mile. Turn left at the sign for Coldoch Road (B8031), and continue for just over 1/2 mile. Wrought iron gates on the left side mark the entrance to Coldoch garden.

Admission: £4.00, children free

SUNDAY 27 JUNE 2:00pm - 5:00pm

Telephone: 01786 841217

The Sandpiper Trust receives 40%, the net remaining to SGS Beneficiaries.

 ♿ ☕ Homemade

6. CULBUIE Buchlyvie FK8 3NY

Ian & Avril Galloway

Spring collection of rhododendrons, azaleas, narcissi, bluebells, primulas and meconopsis. Woodland walk with new planting. Early summer magnolias, cornus and viburnums. Colouful perennial borders. Wild flower meadow. Good autumn colour. Lots of interest throughout this 5 acre garden with splendid views to Ben Lomond and surrounding hills

Route: Take A811 to Buchlyvie, turn up Culbowie Road and Culbuie is almost at the top of the hill on the right.

Admission: £4.00

BY ARRANGEMENT MAY - OCTOBER GROUPS WELCOME

Telephone: 01360 850232

Preshal Trust receives 20%, Macmillan Cancer Relief Fund receives 20%, the net remaining to SGS Beneficiaries.

7. DRUMBROIDER MOSS Easter Greencraigs, Avonbridge FK1 2LF

Alan and Barbara Hunter

Situated in rural countryside and created primarily to encourage wildlife this informal large garden is only six years old. Mixed planting, naturalised ponds, roses and hostas encourage biodiversity. Raised organic vegetable beds. Wonderful views in all directions.

Route: M9. Junction 4. Take A801 at roundabout to next roundabout. Take B825 through Standburn. Proceed through Standburn for 0.9 mile and take a right at crossroads. Unlined road 0.3 miles on right.

Admission: £3.50

SUNDAY 11 JULY 2:00pm - 5:00pm
Telephone: 01324 861159 Email Address: drumbroider@btinternet.com
Strathcarron Hospice receives 40%, the net remaining to SGS Beneficiaries.
   Cream

8. DUNBLANE GARDENS Dunblane FK15
Gardeners of Dunblane
Several creative and different gardens in Dunblane including St Blane's House, High
Street and Glenorchard, Auchenlay Road. Maps and tickets available on day from all
gardens.
Route: Follow yellow signs on entry to Dunblane
Admission: £5.00, Concessions £4.00, Children Free
SUNDAY 04 JULY 2:00pm - 5:00pm
CHAS receives 40%, the net remaining to SGS Beneficiaries.
Partly Homemade at Glenorchard

9. DUNTREATH CASTLE Blanefield G63 9AJ
Sir Archibald & Lady Edmonstone
Extensive gardens with mature and new plantings. Ornamental landscaped lake and
bog garden. Sweeping lawns below formal fountain and rose parterre with herbaceous
border leading on up to an attractive waterfall garden with shrubs and spring
plantings. Woodland walk. 15th century keep and chapel.
Route: A81 north of Glasgow between Blanefield and Killearn
Admission: £4.00
BY ARRANGEMENT ON REQUEST
Web Site: www.duntreathcastle.co.uk
Telephone: 01360 770215
Email Address: juliet@edmonstone.com
All proceeds to SGS Beneficiaries

10. GARGUNNOCK HOUSE Gargunnock FK8 3AZ
By kind permission of the Gargunnock Trustees
Five acres of mature gardens, woodland walks, walled garden and 18th century Doocot.
Snowdrops in February/March, daffodils in April/May. Glorious display of azaleas and
rhododendron in May/June. Wonderful trees and shrubs, glorious autumn colour. Garden
featured in articles in Scotsman and Scottish Field. Good plant sales always.
Guided tours can be arranged for Parties.
Route: On A811 5 miles west of Stirling
Admission: **February - March:** £2.00 Children Free
April - June: £3.00
September - October £3.00
Sunday 26 September: £4.00

STIRLINGSHIRE

SUNDAY 26 SEPTEMBER 2:00pm - 5:00pm
01 FEBRUARY - 11 MARCH, WEDNESDAY'S & SUNDAY'S FOR SNOWDROP
FESTIVAL 11:00am - 4:00pm
MID APRIL - MID JUNE, WEDNESDAYS 2:00pm - 5:00pm
01 SEPTEMBER - 31 OCTOBER, WEDNESDAYS 2:00pm - 5:00pm
ALSO BY ARRANGEMENT GROUPS CONTACT HEAD GARDENER FOR GUIDED TOUR
Telephone: 01786 860392
Email Address: william.campbellwj@btinternet.com
Children's Hospice Association receives 20%, Gargunnock Community Centre receives
20%, the net remaining to SGS Beneficiaries.
✿ At All Times 🐎 ✾ ☕ On 26 September Only

11. GLENORCHARD Auchenlay Road, Dunblane FK15 9JS NEW

Mr & Mrs W Geddes
The garden is a traditional terraced garden dating from 1904, with lots of herbaceaous
borders. It is particularly lovely in May with the azaleas, rhododendron and cherry
blossom. There is a lovely short walk along the banks of the river Allan with spring
flowers. Hardy wild orchids have been allowed to spread freely in the field beyond. In
May the Laighils bank opposite the garden is a carpet of bluebells.
Route: Into Dunblane from A820. Take 3rd turning on left into Kilbryde Crescent (single
track country road) along road for 1 mile, the house is on right hand side.
Admission: £3.50
SUNDAY 23 MAY 2:00pm - 5:00pm
CHAS receives 40%, the net remaining to SGS Beneficiaries.
☕ Homemade

12. KILBRYDE CASTLE Dunblane, FK15 9NF

Sir James & Lady Campbell & Jack Fletcher
The Kilbryde Castle gardens cover some 12 acres and are situated above the Ardoch
Burn and below the castle. The gardens are split into 3 parts: formal, woodland and
wild. Huge drifts of snowdrops are in the wild garden, natural planting (azaleas,
rhododendrons, camellias and magnolias) in the woodland garden. There are glorious
spring bulbs and autumn colour.
Route: Three miles from Dunblane and Doune, off A820 between Dunblane and Doune.
On SGS days signposted from A820
Admission: **28 February:** £3.00 Children Free
9th May: £4.00 Children Free
13 June: £4.00 Children Free
SUNDAY 28 FEBRUARY FOR SNOWDROP FESTIVAL 1:00pm - 4:00pm
SUNDAY 09 MAY 2:00pm - 5:00pm
SUNDAY 13 JUNE 2:00pm - 5:00pm
ALSO BY ARRANGEMENT ON REQUEST
Web Site: www.kilbrydecastle.com

Telephone: 01786 824897
Email Address: kilbryde1@aol.com
Leighton Library receives 40%, the net remaining to SGS Beneficiaries.
♿ Partly ⚲ ☕ Cream and Light Refreshments on 9th May Only

13. KING'S PARK GARDENS Southfield Crescent, Stirling FK8 2JQ NEW
John and Lesley Stein

Southwood, 2 Southfield Crescent, FK8 2JQ (John & Lesley Stein) Walled garden redesigned 1987. Long herbaceous borders within beech hedges, shrubs and lavender border. Well stocked paeony bed on mound. Interesting specimen trees.

3 Southfield Crescent, FK8 2JQ (Mary McCaig) Revamped in 2003, this charming garden has an attractive variegated privet hedge in the front garden, several interesting maples, herbaceous plants and a newly planted monkey puzzle tree. The rear garden is sheltered (semi-walled), with wisteria and other shrubs, raised bed, attractive summer house and several rhododendrons and other plants in pots.

21 Snowdon Place, FK8 2JW (Pauline Leask) Traditional south facing walled garden with fine herbaceous and perennials. Trachelospurmum with buttery yellow flowers on back of house, also cornus Henry Hadden of special note and rockery.

Park Lodge, Park Terrace, FK8 (George & Anne Marquetty) A large and elegant formal garden with good herbaceous borders.

1 Abercromby Place, FK8 2QP (John & Sue Mills) Medium sized walled garden dominated by large 100 year old copper beech. Many mature bushes and 70 year old wisteria on south facing back of house. Clematis grow up various sections of the walls. The garden changes from a colourful spring garden with Azaleas and Rhododrons with spring bulbs and bluebells into a summer garden with an herbaceous bed and a few old-fashioned climbing roses.

Maps & tickets available at all gardens
<u>Route:</u> From city centre signed from Carlton Bingo at Allan Park. From south, signed from St Ninian's Road. From west and north, signed from Drummond Place and Dunbarton Road
<u>Admission:</u> £5.00, Concessions £4.00, Children Free
SUNDAY 20 JUNE 1:00pm - 5:00pm
Telephone: 01786 475735 Email Address: lesley@john-stein.co.uk
Strathcarron Hospice receives 40%, the net remaining to SGS Beneficiaries.
♻ at Southwood   ♿ B&B Southwood   Home-baking, Other Stalls and Attractions at Southwood ☕ Cream at Southwood

14. LOCHDOCHART Crianlarich FK20 8QS
John and Seona Christie of Lochdochart

Walled garden - a variety of fruit, flowers and vegetables. Mature policy woods - a good selection of candelbra primulas, rhododendrons and azaleas. Picnic beach by Loch lubhair, bring your picnic lunch.
<u>Route:</u> A85, 4 miles east of Crianlarich. Take Oban Road, over hill Lixtill garage - 7 miles from garage, Lochdochart two stone pillars on north side of road.

STIRLINGSHIRE

Admission: £4.00

15 MAY - 13 JUNE SATURDAYS & SUNDAYS 12:00pm - 4:00pm
ALSO BY ARRANGEMENT 01 MAY - 30 SEPTEMBER

Telephone: 01838 300274

Email Address: christielochdochart@btinternet.com

Royal Scottish Agricultural Benevolent Fund receives 40%, the net remaining to SGS Beneficiaries.

♿ 🐕 ☕ Homemade

15. MILSEYBANK Bridge of Allan FK9 4NB

Murray and Sheila Airth

Steeply sloping garden with outstanding views, terraced for ease of access. Woodland with bluebells, rhododendrons, magnolias and camellias.

Route: Situated on the A9, 1 mile from junction 11, M9 and ¼ mile from Bridge of Allan. Milseybank is at the top of the lane at Lecropt Nursery and 250 yards from Bridge of Allan train station. Lecropt Kirk is ¾ mile from M9 and ½ mile from Bridge of Allan.

Parking at Lecropt Kirk, disabled parking only at house.

Admission: £4.00

SUNDAY 11 APRIL 1:00pm - 5:00pm
ALSO BY ARRANGEMENT ON REQUEST

Telephone: 01786 833866 Email Address: sheilalecropt@yahoo.co.uk

Strathcarron Hospice receives 40%, the net remaining to SGS Beneficiaries.

✿ ♿ 🐕 ☕ Homemade

16. THE GEAN HOUSE Tullibody Road, Alloa FK10 2EL NEW

Ceteris (Scotland)

The Gean House is an early 20th century Arts & Crafts style mansion. On arrival, the sweeping driveway from the main road takes you through beautiful parkland lined with trees to the Mansion set on top of the hill facing North East. The gardens surrounding the house were originally 40 acres and included a Japanese garden in the woods. All that remains now are seven acres on the southern and eastern aspects of the house. The rose garden is situated directly outside the Dining Room window.

Route: The Gean House is located on the Tullibody Road, Alloa

Admission: £4.00

TUESDAY 27 JULY 2:00pm - 5:00pm

Web Site: www.geanhouse.co.uk

Email Address: ebowie@geanhouse.co.uk

The Scottish Society for Autism receives 40%, the net remaining to SGS Beneficiaries.

☕ Cream in The Gean House

17. THE LINNS Sheriffmuir, Dunblane FK15 4LP

Drs Evelyn and Lewis Stevens

A specialist collection of snowdrops. 3½ acres of woodland and herbaceous garden. A superb Plant Heritage (NCCPG) collection of Himalayan big blue poppies.

Route: Sheriffmuir by Dunblane, telephone for additional directions.

Admission: £3.50

BY ARRANGEMENT 01 FEBRUARY - 11 MARCH FOR THE SNOWDROP FESTIVAL AND BY ARRANGEMENT 19 MAY - 29 JUNE

Telephone: 01786 822295

Email Address: evelyn@thelinns.org.uk

Sophie North Charitable Trust receives 40%, the net remaining to SGS Beneficiaries.

✿ ⚘ NCCPG Himalayan Big Blue Poppies

18. THE PASS HOUSE Kilmahog, Callander FK17 8HD

Dr and Mrs D Carfrae

Well planted medium sized garden with steep banks down to swift river. Garden paths not steep. Camellias, rhododendrons, azaleas, alpines and shrubs. This year will be the 25th opening of this beautiful garden.

Route: 2 miles from Callander on A84 to Lochearnhead.

Admission: £4.00

SUNDAY 02 MAY 2:00pm - 5:00pm

Email Address: carfraede@hotmail.com

Crossroads Care Attendant Scheme receives 40%, the net remaining to SGS Beneficiaries.

♿ Partly 🐕

19. THE TORS AND 33 HIGH STATION ROAD. 2 Slamannan Road, Falkirk FK1 5LG

Dr and Mrs D M Ramsay and Mr and Mrs Roger Findlay

The Tors: 2 Slamannan Road, Falkirk FK1 5LG (Dr and Mrs D Ramsay)

33 High Station Road: Falkirk FK1 5NE (Roger and Alison Findlay)

The Tors is an award winning garden of one acre with a secret woodland garden to the side and an orchard and wild area to the rear. Many unusual maple trees and rhododendrons are the main feature of this garden along with several water features. Bonsai and topiary are features of the small award-winning garden in High Station Road.

Route: The B803 to the South of Falkirk leads to Glenbrae Road. Turn right at traffic lights into Slamannan Road. High Station Road is down steps close by The Tors at the Falkirk High Station. Maps are available at both gardens.

Admission: £3.00 Children Free

SUNDAY 25 JULY 2:00pm - 5:00pm

Telephone: 01324 620877 Email Address: dramsay8@yahoo.co.uk

Strathcarron Hospice receives 40%, the net remaining to SGS Beneficiaries.

✿ ♿ 🐕 ☕ Homemade

STIRLINGSHIRE

20. THORNTREE Arnprior FK8 3EY

Mark and Carol Seymour

Charming cottage garden with flower beds around courtyard. Apple walk, fern garden and Saltire garden. Lovely views from Ben Lomond to Ben Ledi. John MacLean our local bee keeper will be available to answer your questions on bee keeping and will hopefully have an inspection hive on display. An Art Exhibition and Sale by the Byre Art Group from Killearn. In the spring (April) the bank alongside our drive is filled with primroses - you are welcome to come and see them.

Route: A811. In Arnprior take Fintry Road, Thorntree is second on right.

Admission: £4.00

SUNDAY 08 AUGUST 2:00pm - 5:00pm

ALSO BY ARRANGEMENT ON REQUEST

Telephone: 01786 870710 Email Address: info@thorntreebarn.co.uk

Riding for the Disabled receives 40%, the net remaining to SGS Beneficiaries.

❀ ♿ ☕ Cream

21. TOUCH Stirling FK8 3AQ

Angus Watson

Exceptionally fine Georgian House. Walled garden with herbaceous and shrub borders, specie and dwarf rhododendrons, magnolias and interesting shrubs. Woodland walk.

Route: West from Stirling on A811 then take Cambusbarron Road.

Admission: £4.00 Children Free House £2.50

SUNDAY 16 MAY 2:00pm - 5:00pm

Telephone: 01786 448899 Email Address: angus@touchestate.co.uk

Strathcarron Hospice receives 40%, the net remaining to SGS Beneficiaries.

❀ Small ♿ Limited Access ☕ Homemade

22. WEST PLEAN HOUSE Denny Road, By Stirling FK7 8HA

Tony and Moira Stewart

Woodland walks with snowdrops.

Well established garden including site of iron age homestead and panoramic views over seven counties. Woodlands with mature rhododendrons, specimen trees, extensive lawns, shrubs and walled garden with variety of vegetables. Includes new woodland walk with planting of azaleas and rhododendrons.

Route: Leave all routes at Junction 9 roundabout where M9/M80 converge. Take A872 for Denny, travel less than mile, turn left at house sign and immediately after lodge cottage. Carry on up drive.

Admission: £2.00

SUNDAY 07 FEBRUARY FOR THE SNOWDROP FESTIVAL 1:00pm - 4:00pm

SUNDAY 14 FEBRUARY FOR THE SNOWDROP FESTIVAL 1:00pm - 4:00pm

SUNDAY 21 FEBRUARY FOR THE SNOWDROP FESTIVAL 1:00pm - 4:00pm

Web Site: www.westpleanhouse.com

Telephone: 01786 812208 Email Address: moira@westpleanhouse.com

Scottish Motor Neurone Disease Associatiion receives 40%, the net remaining to SGS Beneficiaries.

23. YELLOWCRAIG WOOD BLUEBELL WALK Nr. Causewayhead
Mrs Rosemary Leckie

70 acres of ancient woodland with a mixture of trees including oak, ash, birch, beech, gean, rowan, Scots pines and larches. Carpets of bluebells. Beautiful views from 2 Crags, Witches Crag and Yellow Crag (bring binoculars). Lower part of wood on a steep hill. Also 20 min walk on flat at bottom of wood.

Route: From Causewayhead roundabout, take B998 passing the Wallace Monument on your right. Turn left just before the next roundabout and go straight along this road. The entrance to the foot of Yellowcraig Wood is adjacent to Logie Kirk. Parking in Logie Kirk car park.

Admission: £4.00

SUNDAY 16 MAY 1:00pm - 5:00pm

Telephone: 07906 838205 Email Address: rleckie@tiscali.co.uk

Ataxia Society receives 40%, the net remaining to SGS Beneficiaries.

Church Open for Viewing Homemade Light Refreshments Served in Logie Kirk Annexe

PLANT SALES

10. GARGUNNOCK HOUSE PLANT SALE Gargunnock FK8 3AZ
By kind permission of the Gargunnock Trustees

Large sale of species rhododendrons, azaleas, trees, shrubs, mostly from wild collected seed in India and China all grown on the Estate. See Stirlingshire garden entry no. 10 for details of the garden.

Route: On A811 5 miles west of Stirling

Admission: £4.00

SUNDAY 26 SEPTEMBER 2:00pm - 5:00pm

Telephone: 01786 860392

Email Address: william.campbellwj@btinternet.com

Children's Hospice Association receives 20%, Gargunnock Community Centre receives 20%, the net remaining to SGS Beneficiaries.

Wrap spring bulbs in a thin layer of steel wool. It does not harm the bulbs but will help prevent animals from digging up and eating them.

Adding Brillo pads or old rusty nails will make an improvement to limey soil.

Wigtownshire

'Gardens of Scotland' 2010 is sponsored by **Rensburg Sheppards Investment Management**

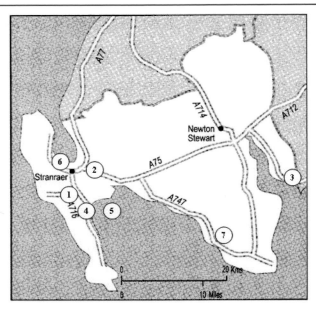

District Organiser: Mrs Francis Brewis Ardwell House, Stranraer DG9 9LY

Area Organisers: **Mrs V Woseley Brinton** Chlenry, Castle Kennedy, Stranraer DG9 8SL

Mrs Andrew Gladstone Craichlaw, Kirkcowan, Newton Stewart DG8 0DQ

Treasurer: **Mr George Fleming** Ardgour, Stoneykirk, Stranraer DG9 9DL

Gardens Open On a Specific Date

Kirkdale, Carsluith	Sunday 14 February	2:00pm - 5:00pm
Smithy Hill Cottage, Leswalt	Sunday 11 April	10:00am - 5:00pm
Logan House Gardens, Port Logan	Sunday 02 May	9:00am - 6:00pm
Smithy Hill Cottage, Leswalt	Sunday 02 May	10:00am - 5:00pm
Smithy Hill Cottage, Leswalt	Sunday 09 May	10:00am - 5:00pm
Smithy Hill Cottage, Leswalt	Sunday 16 May	10:00am - 5:00pm
Smithy Hill Cottage, Leswalt	Sunday 23 May	10:00am - 5:00pm
Logan Botanic Garden, Port Logan	Sunday 30 May	10:00am - 6:00pm
Smithy Hill Cottage, Leswalt	Sunday 30 May	10:00am - 5:00pm
Smithy Hill Cottage, Leswalt	Sunday 06 June	10:00am - 5:00pm
Castle Kennedy & Gardens, Stranraer	Sunday 20 June	10:00am - 5:00pm

Gardens Open By Arrangement

When organising a visit to a garden open by arrangement, please enquire if there are facilities and catering available

Castle Kennedy & Gardens, Stranraer	November – January	Tel: 01581 400225
Smithy Hill Cottage, Leswalt	On request	Tel: 01776 870662
Woodfall Gardens, Glasserton	1 May - 31 August	Tel: 01988 500692

Gardens Open Regularly

Ardwell House Gardens, Ardwell	1 April – 30 Sept.	10:00am - 5:00pm
Castle Kennedy & Gardens, Stranraer	Feb – Mar Sats & Suns	10:00am - 5:00pm
	& 1 April - 30 Oct.	10:00am - 5:00pm
Logan House Gardens, Port Logan	2 Feb. - 21 Mar.	10:00am - 4:00pm
	& 22 Mar – 31 Aug.	9:00am - 6:00pm

1. ARDWELL HOUSE GARDENS Ardwell, Stranraer DG9 9LY

Mr and Mrs Francis Brewis

Daffodils, spring flowers, rhododendrons, flowering shrubs, coloured foliage and rock plants. Moist garden at smaller pond and a walk around larger ponds with views over Luce Bay. Collection Box. House not open.

Route: A716 towards Mull of Galloway. Stranraer 10 miles

Admission: £3.00 Concessions £2.00 Children Under 14 Free

1 APRIL - 30 SEPTEMBER 10:00am - 5:00pm

Donation to SGS Beneficiaries

 Self-pick Fruit in Season, Picnic Site on Shore

2. CASTLE KENNEDY & GARDENS Stranraer DG9 8RT

The Earl and Countess of Stair

Located on an isthmus surrounded by two large natural lochs, these famous gardens extend to 75 acres of landscaped terraces and avenues. The ruined Castle Kennedy is at one end overlooking a stunning herbaceous walled garden; and Lochinch Castle is at the other. In close proximity to the Gulf Stream the gardens contain an impressive collection of rare trees, rhododendrons and exotic shrubs. With over 300 years of tree planting, the collection is mature, featuring many spectacular Champion Trees (tallest or largest of their type) including 6 British Champions, 11 Scottish and 25 for Dumfries and Galloway. The snowdrop walks, daffodils, spring flowers, rhododendrons and magnolia displays, tree trails and herbaceous borders make this a 'must visit' garden throughout the year.

Route: On A75 five miles east of Stranraer

Admission: £4.00, Children £1.00, Concessions £3.00, Disabled Free, Families £10.00 (Two Adults and Three Children)

WIGTOWNSHIRE

SUNDAY 20 JUNE 10:00am - 5:00pm
FEBRUARY - MARCH SATURDAYS & SUNDAYS 10:00am - 5:00pm
1 APRIL - 30 OCTOBER 10:00am - 5:00pm
ALSO BY ARRANGEMENT NOVEMBER - JANUARY
Telephone: 01581 400225
Scots Guards Colonels Fund for injured soldiers and their families receives 40%, the net remaining to SGS Beneficiaries.
❀ ♿ Partial ⚘ ☕ Charming Tea-room Serving Light Lunches and Home-made Teas.

3. KIRKDALE Carsluith, Newton Stewart DG8 7EA
Mr & Mrs Neil Hannay
Fabulous woodland snowdrop walks around historic 18th century property. A chance to view the only working water driven sawmill in South of Scotland and nature trail.
Route: On A75 six miles west of Gatehouse of Fleet. Signposted Cairnholy Chambered Cairn
Admission: £3.00 Children Free
SUNDAY 14 FEBRUARY FOR SNOWDROP FESTIVAL 2:00pm - 5:00pm
Homestart, Wigtownshire receives 40%, the net remaining to SGS Beneficiaries.
♿ Partly ⚘ Working Water-Driven Sawmill ☕

4. LOGAN BOTANIC GARDEN Port Logan, By Stranraer DG9 9ND
The Royal Botanic Gardens Edinburgh
At the south western tip of Scotland lies Logan which is unrivalled as the country's most exotic garden. With a mild climate washed by the Gulf Stream, a remarkable collection of bizarre and beautiful plants, especially from the southern hemisphere, flourish out of doors. Enjoy the colourful walled garden with its magnificent tree ferns, palms and borders along with the contrasting woodland garden with its unworldly gunnera bog. Explore the Discovery Centre or take an audio tour.
Route: 10 miles south of Stranraer on A716 then 2½ miles from Ardwell village
Admission: £4.00 Concessions £3.50 Children £1.00 Family £9.00
SUNDAY 30 MAY 10:00am - 6:00pm
Royal Botanic Garden, Edinburgh receives 40%, the net remaining to SGS Beneficiaries.
♿ Partial   Home Baking and Botanic Shop, Discovery Centre, Guided Tours

5. LOGAN HOUSE GARDENS Port Logan, By Stranraer DG9 9ND
Mr and Mrs Roberts
1701 Queen Anne House. Spectacular woodland gardens with rare and exotic tropical plants and shrubs. Fine species and hybrid rhododendrons.
Route: On A716 14 miles south of Stranraer. 2½ miles from Ardwell village
Admission: £3.00 Children Under 16 Free
SUNDAY 02 MAY 9:00am - 6:00pm

2 FEBRUARY - 21 MARCH 10:00am - 4:00pm
22 MARCH - 31 AUGUST 9:00am - 6:00pm
Port Logan Hall Fund receives 40%, the net remaining to SGS Beneficiaries.
♿ Exhibition of Work by Local Artists ☕

6. SMITHY HILL COTTAGE Leswalt, By Stranraer DG9 0LS

Mr & Mrs Humphreys

A plantsman's alpine and rock garden transplanted from Yorkshire to this site overlooking Loch Ryan over the last 2/3 years. Eight different raised beds provide flowers each month with a broad range of small grafted trees, azaleas, rhododendrons, mountain plants. A small alpine house.

Route: A718 from Stranraer towards Leswalt. One third of a mile after de-restriction sign take the 2nd road on the left. Smithy Hill Cottage is ¼ mile on the left.

Admission: £3.00 Concessions £2.00 Accompanied Children Under 14 Free

SUNDAY 11 APRIL 10:00am - 5:00pm
SUNDAYS 02, 09, 16, 23 & 30 MAY 10:00am - 5:00pm
SUNDAY 06 JUNE 10:00am - 5:00pm
ALSO BY ARRANGEMENT ON REQUEST
Telephone: 01776 870662
St John Patient Transport receives 40%, the net remaining to SGS Beneficiaries.
✿ ♿ Gravel Paths ☕

7. WOODFALL GARDENS Glasserton DG8 8LY

David and Lesley Roberts

A three acre 18th century walled garden undergoing revitalisation. As well as the remains of the original garden buildings there are mixed borders, a woodland area, a parterre and a productive potager.

Route: 2 miles south of Whithorn by junction of A746/747

Admission: £3.00 Concession £2.00 Accompanied Children Under 14 Free

BY ARRANGEMENT 1 MAY - 31 AUGUST
Telephone: 01988 500692
Alzheimers (Scotland) receives 40%, the net remaining to SGS Beneficiaries.
♿

To deter cats add rose thorns onto your flowerbeds as cats hate them, dogs can be deterred by spray perfume or aftershave in your garden. To deter slugs spread egg shells as they will not crawl over them because of the sharpness.

INDEX TO GARDENS

INDEX TO ADVERTISERS

NOTES

"GARDENS OF SCOTLAND" 2011

Order now and your copy will be posted to you on publication in December

---

Scotland's Gardens Scheme
42a Castle Street, Edinburgh EH2 3BN

Please send me _____ copy/copies of

"Gardens of Scotland" 2011

Price £6.50, to include p&p, as soon as it is available
I enclose a cheque/postal order made payable to
<u>Scotland's Gardens Scheme</u>

Name ....

Address ....

....

.... Postcode..................................

Scotland's Gardens Scheme
Gardens open for charity

We welcome gardens large and small and also groups of gardens.
If you would like information on how to open your garden for
charity please contact us at the address below.

SCOTLAND'S GARDENS SCHEME
42a CASTLE STREET, EDINBURGH EH2 3BN
Telephone: 0131226 3714
Email: info@sgsgardensofscotland.co.uk

NAME & ADDRESS: (Block capitals please)

NAME: ....

ADDRESS: ....

....

.... POSTCODE: ....

TEL: ....

EMAIL: ....

Supporting Scotland's Garden Scheme

Savills is delighted to sponsor the Loyalty Awards organised by Scotland's Gardens Scheme. These awards are presented to the owners of gardens which have participated in the Scheme for 25, 50 and 75 years respectively - tremendous achievements!

Savills has been entrusted with the sale of some of Scotland's finest houses and we know the value that an established and cared-for garden brings to a property. I am keen that our sponsorship recognises and celebrates the owners and gardeners who have devoted time and energy to their gardens over the years.

I first became aware of the valuable fundraising work of Scotland's Gardens Scheme some time ago through my mother, Diana Macnab of Macnab, who was chairman of Scotland's Gardens Scheme for 10 years in the 1980's and is still a Vice President.

Savills is a well established business in Scotland, with country house departments in Edinburgh, Glasgow, Perth and Brechin. I have been working for Savills for over 20 years and will be pleased to receive any agency related enquiries. Alternatively, feel free to contact one of my colleagues in an office closer to you.

Jamie Macnab
Head of residential agency in Scotland
Savills
Edinburgh
0131 247 3711